"*Polyvagal-Informed EMDR* is a cutting-edge book that skillfully blends two of the world's leading theoretical trauma models with great sophistication, yet practical steps. This is a must-have book for all EMDR clinicians to bring their clinical practice to the next level. Rebecca Kase demonstrates the power of thinking outside the box to help transform new pathways of healing trauma."

—**Les Aria, PhD**, chief science officer of Menda Health

"*Polyvagal-Informed EMDR* makes perfect sense. As an integrative treatment approach, EMDR therapy focuses on all components of a memory, including the impact of adverse experiences on the nervous system. Rebecca Kase provides a clear description of Polyvagal Theory and specific interventions to apply directly to the eight phases of the EMDR Standard Protocol. She explores the linkages between autonomic responses, the storage of memory, and a variety of clinical presentations. Using PVT interventions, EMDR clinicians can optimize healthy biological responses and utilize them intentionally throughout EMDR therapy."

—**Rosalie Thomas, PhD**, senior faculty, EMDR Institute, past president, EMDR International Association

"Every EMDR trainer, consultant, and practitioner should read *Polyvagal-Informed EMDR*. This clearly-written book brings somatic and attachment lenses and procedures to every part of the EMDR protocol. It reminds us that clients' needs for connection, safety, and safe presence supersede the therapists' needs for immediate trauma processing. It gives us specific language and actions to create and keep the all-important dual attention that allows trauma processing to work. After 29 years in the EMDR world, I see this as the best new lens through which to see and do our good work."

—**Robin Shapiro**, EMDRIA approved consultant, trainer, and practitioner

POLYVAGAL-
Informed EMDR

Polyvagal-Informed EMDR

A NEURO-INFORMED APPROACH TO HEALING

REBECCA KASE

Norton Professional Books

An Imprint of W. W. Norton & Company
Celebrating a Century of Independent Publishing

This book is intended as a general information resource for professionals practicing in the field of psychotherapy and mental health. It is not a substitute for appropriate training or clinical supervision. Standards of clinical practice and protocol vary in different practice settings and change over time. No technique or recommendation is guaranteed to be safe or effective in all circumstances, and neither the publisher nor the author(s) can guarantee the complete accuracy, efficacy, or appropriateness of any particular recommendation in every respect or in all settings or circumstances. All case subjects and dialogues described in this book are composites.

Any URLs displayed in this book link or refer to websites that existed as of press time. The publisher is not responsible for, and should not be deemed to endorse or recommend, any website other than its own or any content that it did not create. The author, also, is not responsible for any third-party material.

Printed in the United States of America

Frontis © krjaki1973 / DepositPhotos

For information about permission to reproduce selections from this book, write to Permissions, W. W. Norton & Company, Inc., 500 Fifth Avenue, New York, NY 10110

For information about special discounts for bulk purchases, please contact W. W. Norton Special Sales at specialsales@wwnorton.com or 800-233-4830

Manufacturing by Versa Press
Production manager: Gwen Cullen

ISBN: 978-1-324-03031-7

W. W. Norton & Company, Inc., 500 Fifth Avenue, New York, NY 10110
www.wwnorton.com

W. W. Norton & Company Ltd., 15 Carlisle Street, London W1D 3BS

1 2 3 4 5 6 7 8 9 0

This book is dedicated to everyone
who has the courage to heal.

Contents

Acknowledgments

This book is the product of the influence of many teachers, healers, and loved ones.

To my husband, who supports me, co-regulates me, and is always cheering me on. You are the most stable, grounding force in my life, and I love you so much.

To my father, who believed in me and always encouraged me to write.

To my mother and my sister, for your endless love and support.

Thanks to Deb Dana for reviewing my chapters and supporting this book. Thank you for your leadership in training and teaching Polyvagal Theory.

Thanks to Stephen Porges for kindly answering my questions and developing Polyvagal Theory for so many people to benefit from.

Thank you to Francine Shapiro for EMDR and for your influence on me personally and professionally. Though I will never have the chance to meet you, you have positively shaped my life.

To Robin Shapiro, who has been a kind and supportive colleague, who introduced me to Norton, and read my pages.

Thank you to Nancy Rubbico, who taught me Polyvagal Theory and helped me find the bridges with EMDR Therapy.

Thank you to Carol Ivanoff, my greatest mentor and guide in my academic development and beyond.

To my clients, who I have the privilege to support, who invite me into their lives, and who have helped me learn the techniques outlined in this book.

To everyone at Norton who supported this book and guided me in the process.

To Crystal Wildes, Jessica Downs, Les Aria, Laurel Thornton, and Rosalie Thomas for reading some or all of the book and offering feedback.

Thank you to my team at Kase & CO. You are a testament to the power of safety amongst colleagues. Thank you for cheering me on, supporting me, guiding me, and being trusted advisors in all of my professional endeavors and creative ideas.

Thank you to everyone who has ever challenged me or left me with pain and hurt. Those wounds have proven to be the greatest lessons and opportunities for growth in my life. Without you, I would know very little about myself and what I'm capable of.

Introduction

Polyvagal Theory and eye movement desensitization and reprocessing (EMDR) are neuro-informed, cutting-edge theoretical models known for their impactful contributions to psychotherapy. Individually, they provide frameworks for conceptualization and pathways for healing. Combined, they deliver a powerful, integrated, neuro-informed approach to foster therapeutic transformation. Polyvagal Theory and EMDR benefit all populations, every age group, every cultural identity, and every clinical presentation. But how do we cohesively integrate these theories? How do we approach the tender work of healing with these models informing both conceptualization and intervention? How do we effectively blend the wisdom and research of these respected models? And what's the benefit in doing so?

As an EMDR trainer and consultant, I often receive questions about the integrative capacity of these theories from consultees. Can I integrate Polyvagal Theory into EMDR? How do I do that? When should I do that? Why should I do that? To date, we as an EMDR community have not deeply explored these questions. No one has explicitly outlined this path—until now.

My love affair with EMDR began in 2006 when I started EMDR basic training. I have experienced EMDR as a life-changing therapy, personally and professionally. It is the most powerful and effective therapy I have ever had the privilege to receive personally, as well as to provide to clients on their healing journeys. EMDR is a neuro-informed therapy, as it focuses on the wisdom and innate healing power of the nervous system and conceptualizes memory storage as a primary contributor to the development of clinical symptoms and diagnoses.

In 2018, I began my dive into Polyvagal Theory and was quickly awestruck to learn this model that described the autonomic nervous system in depth. Polyvagal Theory is a robust framework that explains the science of feeling safe and how the autonomic nervous system responds to danger. This model has inspired thousands of clinicians to connect with their inner neuroscience geek, as it teaches us to befriend the nervous system and remain curious about the adaptive nature of hardwired survival defenses.

I had an intuitive sense that these models complemented each other like peanut butter and jelly. I sensed that Polyvagal Theory could easily integrate into the eight phases of EMDR. So I started experimenting with techniques and approaches. After all, if we never tried new ways of doing things, many of our therapies, including EMDR, wouldn't exist. I curiously explored the points of integration through study and practice, and slowly but surely, I began to see the forest for the trees.

Integrating these models was powerful. Combined, they presented a comprehensive framework, centered on the nervous system, to guide my clinical practice, supporting assessment, case conceptualization, treatment planning, intervention, and tracking outcomes. I felt excited and inspired. Clients stabilized quicker and processed targets with greater ease. My interventions seemed to supercharge or level up in their effectiveness. I had a renewed sense of curiosity and wonder for my job as a therapist. Embracing these models totally worked—and it worked really well.

In the beginning, it was challenging to find the bridge and integrate. I felt like a ping-pong ball bouncing back and forth from one to the other. "How do I combine these?" was a daily mantra and curiosity. Given that both models focused on neurobiology, I knew they complemented each other. Typically, I would look for trainings, books, articles, and experts to learn from. But that wasn't an option here, since no one had explored this before. There are many therapists trained in EMDR, and many therapists who have studied Polyvagal Theory. But I couldn't find someone who was balanced with both. Experts and consultants I spoke to talked about EMDR or Polyvagal Theory, but never both at the same time. In some cases, I even found therapists feeling like they had to choose sides and have allegiance with one or the other. Sadly, this seems to be a common theme in our field of counseling, which leads to silos and "mine is better than yours" limiting mentalities.

Fast-forward to a trip to the grocery store in Colorado in 2020. Denver was emerging from the pandemic lockdown, and my local community had just experienced another mass shooting that took place in a grocery store. I was standing in the ice cream aisle, struggling with the privileged problem of deciding which ice cream to buy, when suddenly there was a loud, startling noise. "Pop!"

"What was that? Was that a gun? Am I in danger? What's happening?" My mind raced. My ears perked up. I froze. I looked up and down the aisle, scanning the environment for information. My heartbeat raced, my blood pressure increased, and my muscles contracted as I tried to figure out what that noise was. A group of teenagers walked by, one of them playfully hitting another. "You jerk! I can't believe you popped that in my ear. I'm going to get you back!" Deep breath. "It's just kids playing and being silly. I'm safe," I thought. I tried to get back to picking out ice cream. But I couldn't.

My heart started to slow, my muscles relaxed a bit, and I refocused on the colorful frozen containers stacked before me. But now memories from my past were flashing through my mind. I recalled a personal incident with gun violence. My mind replayed snippets of scenes from that night a few years ago. I remembered running with the gun I had wrestled away from someone who was about to use it to kill himself or someone else. I could feel the familiar fizzy feeling of adrenalin as I stood in the brightly lit freezer aisle. My mind played images from the news of the local shooting in the grocery store. The survivors, the vigil for those murdered, the gunman. That sound had started a cascade of memories, which I was viscerally reexperiencing in that moment.

I recognized the experience I was having and looked for ways to flexibly maneuver back to a more regulated state. "Breathe. Ground. Just notice," my inner therapist voice coached. I looked around for cues that told me I was safe, a skill I learned from Polyvagal Theory. I put that memory of gun violence from my past into a container, a skill I learned from EMDR. I took a few deep breaths and added some slow bilateral stimulation by swaying side to side, an EMDR intervention, and took a moment to just notice my internal world. I'm sure I looked like an interesting character, standing in that aisle administering some psychotherapy techniques on myself. Regardless, I got regulated again in just a few minutes and went on with my shopping.

That's an awfully dramatic ice cream story, Rebecca. What does it have to do with anything? I share this story because it's the moment that I understood with clarity the overlap of these models. This experience is an example of Polyvagal Theory and the adaptive information processing (AIP) model (from EMDR) happening at once. Neuroception, a polyvagal term you will learn in chapters to come, is the body's internal surveillance system. Neuroception unconsciously scans the environment for cues of danger and safety, activating autonomic alarm bells in response to danger. When I heard the popping sound, my defenses activated based on an environmental cue along with the information held in my unique memories. My nervous system worked its adaptive magic, preparing me with a survival response. A flood of sympathetic arousal quickly prepared me to mobilize. This physiological response is the focus of Polyvagal Theory. Feeling the increase in sympathetic energy along with the potential stimulus of a gun triggered my memory networks, which is the focus of EMDR. Based on the present trigger, AIP began activating memories, reminding me of my own past trauma and my community's recent trauma. Not only was I thinking about those memories, but my body was reexperiencing parts of those memories through autonomic feelings and sensations. The sound hadn't only startled my autonomic nervous system; it also activated my memory networks. The principles of both models were happening simultaneously and interdependently at that moment, as I stood frozen in the grocery aisle, dysregulated. It was a dance of distress between my autonomic nervous system and memory networks.

I am a well-adjusted individual. I've done my work and healed many of my wounds, including the one with gun violence I just referenced. I have invested a lot into myself by developing coping skills, self-awareness, and personal insight. I am fortunate to have a flexible and resilient nervous system. I'm a psychotherapist. I'd better have those attributes if I'm going to teach them to others. Now imagine this chain of events happening to someone without much resiliency or flexibility, someone who has unresolved, maladaptive memories that are easily triggered and cascade into flooding or shutdown. What if I didn't have many coping skills or ways to regulate? That someone is on your caseload. Many of our clients experience chronic activation of defensive states, frequent trauma triggers, and daily challenges regulating stress responses.

Because memories are not just thought but felt, maladaptive memory networks activate autonomic defenses (i.e., fight, flight, freeze, collapse). When a memory is recalled in the mind, it is experienced in state-specific form through the autonomic nervous system. EMDR therapists focus on the storage of memory, and polyvagal-informed therapists focus on the autonomic nervous system. Combining Polyvagal Theory with EMDR means the therapist focuses on both branches of the nervous system and integrates approaches to help the whole system heal.

Both models provide frameworks for conceptualization and outline pathways for healing. The theories are complementary, offering additional depth and breadth to each other in their organization of concepts and approaches. Understanding EMDR will support your understanding of Polyvagal Theory, and understanding Polyvagal Theory will enhance your understanding of EMDR. Both focus on the information processing mechanisms of the nervous system. Polyvagal Theory identifies neuroception as a primary means of information processing, while EMDR focuses on the AIP model. Recognizing the complex yet simple ways the nervous system processes and integrates information, and where the opportunities for intervention lie, is at the heart of this book.

As I've explored the hows, the whys, and the wheres of polyvagal-informed EMDR (PV-EMDR), I've come to a few core principles that guide my practice. We will review these principles throughout this book, supporting you to develop a robust clinical framework to foster healing that holds relevance with all clients and presentations.

- Memory storage and the functioning of the autonomic nervous system are the focus of PV-EMDR therapy.
- The nervous system is the mechanism of assessment, intervention, and outcome of psychotherapy.
- Polyvagal Theory describes the functioning of the autonomic nervous system and the role of the vagus nerve as it mediates autonomic processes.
- The AIP model of EMDR describes the storage of memory.
- Memories are not just thought but are felt through autonomic processes.
- The autonomic nervous system influences the storage of memory.
- The autonomic and central nervous systems have a bidirectional, interdependent relationship. The state of one system directly influences the state of the other.
- Autonomic resiliency is a means to an end and an end itself.

I am writing this book as a PV-EMDR therapist. Integrating these models will shift your conceptual framework away from diagnoses and labels as you become curious about the functioning of the nervous system. PV-EMDR highlights adaptation over pathology, and the innate capacity to heal. These theories describe the intelligence of the nervous system, asking you to explore the significance of the dysfunction rather than the dysfunctional significance. The PV-EMDR model asks you to befriend the nervous system's adaptive nature, recognize clinical complaints as a unique neurophysiological language, and plan interventions accordingly. Clients come to therapy because of dysregulated nervous systems, regardless of the diagnosis or symptoms. PV-EMDR is an advanced, neuro-informed approach to counseling, putting the nervous system at the forefront of assessment, diagnosis, and treatment.

Together we will explore methods to integrate Polyvagal Theory into the eight phases of EMDR, without posing a risk to the fidelity aspects of this evidence-based therapy. It is my belief that the techniques explored in this text enhance the efficacy of the EMDR therapy model. I review key concepts and intervention techniques, I will incorporate composite case examples, with composite dialogue, for reference points.

This book will not serve as a comprehensive examination and review of EMDR therapy. It does not replace any thorough text such as Shapiro's classic EMDR therapy text, now in its third edition (Shapiro, 2018). Neither does this book serve as a comprehensive review of Polyvagal Theory. It is not meant to replace Deb Dana's or Stephen Porges's texts or thorough training in Polyvagal Theory. This book is meant to serve as a bridge to integrate these two theories. It is therefore limited in its coverage of important concepts relevant to each model. There is only so much material that is reasonable to cover in one text if I hope to keep you engaged. Take what supports your practice, dive in deep with concepts that inspire you, and leave what doesn't resonate for your practice. And always, always, always: stay humble, stay curious, and keep learning.

POLYVAGAL-
Informed **EMDR**

Chapter 1

NEURO-INFORMED COUNSELING

Let us rewind to the very eventful decade of the 1990s. The Soviet Union was dissolved, the Hubble Telescope launched, and Google entered our mainstream world. Pop culture was feeding us supersized meals, Destiny's Child, and the Spice Girls. There was a lot going on. The '90s were also designated the Decade of the Brain, as former president George H. W. Bush launched an initiative to advance brain research, examining relevant correlates with disease and illness. The effort was inspired by a call to action from leading health organizations (the National Institute of Neurological Disorders, the National Institute of Mental Health, and the National Advisory Council) in efforts to unlock the secrets of the brain, promote public health, and improve treatment for neurological disorders such as addiction and mental illness. Until the 1990s, the brain remained largely undiscovered territory. Through advances in technology, however, tools became available to study some of the secrets of this complicated and powerful organ.

Polyvagal Theory and EMDR were also emerging in this time, making their grand debuts in the 1990s. Dr. Stephen Porges (the originator of Polyvagal Theory) began his work in the 1960s studying heart rate variability. Dr. Francine Shapiro (the originator of EMDR) made her significant discovery on that famous walk through the park in the late 1980s. Polyvagal Theory and EMDR gained momentum in the 1990s and eventually merged into mainstream clinical practice and awareness. Today these theories are commonly known around the counselors' water cooler as highly researched and respected models.

Thanks to the Decade of the Brain and emerging models, the nervous system is recognized as relevant to psychotherapy—though I would argue that it's not emphasized enough. Neuroscience teaches us that we are our biology. Thoughts, feelings, sensations, behaviors, and symptoms can be understood and explained as products of physiology. The nervous system shapes our inner world and our experience of the outer world. When the nervous system is healthy, we are more likely to be healthy. When the nervous system is unhealthy, we are more likely to be unhealthy. We cannot separate the biology from the person.

When physiological states become traits, there is a tendency to attribute those traits to the individual's personality and moral character rather than their biology. No one wants to grow up an addict; no one truly enjoys depression; struggling with interpersonal relationships is exhausting for everyone; any person with a pulse is attention-seeking at least sometimes, in some way. These are common presentations with stigmatized labels born out of misunderstood physiological processes rooted in trauma, adverse experiences, dysfunctional attachment, racism, prejudice, and neurological disease. Labels do not aid healing and recovery. They stigmatize, pathologize, and shame while distracting from the adaptive neurophysiological processes driving the problem, behavior, or symptom.

Despite these advances in psychology, psychotherapists remain one of the few groups in the medical community that do not look at the organ or system they treat. Isn't that baffling? Counselors treat the nervous system, made up of the brain and nerves of the body. All clinical complaints are expressions of a distressed brain and nervous system. Nevertheless, we rarely send people for MRIs or SPECT scans for purposes of case conceptualization, diagnosis, and mental health treatment. We don't obtain scans for pre- and post-assessments or differential diagnosing, or to identify which psychiatric medications may be best suited to the client. We simply do not look at the mechanism causing the dysfunction that will also be the target of intervention. Can you imagine if a cardiologist tried to treat you for a heart attack without an EKG, or if your dentist diagnosed you with a cavity without an X-ray? You'd probably walk out of their office, because that would be ludicrous and negligent. Yet this is the case for psychotherapy.

Of course, we know why this is. It's the reality of the world we live in. Medical systems and insurance companies do not offer the means, the resources, the standard of care, or the money to do this. If they did, I know you'd probably join me in sending clients to get scans left and right as a standard practice. Mental health is still seen as separate from physical health, and until that changes, different standards will persist. Until then, we can rely on neuro-informed models to guide treatment in the absence of sophisticated equipment and resources.

Neuro-informed counseling reflects the neurobiological correlates of the human experience (Dahlitz, 2015; Luke, 2016). A neuro-informed approach shifts our clinical focus away from pathologizing the dysfunction, toward curiosity for the function of the dysfunction. This approach highlights adaptation over pathology, exploring the meaning of the behavior versus the label and diagnosis. The client's clinical complaints and symptoms are important clues provided by their nervous system that guide us to the root of the problem. Neuro-informed counseling recognizes that dysregulation and dysfunction in the nervous system leads to common clinical complaints like depression, anxiety, addiction, suicidality, personality disorders, and psychosis. Symptom clusters and clinical traits are the nervous system expressing a story, illuminating wounds and areas for growth. When we can identify the wound, we can identify the remedy.

Polyvagal-informed EMDR is a neuro-informed approach to counseling. Integrating these models focuses the clinical work on the nervous system. The nervous system becomes the mechanism of assessment, intervention, and outcome of psychotherapy. Polyvagal Theory is based on neurobiological research. Porges's (2011) research describes the biological and physiological processes of the autonomic nervous system and the function of the vagus nerve. It is the science of feeling safe. This model has evolved from thousands of peer-reviewed articles and academic research that has culminated over decades. EMDR is founded in research on memory and the adaptive information processing system (Shapiro, 2018). EMDR examines the physiological storage of memory and the impact that memory storage has on health, wellness, disease, and pathology.

The brain is resilient and adaptive because neuroplasticity provides us with the ability to heal and transform. The innate drive toward homeostasis and wholeness is a core principle of psychotherapy and any healing profession. EMDR and Polyvagal Theory both highlight the intelligence and adaptive nature of the nervous system. Our biology is geared to work in our favor, and our hardwired survival responses are protective. Problems can arise when our biology gets hijacked, and we get stuck in chronic states of survival. Long-term activation of defensive autonomic states wreaks havoc on our minds and bodies.

When we accept and honor that it's all biology, we can easily be curious about the function and significance of clinical complaints. We can befriend symptoms and explore the problem the system is trying to solve as it tries to adapt. We recognize behaviors as attempts to compensate and soothe. Clinical complaints and symptoms can be accepted as a unique language the nervous system is speaking, pointing out the areas needing intervention.

Symptoms are data points. When you get physically ill, you likely assess your symptoms to figure out what illness you might have. Based on that assessment, you choose how to take care of yourself. If you're getting a migraine, you might go to a dark, quiet room. If you think you have appendicitis, hopefully you get to the emergency room. Or if you think you're getting a cold, you might drink a lot of fluids and take some vitamins. If you didn't get symptoms, you wouldn't know you were sick and in need of an intervention. The body communicates through symptoms. The nervous system is no different. After all, it's part of your physical body. Getting curious about symptoms often reveals the interventions needed to help the body heal. Let's explore this with the case described below.

Jane (she/her) is a 32-year-old, white, gay client. She presents to therapy with chronic anxiety, racing thoughts, difficulties with sleep, and irritability. Jane drinks around four to six drinks per day, and more on the weekends. She discloses binge eating behaviors, which are typically triggered when alone at night, while watching TV. Jane discloses a history of emotional neglect and family dysfunction growing up. She shares that her parents were absent in her childhood, that they were "there but not there." Jane's father kept to himself, "drinking beer and watching TV," and her mother was often depressed and in bed. Jane says she didn't feel loved or nurtured as a child. When asked how her parents managed stress, she reports, "They didn't. They just shut down. Mom would sleep. Dad would drink and watch TV."

I invite curiosity and explore the function of the alcohol use and binging. "What does drinking do for you? What does it help?" Jane quickly responds, with judgment and rationality, "Well, it doesn't. I know I drink too much." I encourage Jane to lean in a bit more and get curious about the drinking. "Let's get curious. It must help something, or you wouldn't do it," I say. As we slow down and explore her experience with more depth, we start to uncover some critical information. "I think it's just when I get to drink six or so, I feel warm and quiet inside. It's like a bubble goes up around me. I feel safe. I also feel that way when I overeat and binge. I go into a bubble. I'm not real in that moment. Everything disappears and feels fuzzy. I never remember eating so much. I zone out." These insights are priceless.

Integrating PV-EMDR, I tune in to some very important information that builds conceptualization and identifies a path for intervention. First and foremost is the golden rule of creating a safe therapeutic relationship, or building the therapeutic soil, as I describe later in this book. Safety in the relationship allows Jane to explore the meaning behind her alcohol use and binge eating. Curiosity is available only when we are safe enough to be curious.

As I gather information from Jane, I also track the state of her autonomic nervous system. Jane's autonomic nervous system is chronically dysregulated, based on her descriptions of sympathetic overwhelm and dorsal disconnection. Sympathetic states are evidenced by racing thoughts, anxiety, and irritability. Jane appears tense and tight in sessions, talks at a rapid pace, and fidgets, which are also signs of sympathetic arousal. She describes times of dorsal dissociation, as she goes into a trance, consuming massive amounts of calories, dissociating, feeling fuzzy, and losing track of time. These are all defenses of the dorsal circuit. Jane is missing the skills to navigate this distress because she didn't learn self-soothing techniques in childhood. She doesn't know how to regulate her internal world because her parents never taught her how. But her nervous system is clever and adaptive, and has found ways to compensate with chemically and behaviorally induced soothing via drinking and binge eating.

Treatment starts with coregulation so that Jane can experience reliable safety and soothing. I coregulate Jane by using my own regulated nervous system to guide her through various regulation strategies, and in doing so increase her access to her ventral circuit, expanding her window of tolerance. I begin each session with a regulating activity to support learning and use of techniques outside of session. I use coregulation periodically throughout sessions when Jane begins to get overwhelmed, flooded, or dissociated, helping her build adaptive neural pathways to flexibly maneuver between states of activation and calm. Our work together also teaches Jane how to notice and name feelings, sensations, thoughts, and experiences. These steps all help to build resiliency in Jane's autonomic nervous system, enhancing day-to-day stability and preparing for EMDR reprocessing of memories.

Once the autonomic nervous system is prepared, we develop an EMDR treatment plan and prepare for reprocessing. Without EMDR reprocessing, maladaptively stored memories will continue to elicit responses of the autonomic nervous system regardless of how good Jane gets at coping. EMDR treatment planning with Jane revealed memories of feeling abandoned, she said, "when Mom wouldn't get out of bed to cook me dinner" and "the time Dad gave me my first beer, and I felt loved by him." We reprocessed memories with the EMDR protocol, and I tracked her symptoms and nervous system to determine progress and plan interventions. Jane quickly reported a decrease in sympathetic distress. As her sympathetic nervous system became less activated, she felt more peace and happiness in her life and began to trust her ability to take care of herself. She also reported the urges to binge and drink greatly subsided. Over a few months she showed improved self-esteem, and symptoms of sympathetic and dorsal activation decreased. She had more access to the ventral state and overall stated she felt "so much better."

This brief vignette describes the application of an integrated model for conceptualizing, intervening, and tracking progress. PV-EMDR therapy is an advanced psychotherapeutic approach that asks the therapist to befriend the nervous system by integrating two neuro-informed, evidence-based theoretical models. Polyvagal Theory offers a method for conceptualizing and making sense of the autonomic nervous system as it appraises and responds to cues of danger or safety. EMDR helps the clinician understand the role of memory storage in clinical symptoms and outlines an evidence-based protocol to reprocess maladaptive memories. Integrating these theories allows the clinician to conceptualize the bottom-up and top-down processes that shape the client's experience.

Polyvagal Theory is a theoretical model, not a specific therapy. The culmination of Porges's research and thousands of peer-reviewed articles has shaped a robust scientific model with significant implications for clinical practice. Polyvagal Theory outlines a framework for understanding the adaptive defenses of the autonomic nervous system and the function of the vagus nerve. The model explains how the vagus nerve acts as a mediator between the three circuits of the autonomic nervous system and describes the adaptive characteristics of each circuit. This model also highlights the wisdom of the autonomic nervous system, as it has evolved over millions of years, with the number one goal being survival. Polyvagal Theory also explains the biological imperative of social bonds, and how the vagus nerve influences our capacity for connection.

EMDR is both a theoretical model and a specific therapy. Because of the adaptive information processing model, EMDR provides a means to conceptualize and plan interventions. EMDR focuses on memory storage and how memory storage contributes to health and wellness or dis-ease and pathology. The model outlines techniques for identifying specific memories that hijack the autonomic nervous system and lead to clinical symptoms and diagnoses. These memories are targeted via the protocol and reprocessed to a point of adaptive resolution.

This book presents a polyvagal-informed framework for EMDR. We review the many ways that Polyvagal Theory is alive and well within EMDR therapy and examine opportunities to expand its influence. You will learn to look beyond symptoms and diagnoses, relying on neurophysiological processes as the informers of case conceptualization and treatment planning. The combined approach of PV-EMDR is an integrated therapy model that supports the nervous system to heal and become more resilient. This is a book about neurobiology, and how to apply neurobiology to counseling. While neurobiology can be complex and overwhelming to study, I will do everything I can to translate the most relevant information in a clear and simplified manner, to support your practice.

Chapter 2

THE NERVOUS SYSTEM AND TOXIC STRESS

To orient to the techniques and approaches described in this book, we must begin with a brief overview of the nervous system. The nervous system is intelligent, complex, and resilient. While we know much about human neurobiology, we have yet to learn even more. This chapter oversimplifies very dense and complex concepts. I believe that having some understanding of the nervous system, even if minimal to moderate in scope, can significantly contribute to your clinical practice. You don't need a neuroscientist's level of expertise to use these concepts in meaningful ways.

The nervous system is one entire system with many subsystems and functions. We often talk about the nervous system in parts or branches because it's a way to divide very complex structures into easier-to-understand sections. But do not forget, it's all one system pulsing with energy at the heart of our day-to-day experience.

The nervous system originates from the same cells as the skin (Kiernan & Barr, 2009). Both originate from a layer of cells called germ cells, which form in embryonic development. Germ cells develop into the ectoderm, which becomes the skin and the nervous system. Like the skin, the nervous system is a sensing organ that covers a lot of surface area and processes a lot of information. You may even consider the nervous system to be your inner skin, as the two share similar functions of protection, regulation, and sensing.

The nervous system contains billions of cells and has an array of important functions. It protects us in times of danger and adversity. It is also a regulator, as it regulates the internal environment (e.g., feelings, sensations, body temperature, blood pressure, heart rate). As it senses, processes and responds to stimuli, it influences physiological states with correlated responses. Because of the nervous system, we experience things like hunger and fullness, anxiety and depression, concentration and distraction. The nervous system is always working and sensing, constantly firing off electrical impulses throughout the body. It is the mechanism through which we experience our life. We perceive and interpret everything via the flow of energy moving through this system.

The nervous system consists of thousands of connection points that send information through neurons, synapses, axons, and dendrites (Brodal, 2016). Neurons (i.e., nerve cells) communicate by sending electrical impulses through synapses, from one cell to another. Some cells control voluntary movements, and some control involuntary movements. Some cells tell you you're hungry, and some cells tell you you're in pain. Some cells help you form memories, and others help you to learn. The specific cells that fire together effect physiology, which activate thoughts, feelings, sensations, and behaviors. Every aspect of your experience is an outcome of the lightning show taking place in your nervous system.

Consider that the nervous system is a communication superhighway, in constant motion. This system is a bundle of energy, held together by tissue and bone, informing every moment of your life. Though the synaptic impulses may be tiny, they are experienced in very big ways. The functioning of your nervous system governs your life, and shapes your experiences and perceptions. We could say your nervous system is the center of your universe.

The two main branches of the nervous system are the central nervous system and the peripheral nervous system. The central nervous system includes the brain and spinal cord. The peripheral nervous system is composed of several subbranches, one being the autonomic nervous system. For this book, we discuss components of both the central nervous system (specifically the brain) and the peripheral nervous system (specifically the autonomic nervous system) as they relate to PV-EMDR. The central nervous system includes the relevant subject matter pertaining to EMDR's model of adaptive information processing. The autonomic branch of the peripheral nervous system is the focus of Polyvagal Theory.

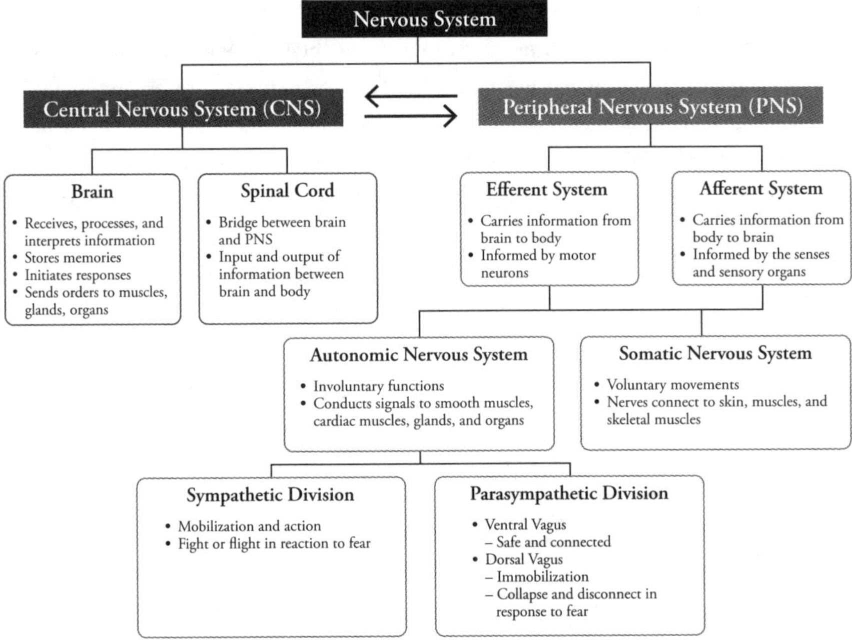

Figure 2.1: The Nervous System. Toxic Stress and Trauma.

What comes to your mind when you think of stress? Something terrible and uncomfortable? Do you think of yourself with a to-do list that won't quit and a fast-approaching deadline? Do you think of something traumatic? Do you get an image of yourself looking frazzled, strung out on caffeine? What if I asked you to picture yourself on a brisk walk or running on a treadmill? Would those be forms of stress? Is traveling through an airport on your way to a fabulous vacation a form of stress? Is giving birth a form of stress? Yes, yes, and yes. It's all stress. But it's not all the same flavor of stress, is it?

Stress comes in many forms and flavors. Stress is any event that taxes an organism's normal abilities to cope and perform, producing physiological changes beyond those of homeostasis in response to the stressor. Stress has two facets: a stimulus and a physiological response (Porges, 2011). Stress can stem from an internal or external stimulus that demands a change in our physiology in response. The response may be to upregulate with mobilization strategies or to downregulate with immobilization strategies. The stressor is ideally temporary, and when it ends, physiology returns to homeostasis, or a state of health and wellness.

Stress is a normal part of life and isn't necessarily bad. Being alive on this planet is a stressful experience. We experience physical stress when working out, taking a test, or giving birth. You probably experienced stress when you learned to drive or made your way through graduate school. These are all examples of a stimulus demanding something of your physiology beyond the regulated and peaceful state of homeostasis. However, in these examples it is evident that the stressor led to desired growth. We exercise for health and wellness. You put yourself through grad school because you wanted to be a therapist. Learning to drive leads to independence and autonomy. Stress, therefore, isn't always a bad thing. In fact, it's necessary for adaptive development (Aschbacher et al., 2013). Stress becomes toxic when it exceeds capacity and duration thresholds. How great the stressor is and how long it lasts are relevant variables of toxicity. Stress that overwhelms the nervous system and goes on for a prolonged period wreaks havoc on the mind and body.

Post-traumatic stress disorder (PTSD) is listed under "trauma and stressor-related disorders" in the *Diagnostic and Statistical Manual of Mental Disorders* (American Psychiatric Association, 2017). The psychiatric world has a whole category of diagnoses dedicated to stress, which is enough to show that stress can be incredibly harmful. You know, and I know, from personal and clinical experience, that too much stress for too long is a bad thing. Toxic stress is commonly at the root of addictions, anxiety disorders, depressive disorders, personality disorders, and psychotic disorders. Stress can harm us and lead to a plethora of complex biopsychosocial challenges, creating risk of an early death (Felitti et al., 1998). Toxic stress can be so harmful it can kill us.

It can be difficult to define what events will cause trauma and toxic stress. It's difficult because we've been taught to assess the wrong variable, which is the event or what happened. Assessing how your client experienced an event is more important than what happened. The term "trauma" as we know it in psychology can be limiting, because trauma is defined by an event rather than the response. Assessing for trauma, as most of us have been trained, requires the clinician to objectively assess someone's subjective experience. How one person responds to a traumatic event can vary dramatically from another. Therefore the response is more important than the event itself.

Physical and sexual assault, war, and natural disaster are commonly identified human traumas. These have historically been referred to as "big-T traumas," as experiences that professionals and nonprofessionals readily identify as traumatic. They are extreme and overwhelming events. Asking a client,

"Do you have a history of trauma?" will likely result in their examination and reporting of big-T traumas. But this is only one type of trauma. The counseling field has also historically used the term "small-t trauma" to label experiences that are also stressful and harmful, but less extreme and sudden. Possible examples include bullying, emotional neglect, and verbal abuse. These highly common traumas can be easily overlooked by professionals and clients. Asking a client, "Do you have a trauma history?" is unlikely to elicit their self-disclosure of small-t traumas. While big and small traumas may be objectively different, they can both be impactful and harmful, depending on the individual's experience and response. In fact, experiencing multiple small-t traumas can be more damaging than one or two big-T traumas (Shapiro, 2018), because the event is only one part of the story, and the response is the other.

Based on this knowledge, be mindful of your questioning techniques. Asking a client if they have a trauma history will yield limited information This type of questioning fails to examine all forms of toxic stress and, most importantly, the client's reaction to stressors. How often have you had the experience of being a couple of months into the therapeutic work, and your client tells you about a traumatic experience they had, which they don't label as trauma? You reflect and educate: "Did you know that is considered to be trauma?" Your client responds by looking at you like you just said chocolate cake is the new health fad. Rather than asking about trauma, assess for adversity and toxic stress. This change can free clinicians from limiting definitions and lets us refocus assessment on the nervous system's experience.

The Adverse Childhood Experiences Study (ACE Study) was first published in 1998 (Felitti et al., 1998). Today, this study is widely known and is considered the birthplace of trauma-informed care (Goddard, 2021). The ACE Study began as a partnership between the Centers for Disease Control and Kaiser Permanente. It is a longitudinal study with over 13,000 participants, still being conducted today through phone screenings. The ACE Questionnaire asks about 10 traumas in childhood, or adverse experiences, before the age of 18, and the influence of childhood adversity on well-being throughout the lifespan

The ACE study is one of the largest longitudinal studies to investigate the negative consequences of early childhood trauma on health and well-being. The study found that ACEs in childhood impact neurodevelopment which may produce social, emotional, and cognitive impairments. These factors can then lead to the adoption of high-risk health behaviors (i.e., drugs and alcohol, smoking, truancy) which increases the risk of disease and disability and an early death (CDC, 2022). The study also highlighted that almost two-thirds of the U.S. population reported at least one ACE, with one in five participants reporting five or more ACEs (Felitti et al., 1998). As ACE scores increase, so does biopsychosocial risk. Exposure to one ACE significantly increases the risk of exposure to another. ACEs do not occur in isolation, and there appear to be relationships between ACEs. For example, growing up in a family with substance use increases the risk of sexual abuse. With higher ACE scores come a host of physical, psychological, and sociological health risks including, but not limited to, addiction, heart disease, diabetes, stroke, autoimmune disorders, unintended pregnancy, early death, depression, PTSD, personality disorders, psychosis, suicide, anxiety, OCD, truancy, legal troubles, homelessness, unemployment, and learning disorders, to name a few (Kalmakis & Chandler, 2015; Monnat & Chandler, 2015; Petruccelli et al., 2019).

There is much to appreciate about the ACE Study. It was revolutionary for its time and remains impactful as longitudinal data continues to be collected. This study also used the term "adverse experiences" as opposed to "trauma" to capture a multitude of stressful experiences in childhood ("T" and "t") and examined their potential psychological and physical impact. The ACE Study identified the complex biopsychosocial risk factors throughout the life span in correlation with high ACE scores. Its message is simple. Toxic stress in childhood is incredibly damaging throughout the life span in many ways and can lead to an early death because a chronically dysregulated nervous system cannot thrive. In response to chronic stress, one attempts to adapt and cope, sometimes in unhealthy ways. Maladaptive coping skills and chronic physiological dysregulation increase the likelihood of social risk and disease, ultimately shortening one's lifespan.

The nervous system does not put a label on what is or is not traumatic. The nervous system reacts to stimuli and stressors with adaptive physiological defenses in the name of survival. When autonomic responses are activated, the system is not consciously appraising: "Is this traumatic? Let me get out the checklist." The nervous system unconsciously appraises a stimulus that it perceives to require a particular survival response. Survival physiology is evolutionary brilliance, and the response to the stressor itself is not problematic. Autonomic responses become problematic when they are maintained for long periods of time, or when they hijack us out of context.

To develop a thorough case conceptualization, don't only examine your client's trauma history. Examine their history of toxic stress and adverse experiences. Put your client's reaction to experiences before definitions and categories, assessing for stressful experiences that continue to impact and hijack them. Trauma speaks to the experience, and toxic stress sums up the physiological toll. Dr. Shapiro (2018) perhaps summed this up best when she defined trauma as any experience that has a lasting negative effect on an individual.

HOW TO TAME YOUR DRAGON

Imagine a fierce dragon and a dragon rider who has yet to learn how to ride their dragon. The rider attempts to ride their wild dragon without any knowledge and with little information to guide them. In the beginning, it's utter chaos and confusion. The dragon won't go where the rider wants it to, nor does it listen or obey commands. The rider knows neither how to steer nor direct the dragon. It's a mess. The dragon becomes unruly and out of control without the rider to tame and corral it. It swoops around scaring people, breathing fire, burning down villages, and leaving destruction and terror in its wake. With learning, patience, and practice though, the rider learns how to ride the dragon, and the dragon is tamed. They learn to trust and sense each other's moves and needs, and function in harmony. There is a sense of interdependency that develops, for together, they are stronger and more resilient to face challenges and adversities.

This dragon-rider dynamic represents the relationship between the cognitive brain (the rider) and the sensing autonomic nervous system (the dragon). We are challenged in this lifetime to learn to tame our autonomic nervous systems so that mind and body can experience harmony, health, and wellness. No one comes into this world with a regulated, tamed dragon (i.e., the autonomic nervous system), for no one is born knowing how to self soothe or regulate. Those are skills and resiliencies learned and acquired with practice. If we don't know how to tame our dragon life can be incredibly challenging. We feel volatile and scared; our relationships suffer; we find the world overwhelming, and our physiology is akin to a charred landscape. We may feel helpless because of our physiological experiences, collapsed into a state of despair and immobilization, or activated and overwhelmed with the fear and panic of fight and flight. Life is hard when we don't know how to interact with our autonomic responses, and suffering ensues.

Clients often present in therapy feeling out of control of their internal world. They feel powerless toward triggers, feelings, and sensations. They say things like, "I know I'm a good person, but I don't feel it," or "I just need to get over it—it was so long ago." They may report panic attacks "which come out of nowhere," getting stuck in depressive episodes for extensive periods of time, and many other chronic states of stress. These are the cries of a dragon and a rider at odds, of a dysregulated mind and body relationship due to adversity and toxic stress. So how do we learn to tame our dragons? By befriending our biology and learning the ways of the autonomic nervous system.

THE AUTONOMIC NERVOUS SYSTEM

How often have you been successful in helping clients talk or think their way out of feelings and sensations? Rarely, and in these cases, change is often temporary and doesn't stick. If we could think our way out of feelings and sensations, psychotherapists would quickly work their way out of a job. Emotions and sensations are not always rational or logical. While the mind says one thing, the heart and the body can say something very different. We often hear this from clients who say they consciously and cognitively know one thing, but their body doesn't align. "I need to get over her, but I just can't." "I know I need to stop using, but those urges get me every time." These are examples of a cognitive, rational brain that says one thing and a dysregulated autonomic nervous system that tells a different story. Therapy cannot solely focus on the cognitive components of experience (thoughts, facts, events), for doing so abandons the role of the autonomic nervous system as it relates to present-day feelings, sensations, and behaviors. The autonomic nervous system must be involved in therapy if we are to produce long-term, sustainable change for our clients.

The autonomic nervous system is a branch of the peripheral nervous system and the focus of Polyvagal Theory. It is autonomic, as it is automatic and unconscious. It is a sensing and perceiving system composed of two subsystems: the sympathetic nervous system and the parasympathetic nervous system. "Sympathetic" means "with emotions," as this branch of the nervous system mobilizes emotional and physiological responses (van der Kolk, 2014). "Parasympathetic" means "against emotions." This branch is where rest, relaxation, and immobilization responses lie. It is also within this branch that dissociation and depression live. The vagus nerve is part of the autonomic nervous system and plays a critical role in the expression of sympathetic and parasympathetic states.

Imagine that you are living thousands and thousands of years ago. While you're out gathering food one day, a tiger decides you might make a nice lunch and starts to chase you. Your autonomic nervous system mobilizes into flight, and you take off running as fast as you can. Unfortunately, you are no match for this predator, and it is quickly swinging at you with its claws and snapping with its sharp teeth. As your sympathetic nervous system is still activated, you pick up a tree branch and begin to fight back. Sadly, your efforts fail, and soon you are pinned down with tiger on top of you. The end appears to be near. You can no longer fight or flee, so your nervous system attempts to rescue you with the parasympathetic response of the dorsal branch, moving you into a state of collapse, numbness, and disconnection. This allows you to dissociate from the terrifying, painful experience.

Both branches of the autonomic nervous system, the sympathetic and parasympathetic, are necessary for surviving and thriving (Porges & Dana, 2018). These circuits of neurobiology are always on, always functioning, and always firing. Each system is needed throughout the day to execute the functions of human living. The sympathetic nervous system is needed to wake up and get going, exercise, move, make that deadline, give a speech or presentation, and get the list of chores done. Sympathetic mobilizes us to act or do. We need the parasympathetic nervous system to do the opposite—digest our food, sleep, lie still while getting a massage, and snuggle with a loved one or pet. The parasympathetic system stills or immobilizes us to rest. These systems support functioning, health, and wellness and provide incredible survival skills, such as fight, flight, freeze, and collapse. These circuits keep us alive, whether by allowing us to rest and digest in times of peace or helping us defend and survive in times of threat. However, when the survival defenses of these circuits get hijacked or stuck on overdrive, our mind and body suffer. Sustained activation of stress responses, quite plainly, is a very bad thing.

The sympathetic nervous system is responsible for mobilizing responses and behaviors. Activation of the sympathetic nervous system produces an increase in heart rate, blood pressure, and respiration (Brodal, 2016). Pupils dilate, and the digestive system constricts. The skin, arteries, and muscles also constrict and tighten. This system inhibits the bladder from voiding, represses salivation, and decreases intestinal motility (Presti, 2016). This circuit is also where anxiety, panic, rage, hypervigilance, rumination, physical irritability, and nightmares fall. Activation in this circuit in response to danger mobilizes fight and flight responses.

The parasympathetic nervous system consists of two branches, ventral and dorsal. The ventral system is where homeostasis lives and is a circuit that supports rest and rejuvenation. When the ventral circuit is leading the way, we feel relaxed, calm, and focused. We can concentrate and learn. Heart rate and respiration operate at a normal, healthy rate (Presti, 2016). The pupils constrict, and digestion and salivation are stimulated.

If the parasympathetic nervous system activates in response to danger or fear, the dorsal circuit produces an immobilization response. Dorsal is where depression, dissociation, derealization, catatonia, lethargy, and despair reside. The parasympathetic system, therefore, has two branches. One branch is the just-right zone of ventral, and the other is the collapse and immobilization zone of dorsal.

These three circuits (sympathetic, ventral, dorsal) collectively make up the autonomic nervous system. They produce automatic responses based on the appraisal of sensory information. The three circuits are always operating. They are not on or off. When one has more energy than another, physiology changes, along with emotions and behaviors. Because these circuits produce adaptive survival defenses, they are undeniably important to the counseling process.

The autonomic nervous system responds to sensory input, as well as input from memory networks. While a novel stimulus in our environment can trigger an autonomic response, a memory recalled can also trigger autonomic states.

TOXIC STRESS AND MEMORY

Psychotherapy is completely reliant on memory. Therapists focus on client memory and correlated symptoms in the counseling process. Whether sharing the events of their day, their childhood history, or specific symptoms or experiences, therapy revolves around client memory.

Memories are physically stored bits of data about our life, stored in the brain. They inform our perception of ourselves, others, and the world and provide us with knowledge and context (Shapiro, 2018). No one is a blank slate, for our memories inform every facet of our lived experience. Memories consist of components, or data points, which may include images, sounds, smells, sensations, feelings, thoughts, and beliefs (Shapiro, 2018). Some experiences are committed to long-term memory, though many of our day-to-day experiences are forgotten. Whether or not we create an emotional long-term memory for an event is dependent on how personal and emotional the event is to us (van der Kolk, 2014).

When a memory is recalled, it is remembered along with its stored components and associations. For example, if you think of cut grass, you can probably get a whiff of that associated smell because it's part of a memory. Or if you think about a deeply happy memory, you can probably feel some of those feelings and sensations right now because they are stored in a memory. We think our memories, and we feel our memories.

Toxic stress, or trauma, can disrupt the normal storage and integration processes of memory (Cozolino, 2017; van der Kolk, 2014). Stress responses produce hormonal changes as part of the body's hardwired survival response. Moderate levels of stress hormones can help create a memory imprint (McIntyre et al., 2012; van der Kolk, 2014). However, when the nervous system is overwhelmed with fear and terror, the system surpasses a threshold, and memory integration, along with learning, is negatively impacted (Chamberlin, 2019; Cozolino, 2017). This is because of the effect that toxic stress has on the limbic system and neocortex, which are both necessary structures for adaptive memory storage and integration.

The limbic system is made up of several important brain structures that influence emotions and survival responses (Brodal, 2016). This system is known as the emotional brain due to its role in regulating and processing emotions and responding to cues of danger. Two very important structures of the limbic system include the amygdala and the hippocampus. The amygdala and hippocampus are involved in the storage and creation of emotional memories, or memories that elicit emotional responses of the autonomic nervous system (Cozolino, 2017).

The amygdala is the smoke detector of the brain, as it is tasked with assessing danger and activating an alarm response in times of threat (Brodal, 2016; Cozolino, 2017). This structure rapidly assesses stimuli and triggers an autonomic response based on its appraisal. The amygdala functions without conscious thought and therefore works faster than the logical, rational, intellectual cortex. After all, thinking time is surviving time. If you had to spend time consciously evaluating the danger or safety of a stimulus, it might be too late to react by the time you've reached a conclusion.

The amygdala activates an autonomic response by stimulating a nerve that runs to the adrenal glands, producing epinephrine and norepinephrine (Bergmann, 2020). The stimulation of these hormones activates adaptive responses of the autonomic nervous system and causes physiological changes in the body to protect and defend. The survival response is encoded within the memory and can be reactivated and relived in response to a reminder or trigger.

The hippocampus is linked to the amygdala and maintains a role in the processes of learning and memory (Brodal, 2016). The hippocampus is responsible for encoding memories, integrating emotions, and connecting cognitive information from the neocortex to the limbic system (Badenoch, 2008; Bergmann, 2020). It is this structure that helps us to consciously appraise a stimulus beyond the rapid and reactive appraisal that happens in the amygdala. A heightened amygdala response blocks the hippocampal pathway, which interferes with the encoding of the experience (Cozolino, 2017). This leads to the adverse experience being stored without perceptual context or semantic representation (Bergmann, 2020). This impairs integration and results in fragmented memories with strong sensorimotor components.

The neocortex is also important in the discussion of trauma memories, as this section of the brain makes logic, consciousness, and cognition possible. Structures of the neocortex interpret sight, smell, taste, sound, and somatic sensations. The neocortex is the part of the brain that makes us human, allowing us to think about our thoughts and feelings, plan our day, and problem solve with logic and reasoning.

The prefrontal cortex, a specific area of the neocortex, processes emotions and is the seat of goal-directed behavior (Brodal, 2016). It is also the inhibition center of the brain (Cozolino, 2017). This structure allows us to regulate emotions, behaviors, and impulses. Cortical processes let us consciously choose a response and suppress unwanted behaviors (Brodal, 2016), which is important for establishing healthy relationships, accomplishing tasks, and living an overall functional life. The "damper switch" for the amygdala is also located in this area of the brain, which dampens our emotional impulses and autonomic reactions (Bergmann, 2020). When the nervous system is overwhelmed in response to a trigger or threat, these functions are impaired. The whole system breaks down, and the brain can't access the information it needs to internally resolve the distress, manage impulses, and moderate autonomic activation (Chamberlin, 2019).

As an example of these integrated processes, imagine being out on a walk one day, and you see a snake slither across the path in front of you. Your amygdala triggers a startle response, causing you to jump back quickly and reactively from the perceived danger. But then you recognize what kind of snake it is. Based on your knowledge of snakes in the area, you remember that this specific snake is not poisonous. While you don't care for snakes, you know this one is not dangerous. You calm down, watch it slither away, and move on with your day. This ability to consciously assess the threat based on your knowledge, and then dampen the automatic fear response, is made possible via cortico-hippocampal processes. The capacity to exchange information between structures of your brain is extremely important to be able to incorporate knowledge and context to dampen autonomic defenses triggered by the amygdala.

When the amygdala sounds the alarm in response to danger, cortico-hippocampal functioning and memory storage can be negatively impacted. The high arousal response produced in the amygdala impairs the cortex and hippocampus from reality testing (e.g., is that snake poisonous?), adding context (no, I have learned that snake is not poisonous), and dampening the emotional response (chill, it's not dangerous). A high arousal response can lead to a memory being stored in sensory fragments with strong emotional imprints (van der Kolk, 2014). Prime examples of these charged fragments are evident in the common trauma symptoms of flashbacks, panic attacks, negative self-talk, and nightmares. These sensory fragments are maladaptively stored, which leads to present-day triggers activating the stored trauma memory, and reinforcing the maladaptive memory network (Shapiro, 2018).

The limbic system has a greater influence on autonomic responses than the cortex, which is why it's nearly impossible to think your way out of triggers and symptoms (Arnsten et al., 2015). Survival biology is powerful, evoking physiological changes that bypass logical thought in response to perceived danger. The perception of threat or danger sets off a cascade of neurochemicals that activate autonomic responses. The release of adrenaline mobilizes the sympathetic responses of fight and flight, while the release of acetylcholine leads to the dorsal response of immobilization. The survival response can define the memory, as sympathetic or dorsal responses are stored within the memory network. These processes happen without conscious awareness and faster than the logical, rational neocortex can process. When we move into a survival state, activity in the prefrontal cortex diminishes as resources and energy are channeled to areas of the body necessary for survival (van der Kolk, 2014).

WHY PV-EMDR?

Why is polyvagal-informed EMDR important and beneficial in our work with clients? Because trauma responses are defined by maladaptive memory storage and hijacked autonomic responses. The brain and the autonomic nervous system are the systems under duress for the majority of those who present for counseling, and certainly for those we provide trauma treatment to. Therefore, we need an integrated model that incorporates ways to work with both systems.

Memory networks and the autonomic nervous system have an interdependent, bidirectional relationship. Memories influence the autonomic nervous system, and that system influences memory storage. Hardwired survival responses are needed and adaptive. But too much overwhelm in the system interferes with memory storage, which produces overwhelm in response to triggers, which activates the memory and causes more overwhelm, and on and on the cycle goes.

The central and autonomic nervous systems do not function in silos. These systems are constantly engaged in a dynamic feedback loop, and the processes in one influence the processes in the other. The autonomic nervous system influences the central nervous system, and the central nervous system influences the autonomic nervous system as information flows from mind to body, and body to mind. They are forever engaged in a feedback loop.

Many leading theories and therapies offer effective and powerful interventions targeting autonomic responses or the storage of traumatic memory. But few therapies offer the tools to work with both. Working with autonomic states is a goal of therapies that focus on coping skills and regulation tools. Working with the storage of memory is the goal of therapies that work with the adverse, traumatic experience itself, often through narrative means or memory activation. Both approaches are necessary to support the nervous system to integrate an experience and resolve the autonomic hijacking that clients otherwise feel powerless to stop.

Polyvagal Theory offers insights and pathways to work with the autonomic distress that toxic stress can leave behind in its wake. EMDR offers insights and pathways for reprocessing maladaptively stored memories, which hijack the autonomic nervous system. Combined, these theoretical models offer a comprehensive approach to healing and integrating adverse experiences and resolving trauma. We cannot treat only the autonomic nervous system, nor only the memories. We must work with both if we are to support clients to achieve their goals of health and wellness, and truly heal. Neuroscience teaches us this. The integration of these models supports case conceptualization, treatment planning, and intervention. Both models focus on the nervous system, associated symptoms, and health and wellness as the therapeutic outcome. PV-EMDR is a comprehensive framework for a comprehensive, neuro-informed therapeutic approach.

Chapter 3

POLYVAGAL THEORY

I begin this chapter with a deep, humble bow to Stephen Porges and Deb Dana. Dr. Porges's dedication to his research over many years has culminated in what we know today as Polyvagal Theory. Deb Dana has led the way in translating Porges's research into clinical practice. Dr. Porges is the original discoverer and researcher of Polyvagal Theory, and Deb Dana the clinical pioneer. Porges and Dana have offered those of us in the mental health field new, better, smarter ways of doing our jobs and helping people heal.

Polyvagal Theory emerged from Porges's research, which began in 1969 (Porges, 2011). His work started with an interest in heart rate variability and his belief that understanding neurophysiology would support the counseling relationship (Porges, 2011). His research on heart rate variability uncovered the influential role of the vagus nerve on autonomic responses. The vagus nerve influences heart rate and therefore sympathetic arousal. It is the physical mechanism behind the clinical terms "hyperarousal" and "hypoarousal," and contributes to the window of tolerance. Porges's theory describes the adaptive defenses of the nervous system in response to appraised cues of danger or safety. The theory describes the "bidirectional communication between the brain and the visceral organs represented in the autonomic nervous system" (Porges, 2021b, p. xvii).

Polyvagal Theory is like a love letter to the autonomic nervous system. It highlights the protective predisposition of the autonomic branch, as its number one priority is our safety and well-being. The theory embraces the evolution of the nervous system as it has learned, over millions of years, incredibly adaptive and clever ways to survive and thrive. If the therapist recognizes the nervous system's responses as attempts to help, there is opportunity to reframe pathology and befriend biology. Instead of focusing on labels and diagnostic categories, we can learn to recognize and respect the nervous system's defensive accommodation strategies to cope and survive. We can acknowledge that autonomic processes are the result of activated neurological circuits and functions of our biology. This path is one of compassionate curiosity for the nervous system and your client's symptoms.

KEY PRINCIPLES OF POLYVAGAL THEORY

Polyvagal Theory is robust, with multiple principles and implications based on thousands of peer-reviewed and academic sources. Here are some of the fundamental principles of Polyvagal Theory (Porges, 2011):

- *Three circuits:* The autonomic nervous system is composed of three circuits: the dorsal vagal circuit, the sympathetic nervous system, and the ventral vagal circuit.
- *Evolution:* Evolution is the reason for these three circuits. Because humans evolved, we have a sophisticated nervous system that has developed over millions of years.
- *Hierarchy:* The three circuits have an evolutionary hierarchy. The autonomic circuits function in a specific order in response to cues of danger and safety.
- *Neuroception:* Neuroception is the body's internal home surveillance system. Defined by Porges, "neuroception" means perception without awareness and is a process of the autonomic nervous system. It is the process by which the nervous system persistently and unconsciously scans for cues of danger and safety.
- *The social engagement system:* Humans are social creatures, with a biological imperative to connect and form healthy social bonds. The social engagement system is innervated by the vagus nerve and represents a unique biological language for connection.

Let's dive into these core principles further and explore their relevance in your work. Grab some popcorn and a highlighter and get ready to geek out on neuroscience.

THE VAGUS NERVE

The vagus nerve is the 10th cranial nerve. It mediates responses of the parasympathetic and sympathetic nervous systems and acts as a cardiac pacemaker influencing heart rate (Porges, 2011). The vagus nerve is a truly incredible, multifaceted nerve. The vagus is the neurological mechanism underlying the experience of feeling safe and plays a critical role in responding to fear and danger. When we perceive threat or danger, this nerve activates physiological responses of hyper- or hypoarousal, as traditionally referred to in the counseling field. Hyperarousal responses are the physiological effects of the sympathetic nervous system, while hypoarousal responses are the physiological effects of the dorsal vagus.

The vagus nerve is the longest of the 12 cranial nerves. "Vagus" means "vagabond" or "wanderer," to capture this nerve's many destinations and functions. I think of this nerve as the wanderlust nerve, because it wanders to so many areas of the body. The vagus nerve innervates muscles of the face, eyes, inner ear, viscera around the abdominal organs, heart, and lungs. It is a bundle of afferent and efferent nerves. Afferent nerves, or sensory nerves, carry information from the body to the central nervous system. Efferent nerves carry signals from the brain to the body. Eighty percent of the vagus nerve is composed of afferent fibers, and 20% is efferent (Porges, 2011). Thus, the vagus is the body-to-brain and brain-to-body connection.

The vagus consists of a dorsal (backside) vagus and a ventral (front side) vagus. These two branches of the vagus make up the parasympathetic nervous system. The sympathetic nervous system is the other branch of the autonomic nervous system, composed of nerves originating from the lumbar and thoracic spine (Brodal, 2016). The sympathetic nervous system is influenced by the vagus nerve and its influence on heart rate. These three circuits (dorsal vagus, ventral vagus, and the sympathetic nervous system) collectively make up the autonomic nervous system. How these three circuits respond to cues of danger or safety, via the vagus nerve, is the focus of Polyvagal Theory.

THREE CIRCUITS

As we've reviewed, the autonomic nervous system consists of the parasympathetic and sympathetic nervous system. The parasympathetic nervous system is composed of the two branches of the vagus, which are dorsal and ventral. A single branch of nerves represents the sympathetic nervous system. These three circuits (dorsal vagus, ventral vagus, sympathetic) compose the autonomic nervous system.

The dorsal vagal circuit is the most primitive, sharing ancestral evolutionary lines with reptiles (Porges, 1995). The dorsal vagus is unmyelinated (i.e., unprotected by a myelin sheath) and is over five hundred million years old (Porges, 2011). It originates from the dorsal motor nucleus of the vagus (Porges, 2011). For comparison and context, consider this part of the nervous system to cause hypoarousal, as you have learned in your professional career. When this circuit is recruited in response to fear and danger, it activates physiological processes of immobilization, increasing energy conservation and preparing the organism for potential death or severe harm.

When the dorsal vagal pathway is leading the way, digestion and the immune system are depressed, and the body moves to conserve and store energy and calories. Heart rate and breathing slow, and a decrease in oxygen to the brain impairs cognitive functions. Acetylcholine and stress endorphins enter the bloodstream, producing numbness and disconnection. There is a loss of muscle tone in the face, resulting in flat facial expression and vocal tone lacking in prosody.

Psychological responses produced by the dorsal vagal circuit include dissociation, depression, depersonalization, and derealization. We may experience a loss of interest in activities and collapse into isolation. Anhedonia, hopelessness, powerlessness, and disconnection exist in this circuit. The capacity to orient to the present is diminished, along with the ability to concentrate, learn, and engage with others.

In the field of psychotherapy, we have traditionally used the term "freeze" to describe a hypoarousal state. However, this is not entirely accurate when we examine the physiological mechanisms of hypoarousal and freeze. Freeze is not a pure hypoarousal, dorsal vagal function. Freezing is much more complex than just immobilizing. Freeze responses also have a great deal of tension, rigidity, and mobilizing energy mixed into them. To freeze is to be immobilized with tension and energy, not to faint or pass out. Therefore, freeze is a mixture of dorsal vagal and sympathetic energy rather than a pure hypoarousal response. We will discuss the mixed state of freeze in sections to come. For now, recognize that a dorsal response is one of immobilization and not purely freeze.

The next circuit to develop along the lines of evolution was the sympathetic nervous system, which is approximately four hundred million years old (Porges, 2011). This branch of the nervous system emerges from the spinal cord and is a system of mobilization. The sympathetic circuit can be compared to hyperarousal, for this is where fight and flight responses are activated. When recruited in response to fear and danger, this system cues an influx of energy to mobilize to safety.

Physiological changes that accompany this circuit are those that come along with an influx of energy, including increased heart rate, blood pressure, and respiration. A flood of adrenalin increases the flow of oxygen and blood to vital organs and extremities needed to fight or flee, along with increased capacity for blood clotting. The digestive and immune systems are depressed, and the sensation of hunger dissipates, along with the production of saliva, which causes dry mouth. We may have an urgency to void bowels or bladder as the body moves resources to quickly burn calories and energy.

Psychological responses correlated with this circuit in response to fear and danger include anxiety, overwhelm, rage, fear, panic, racing and intrusive thoughts, and hypervigilance. We may have difficulties sleeping and experience various forms of reliving through flashbacks or nightmares. We experience diminished abilities to orient to the present, focus, learn, and concentrate as attention shifts to the stressor at hand. These physiological changes also impact the capacity to socially engage and form relationships.

The most recent circuit to evolve is the ventral vagus, which is also a part of the parasympathetic nervous system. The ventral vagus is myelinated, coated in a protective protein sheath (Porges, 2011). Myelin allows nerves to transmit signals quickly and efficiently. The ventral vagus developed around two hundred million years ago and originates from the nucleus ambiguus, which innervates the soft palate, larynx, esophagus, and heart (Kiernan et al., 2013). This circuit supports human evolution, as the ventral vagus allows mammals to socially bond and cooperate. This circuit is the just-right zone where homeostasis, health, and wellness live, and is a component of the window of tolerance. When a client is within their window of tolerance, the ventral circuit is leading the way.

Physiologically, the ventral vagus allows systems to function as they should at rest. The digestive and immune systems function as they should, doing their jobs of digesting and protecting from illness. Heart rate is normal, along with respiration and blood pressure. Blood is oxygenated and flowing to all parts of our bodies.

Similarly, psychological faculties are in their optimal zone in the ventral circuit. We are grounded, present, curious, and able to learn in this circuit. We can form relationships and engage socially with others in ventral. We can tolerate our lives and stressors, and experience a sense of peace and calm.

These three circuits make up the autonomic nervous system and are always on and always functioning. Humans need these three circuits to live an evolved, social, functional life. All these states are good. However, when recruited in response to danger and fear, they can take on different flavors as they activate millions of years of survival physiology in efforts to keep us safe and alive. The autonomic nervous system allows us to survive, form social bonds, and thrive. The system responds to cues of danger and safety by giving more energy to the circuit it appraises is needed in the moment, allowing the survival functions of that circuit to take over. The vagus nerve mediates this process.

THE AUTONOMIC HIERARCHY

Evolution is the reason there are three autonomic circuits. The oldest or most primitive is the dorsal vagus, followed by the sympathetic nervous system, and finally, the most evolved being the ventral vagus (Porges, 2011). These circuits offer an array of survival tactics and opportunities for health and wellness. But first, let us explore the adaptive nature of these three circuits.

When the ventral vagus is leading the way, we thrive. This circuit's physiological and psychological properties support health, wellness, and optimal functioning. The ventral vagus supports connection, which is important for social bonds and collaborative relationships. We can most easily access ventral when our external and internal worlds are free of threats and danger, allowing us to be in an optimal zone of arousal. Let's say something scary happens, and a defensive state is triggered as an adaptive response. Autonomic states move us down the evolutionary hierarchy, away from ventral toward the sympathetic nervous system as the first line of defense. Consider the wisdom of the sympathetic system being the first survival response, in that you are most likely to survive a threat if you can fight or flee. As the sympathetic circuit takes over, physiology shifts away from feeling safe and connected to defensive mobilization. The body prepares with an influx of energy and resources to fight off a predator or flee from threat. If the body cannot fight or flee, or if those tactics prove futile, the lowest circuit of the hierarchy takes over. With dorsal leading the way, the nervous system shifts to immobilization, numbness, and collapse. After all, if you cannot fight or flee, numbing out and shutting down are incredible survival tools. The dorsal vagal circuit is the pathway of last resort. In this circuit, the body stores resources, conserves energy to protect and defend, and prepares for potential death.

MIXED STATES

We have defined the three circuits of the autonomic nervous system and described each circuit's corresponding responses. However, these states don't exist in separate blocks, nor are they "on" or "off." Each circuit is always active and functioning, and therefore you are always experiencing each circuit to some degree. What's important to assess in clients is which circuit has the most energy and is most activated. Exploring which circuits are leading the way illuminates the neurophysiological correlates of symptoms and clinical complaints. Most people spend their days moving up and down the autonomic hierarchy in response to daily life cycles, stressors, and demands. The circuits are not absolute or mutually exclusive, with most of us spending most of our time in mixed states. Consider mixed states to be blends or mixes of the three autonomic circuits.

To conceptualize mixed states, I like to use the analogy of the primary colors. The three primary colors are red, blue, and yellow. Combining colors creates new colors. For example, mixing red and yellow makes orange, and blue and red make purple. Combined autonomic states provide additional physiological states, as we experience the protective and adaptive effects of their mixed qualities.

Dorsal Vagal + Ventral Vagal = Immobilized With Safety; Stillness

This mixed state is defined by the immobilization qualities of dorsal, though in the absence of fear. The presence of ventral offers connection to safety. This state allows one to be still while feeling safe. Stillness could be experienced when snuggling with a pet or loved one, getting a massage, or after meditation. This state is quiet, peaceful, still, and safe.

Dorsal Vagal + Sympathetic Nervous System = Mobilized and Immobilized With Fear; Freeze

This mixed state produces the freeze response. An immobilization response is mixed with a mobilization response, in the presence of fear or terror. The result is an inability to move or speak, while also feeling tension, constriction, and urgency to mobilize.

Sympathetic Nervous System + Ventral Vagal = Mobilized With Safety; Play and Performance

This mixed state is defined by the mobilizing qualities of sympathetic, though in the absence of fear. The presence of ventral offers connection to safety. This state may be experienced in exercise, play, or performance situations.

Exploring mixed states paints the picture of a dynamic nervous system. Mixed states add a survival response (freeze) and offer the opportunity for play and stillness. The nervous system is artful in its blending of energies that contribute to a rich and dynamic life.

THE VAGAL BRAKE AND VAGAL TONE

The vagus nerve acts as a pacemaker, influencing cardiac output (Porges, 2011). The specific mechanism of the vagus nerve that influences cardiac output is known as the vagal brake, a mechanism of the ventral vagus. The vagal brake influences sympathetic and parasympathetic energy by increasing or decreasing heart rate. When the vagal brake engages, heart rate slows, and the sympathetic circuit dampens. Conversely, heart rate accelerates, and the sympathetic circuit engages when the vagal brake releases. Without the vagal brake, the heart would beat dangerously fast on a regular basis.

Dana (2018) uses a bicycle analogy to conceptualize the vagal brake. Imagine riding down a hill on a bicycle. As you apply the brakes the speed slows, and as you release the brakes the speed increases. Similarly, when the vagal brake engages heart rate slows, and when it is released heart rate increases. One could also use the analogy of a dam of water, with the flow of water increasing as the dam opens, and the flow of water decreasing as it closes. When the vagal brake works efficiently and flexibly, we can smoothly transition between states in the nervous system. Such flexibility contributes to well-being. If the vagal

Window of Tolerance	**Safe & Connected** **Parasympathetic Ventral Vagus**
Psychological Responses	Physiological Responses
In the present moment; calm and regulated; managing stressors effectively; able to tolerate stress and regulate emotion; able to self-soothe; comfort zone, things just "feel right"; able to be curious and engaged; able to connect with others	Digestion and immune system are functioning; engagement in eye contact; heart rate and blood pressure regulated; circulation in non-vital organs; normal breathing
Hyper-Arousal	**Mobilize/Fight Or Flight** **Sympathetic Nervous System**
Psychological Responses	Physiological Responses
Increase of energy; urge to fight or flee; overwhelm; anger and rage; fear; panic; busy mind; obsessive thinking; distracted; difficulty concentrating; diminished ability to connect and engage with others	Increased heart rate and blood pressure; adrenaline secretion; increased flow of oxygen and blood to vital organs; decreased blood low to non-vital organs; increased capacity for blood clotting; decrease in digestion and production of saliva; depressed immune system; increased breathing; restlessness; muscle tension
Hypo-Arousal	**Immobilize/Collapse** **Parasympathetic Dorsal Vagus**
Psychological Responses	Physiological Responses
Loss of energy; disorientation; derealization; depersonalization; depression; numbness; loss of interest in activities; isolation; helplessness and hopelessness; shut down; loss of orientation; flat emotion; diminished capacity to engage with others; despair; disconnection to self and others; blank mind	Immobilization; preparing for death; increase in pain-reducing endorphins; numbness; depressed heart rate and blood pressure; slowed breathing; fatigue; depressed immune response; diminished eye contact with others; diminished muscle tone and facial expression; increase in storage of fuel

Figure 3.1: Autonomic Nervous System Graphic. Adapted from TRAUMA AND THE BODY: A SENSORIMOTOR APPROACH TO PSYCHOTHERAPY by Pat Ogden, Kenkuni Minton, Clare Pain. Copyright © 2006 by Pat Ogden. Copyright © 2006 by W. W. Norton & Company, Inc. Used by permission of W. W. Norton & Company, Inc.
Adapted from POLYVAGAL FLIP CHART: UNDERSTANDING THE SCIENCE OF SAFETY by Deb Dana. Copyright © 2020 by Deborah A. Dana. Used by permission of W. W. Norton & Company, Inc.

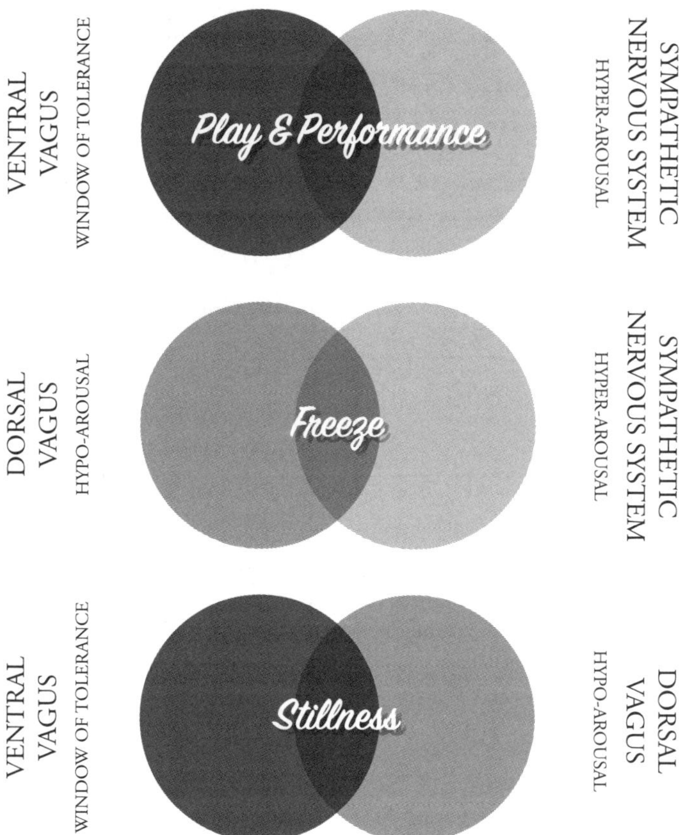

Figure 3.2: Mixed States Graphic. Adapted from POLYVAGAL FLIP CHART: UNDERSTANDING THE SCIENCE OF SAFETY by Deb Dana. Copyright © 2020 by Deborah A. Dana. Used by permission of W. W. Norton & Company, Inc.

brake lacks flexibility, life can be quite challenging. Returning to the analogies provided, we can get stuck in states of going too fast or too slow or having too much or too little energy, which can leave us feeling out of control and unable to manage or cope.

You can try an at-home experiment to experience the vagal brake. First, locate your carotid pulse on the side of the neck. Push your three middle fingers gently against the outer edge of either side of your windpipe to find your pulse. If you have a stethoscope or a heart rate monitor, even better. Take a long breath in, and a long breath out. Repeat this several times and observe your heart rate. What do you notice happens to your heart rate as you breathe in and out?

What should happen is that your heart rate accelerates on the inhalation and slows on the exhalation. That's your vagal brake at work. The vagal brake produces the acceleration and deceleration of heart rate in response to breath. On the inhale, the vagal brake disengages, resulting in an increase in heart rate and engagement of sympathetic energy. On the exhale, the vagal brake engages, dampening heart rate and decreasing sympathetic energy. Stress, illness, and physiological factors can influence the functioning of the vagal brake, and this exercise may not produce the same effects for everyone. If your heart rate did not respond this way, you might discuss this at your next doctor's appointment.

A common theme of talk therapy is working with client dysregulation by teaching and using skills that influence the vagal brake. Using skills to moderate arousal contributes to neural integration via activation of emotional and cognitive content, alongside techniques that dampen stress responses in a manageable way. Whether through breathing, journaling, mindfulness or movement, most therapies invite opportunities to exercise the vagal brake. Coping and self-soothing strategies help clients learn to flexibly work their vagal brake, decreasing and increasing arousal in response to stressors and life demands.

The vagal brake exists within everyone. Because humans are resilient beings and neurons have neuroplasticity, we can learn to influence the brake in ways that support health and wellness. The more skillful we become at engaging and dampening the vagal brake, the more health and wellness we have. Learning to engage the vagal brake requires the use of skills that regulate physiology and increase connection to the ventral circuit. When you feel overwhelmed and begin to practice a breathing technique, you are exercising your vagal brake. When you feel flat or shut down and decide to go for a walk, you exercise the vagal brake. When you feel lonely and turn to play with a pet, you are exercising the vagal brake. We make choices, every day, all day, which influence our neurobiology for better or worse. Everyone has the innate capacity to influence their nervous system in pursuit of peace and wellness. Becoming skillful at this takes time and practice.

Vagal tone is an important concept related to the vagal brake. In simple terms, vagal tone is how efficient the vagus nerve is at influencing cardiac rhythm over a period time (Laborde et al., 2017). Vagal tone is a marker of health and wellness, as it is an indicator of how efficient the vagal brake is. High vagal tone is associated with emotion regulation and adaptive coping (Park & Thayer, 2014). Conversely, low vagal tone is associated with difficulties in emotion regulation, poor interpersonal skills, and psychological and physical suffering (Park & Thayer, 2014; Porges, 2011).

Vagal tone is measured through heart rate variability, which is a way to measure the variation in time between heartbeats. The ideal heart rate is not steady, even-keeled 24/7. Instead, heart rate needs to vary in response to day-to-day demands and tasks of living. For example, ideally heart rate increases when you're on a brisk walk and decreases when you're going to bed. If that doesn't happen, these daily activities become challenging. High vagal tone is indicative of a nervous system that can increase and decrease heart rate throughout the day in response to demands and biological rhythms. This is made possible with a flexible vagal brake.

Consider your clients who struggle with emotion regulation and distress tolerance. How efficient is their nervous system at applying the vagal brake when they feel overactivated, anxious, fearful, or worked up? Can they disengage the vagal brake when they need more energy to meet a demand like getting out of bed, working out, or finding motivation to get through the day? Likewise, how efficient are you, the therapist, at engaging and disengaging your vagal brake as you meet the demands of your day-to-day? What might the implications be for your own relationships, your mood, and your clinical work? These concepts are applicable to everyone, and the best way to learn them is to get curious about your own nervous system and lived experience.

Vagal tone starts with attachment and coregulation in childhood. We learn to exercise the vagal brake and regulate autonomic states from someone teaching us skills. No one enters life with an instruction manual that explains the most efficient skills for coping and managing stress. We aren't born hardwired to self-soothe and cope. Instead, we learn how to manage stress and our autonomic reactions through a caregiver who teaches us. Coregulation paves the way to self-regulation (Dana, 2018). This is also a staple of the therapeutic process, as we help clients learn to work with triggers and develop coping skills. The therapeutic process revolves around learning to flexibly maneuver between autonomic states and integrate experiences in the process.

There are organic, biological deficits that can influence vagal tone, such as genetics, organic deficits, and temperament. These physiological limitations are hard to influence within the clinical space. However, most causal factors that negatively influence vagal tone respond positively to clinical intervention. The nervous system is resilient and adaptive, and neuroplasticity allows opportunities to gain experience of new ways to manage stress and regulate autonomic responses. The nervous system is adaptive and is always transforming. The counseling space can serve as a rich learning environment for clients to receive consistent, dependable coregulation and to exercise their vagal brake. With enough time and practice, skills practiced in coregulation transmute to the practice of self-regulation, which in turn build vagal tone and increase autonomic resiliency.

Chapter 4
SAFE AND CONNECTED

Humans are social creatures. We are wired to connect and form social bonds. Connecting and forming social bonds is a biological imperative that contributes to human survival and evolution. Without this disposition to attach, humans would be able to easily abandon each other without remorse, making it impossible to form functional family units or societies. Breakups wouldn't be a visceral experience; loneliness wouldn't be a problem; we'd abandon our children when we got frustrated and burned out on parenting; we wouldn't date again after having our hearts broken. The biological drive to bond consistently urges us toward connection, because of the evolution of the autonomic nervous system and the vagus nerve.

Relationships are not simply social constructs; they are products of physiology. Incredible neurological processes occur between synapses and neurons when we bond and connect. It is biological alchemy. The most crucial ingredient on the list for the wondrous human experience of connection is safety. Without safety, our capacity for bonding and connection is limited. Safety is a requirement for healthy relationships.

The autonomic nervous system is a sensing system, always sensing and assessing stimuli it encounters. It scans for cues of danger and safety without our conscious awareness. Based on the unconscious appraisal of cues, autonomic responses of dorsal, sympathetic, or ventral circuits are activated. So how does the nervous system determine who or what is and isn't safe? What data is it reviewing to sound the alarm or cue the calm? It all starts with something called neuroception.

NEUROCEPTION: THE BODY'S HOME SURVEILLANCE SYSTEM

Your nervous system's number one priority is survival. This fact is true for every human. Your nervous system is always working in your favor, with the goal of keeping you alive. The autonomic nervous system's job is to survive in times of danger and thrive in times of safety (Dana, 2018). The system appraises danger and safety through a process Porges terms "neuroception" (Porges, 2011). Neuroception is a function of the autonomic nervous system, by which it scans the environment for cues of safety or danger. As defined by Porges, neuroception is perception without awareness, as this neurophysiological process happens without our conscious awareness.

Picture a beautiful house full of beautiful, expensive things. To keep the house and all the belongings safe, a state-of-the-art security system is installed to scan the internal and external perimeters. The security system is up and running 24/7, always on, and always scanning for threats. A security system like this allows the owner to go about their day without having to consciously assess and reassess the safety of the home. The owner can trust that if a threat is detected, an alarm will sound and the system will activate an automated response.

The body has a mechanism similar to this home surveillance system, called neuroception. Like the home security system, neuroception constantly monitors for safety and assesses for danger without our conscious awareness. That is, you don't have to constantly check on your safety throughout the day. If you had to always be on conscious safety patrol, it would be challenging to go about day-to-day tasks, and forming relationships would be nearly impossible because you would be constantly distracted. Neuroception unconsciously scans your environment, alerting you when it perceives a cue of danger by triggering an autonomic response. The response may be to mobilize through sympathetic energy or immobilize with dorsal energy. When enough cues of safety and security are present, we can access the ventral circuit, where we thrive and connect.

There are three environments that neuroception continuously, unconsciously scans: within, without, and in-between. "Within" encompasses your internal world; "without" encompasses your external world; and "in between" pertains to those you are in contact with. Neuroception is an automatic and wordless process, and the autonomic state it elicits shapes our behavior and response (Dana, 2018).

Neuroception scans within the body for cues of danger or safety, including hunger and thirst, energy, physical pain or discomfort, or signs of sickness. As an example, think about what it's like when you get sick. We often identify warning signs that trigger the awareness that we may be coming down with something before the sickness really hits us. We may notice that our throat feels scratchy, our energy feels off, our stomach feels crampy. This awareness is provided by neuroception catching your attention, saying, "Something's not right here." You probably use that information to your advantage and change your behavior to align with your awareness. That may include getting extra rest, taking medication, drinking extra fluids, or going to the doctor.

Neuroception also scans "without," which is your external environment. Are you safe in your physical space and environment, or are there cues of danger? How's the light in this space? Where's the exit? Is this space cluttered or clean, and what value does your system put on that? Are there scary sounds? Is anything on fire or exploding? Are there any cues that signal safety, such as access to the door or a sleeping pet at your feet? The cues in your environment inform neuroception, and the appraisal of those cues elicits autonomic responses.

Neuroception also scans in between, which is the interpersonal space. Is that person a threat, or are they safe? Does their eye contact communicate they are friend or foe? Does their tone of voice make you feel at ease or suspicious? What do their body posture and facial expressions communicate? How does this person make you feel? Think about a time when you felt an internal sense of unease or dislike for someone, but you couldn't consciously put your finger on why. Or think of a person who makes you feel calmer just being around. Those responses are autonomic states activated based on the appraisal of neuroception. The saying about "feeling someone out" captures this process, along with the tendency to rely on the felt sense you experience with another.

Scanning Neuroception Exercise

Let's practice together and bring the passive process of neuroception into active awareness. Begin by checking in with what you notice inside, scanning within. What do you perceive within your physical body? What cues of danger or alarm can you identify? What cues of safety or security do you notice? Examples could be feelings, sensations, pain, hunger, thirst, and energy. As you become aware of your internal world, be empowered to make any changes that feel appealing to you. For example, if you notice you are thirsty, perhaps you choose to get some water. Or if you are cold, perhaps you grab a blanket.

Move on to scanning without. What are you aware of in your surrounding environment that sends cues of danger or safety? Notice what you see, hear, smell, and perceive in your external surroundings and the value your system assigns to that information. As your awareness grows, take a moment to make any changes that feel appealing, such as turning on a lamp for light or straightening a crooked picture on the wall.

Finally, consider the space in between and bring to mind a recent social interaction you had that you can think of clearly. Bring the experience to mind and notice how that interaction makes you feel now. Explore the in-between cues that were present, such as eye contact, tone of voice, gestures, prosody, intonation, and body language. Perhaps you can recall how a person's eye contact sent cues of safety and security or how a person's tone of voice communicated a cue of danger and alarm. Get curious about the physiological cues that made that a pleasant or unpleasant interaction. What was your felt sense of that person? How did they make your nervous system feel?

Were you aware of all this information before taking a moment to make neuroception conscious? Did anything change in your experience as you became aware of these cues? Did you notice anything that surprised you? Because neuroception is an unconscious process, there will always be data that is just below our conscious awareness informing our states. But as we can bring the unconscious to conscious awareness, we can then make changes and intentionally manage our responses.

The body's internal home surveillance system, neuroception, is truly amazing. This process allows you to move through your day and focus on tasks such as conversations, reading, driving, eating, and sleeping without sacrificing safety. Without neuroception, humans likely wouldn't make it far in life. We would be completely unaware of the dangerous animal about to attack us, the smell from the kitchen that something is on fire, or the person following us in the parking lot. We wouldn't get much done, as we would repeatedly have to scan to check our safety. "Am I safe? . . . . How about now? And now? . . . How about now?" Neuroception allows us to live our lives while staying alive.

This is a beautiful practice for therapist self-care and clinical intervention. Instructions for integrating this exercise with clients are outlined in chapters to come, as it is a wonderful exercise to teach clients in Phase 2, Preparation. In the meantime, allow yourself to remain curious about the influence of neuroception on your day-to-day and moment-to-moment experience. Next time you notice yourself feeling really calm and peaceful, scan your neuroception and identify some of the cues that elicit that experience. Similarly, next time you feel a rise in stress levels, scan and identify the cues informing that response. With greater self-awareness and insight, we can better regulate our states and keep ourselves safe.

NEUROCEPTION AND PSYCHOTHERAPY

Neuroception is always working, scanning within, without, and in between. Its assessment is informed by hardwired evolutionary cues of danger, as well as personal lived experiences. Past experiences create memories that inform present-day attitudes, behaviors, and perceptions (Shapiro, 2018). This is a core premise of the adaptive information processing model, which is the cornerstone of EMDR. Past experiences form memory networks that shape present-day perception.

The autonomic nervous system responds to neuroception's appraisal with coordinated physiological responses. If the system senses cues of danger or alarm, it moves into sympathetic or dorsal defenses. If it appraises enough cues of safety and security, it provides access to ventral. Just like the home security system, though, false alarms can happen. Cues can be misinterpreted, appraised as dangerous when they are safe, or appraised as safe when there is in fact danger. Such is the case of miscalibrated or faulty neuroception. Miscalibrated or faulty neuroception happens when the nervous system's ability to assess threats and safety is compromised by past experiences. Faulty neuroception is a common presentation in those with complex trauma histories. Adversities stored as maladaptive memories inform neuroception's appraisal, producing chronic defensive states that manifest as PTSD, anxiety, panic, dissociation, and so on.

Let's explore this concept with a client example. A 45-year-old male (he/him), white, heterosexual, veteran, disabled client one day shared how triggered he felt at the grocery store. We got curious together and brought the unconscious process of neuroception into conscious awareness. I shared the home surveillance system analogy with him, and we explored cues of danger and safety at the grocery store. I asked, "What do you think your nervous system is picking up on in the store that tells it to sound the alarm?"

He thought about the question for a moment and shared his reflections. "There are too many people. When there are that many people, I can't tell who could be a threat. You learn in the military to always be reading people. The way they walk, how they hold themselves, where they're looking. There's too much to read at that store."

"That makes perfect sense," I responded. "What other cues do you think your nervous system is reading?"

"I don't know where all the exits are. I just moved and have to go to a new grocery store I'm not used to. I don't know the layout. I always need to know the exits," he reflected.

I said, "Of course. Knowing the exits is important for you to feel safe. This is all really important information. You're doing great. Just stay curious. What else?"

We identified several other cues his system was reading at the store. The grocery store was full of "without" cues, including the crowd, exits, overhead lighting, noise, and the smell of fish. The smell of fish was a trauma trigger, and he described how he went to extremes to avoid the fish counter at the store. This was something the client had never shared before this exercise.

"Within" cues included the physical pain he experienced when walking and standing. This client struggled with chronic back and knee pain, and also experienced frequent migraines due to a brain injury. Shopping exacerbated his pain and often triggered migraines, which were all cues of danger to him.

There were many "in-between" cues related to store staff. "They all look unhappy and overworked," he reflected. He identified that staff often did not make eye contact and rarely smiled at him. "They don't talk to you, and they all look miserable." He also stated that being around so many strangers and in crowds was a trigger. "I don't like crowds or groups of people," he shared.

Taking time to get curious and explore neuroception with this client provided insight and information. The client identified the many cues he was unconsciously perceiving, which triggered visceral responses of fight or flight. This discussion also uncovered the trigger of the smell of fish, which stemmed from a specific memory. As an EMDR therapist, I made a note of this memory as a potential target to reprocess. We remained curious about where he learned that these cues were unsafe, which was information that informed an EMDR treatment plan. Additionally, the physiological distress he reported and the cues we uncovered in this conversation identified focus areas for Phase 2, Preparation Work. We were able to build internal and external resources to manage these triggers. He learned to practice scanning neuroception on his own and identified ways to increase cues of safety when needed. We explored how he could use conscious choice and empowerment to change his experience. I asked, "What is within your control to change in this situation to help you feel more safe and secure?" This question led to curious discussions about shopping at another grocery store, what time of day was best for his pain to go to the store, and alternative ways of securing food and household goods such as ordering online. He decided to switch grocery stores, shop early in the morning on a weekday, and order some items online. He also chose to do some of his shopping at the local farmers market because "people are really friendly there." He could bring his dog to the farmers market and enjoyed being outside, which were both cues of safety for him.

Going to the grocery store is anxiety provoking for many people. There is a lot of information the nervous system is processing as we do something as seemingly simple as picking out produce and toothpaste. Stores are full of cues for the nervous system to appraise and interpret. The majority of what we are appraising and processing is outside of our conscious awareness as we go about this simple yet neurobiologically complex chore. Taking time to consciously think about what the nervous system is reading moves the unconscious to the conscious, and offers an opportunity for choice, empowerment, and discernment.

THE SOCIAL ENGAGEMENT SYSTEM

"To connect and co-regulate with others is our biological imperative" (Porges, 2017). Humans are biologically wired to connect, form bonds, and create social groups of cooperation and reciprocity. Doing so supports human evolution and survival. Whether an extrovert or an introvert, everyone is wired for relationships. Just like a plant needs sun, humans need relationships. The neurobiological mechanism that is at the heart of our social nature and our relationship-building skills is something known as the social engagement system.

The social engagement system is described in Polyvagal Theory. It is influenced by the vagus nerve and neuroception. The social engagement system is composed of five cranial nerves that control muscles in the face, head, and heart (Porges, 2003). The system represents a unique biological language of connection and attachment, communicated through physiology, specifically via the eyelids, facial muscles, vocalizations, vocal prosody, and head movements (Bergmann, 2020).

The vagus nerve plays a significant role in feeling safe, which is a necessary ingredient for connection (Porges, 2021). Without safety, we cannot bond. Safety is appraised through neuroception, as it scans within, without, and in between. When defense circuits are recruited in response to danger, capacity for connection dwindles. In sympathetic activation, the ability to accurately read the expressions of others is impaired, and we are prone to misinterpret people as dangerous or angry (Porges, 2011). We move to defend and disconnect. In the dorsal vagal circuit, we lose muscle tone in the face, appear flat, lose prosody of voice, and avoid eye contact. Dorsal moves us away from connection and toward isolation, with its collapsing and immobilizing traits. It is easy to recognize that autonomic defenses impact connections and social bonds in either case. In defensive states, we can't relate.

As therapists, we know that a great deal of communication happens outside of spoken words. Words are only a piece of the picture. How we communicate and express ourselves through body language carries much greater weight than the words themselves. Emotions and intentions are communicated through our eyes, face, head tilts, and body language. Imagine telling a friend you just got a big promotion, and they respond with a flat face, flat voice, and no eye contact, and say, "That's great." Alternatively, imagine that friend responds by lifting their eyebrows, and their eyes get big. They genuinely smile, and as they throw up their hands in celebration, they say, "That's GREAT!" Same two words, communicated in very different ways.

The social engagement system communicates through the body. As a compassionate clinician, consider precisely what you do with your body, consciously or unconsciously, to express care and positive regard to a client. When I ask clinicians to reflect on this in training, I often hear characteristics that make a good therapist, such as compassion, approachability, kindness, good listening skills. Try to deepen that awareness and explore the specific body expressions of those characteristics. What specific body cues give your client the felt sense of safety and connection? How do you influence someone's neuroception with your physiology to tell them you are a safe person? How do you physically express care and compassion? What are the specific physical expressions of these attributes? As you consider these physiological traits, also remain mindful of cultural differences that can impact how a person may experience those traits. Eye contact and physical proximity, for example, can be cues of safety or danger depending on one's cultural background.

While remaining cognizant of individual differences, some typical cues of safety observed in many cultures include a motherly or soothing tone of voice, caring and compassionate facial expressions, open and inviting body language, physical proximity, maintained eye contact, and timely head tilts. These expressions represent the unique language of connection in humans. The interpersonal process of psychotherapy enlists the social engagement system as the vehicle for healing. The autonomic nervous system and the social engagement system are the reasons that the therapeutic relationship is so important and so powerful.

Childhood attachment shapes the social engagement system (Cozolino, 2017). This system makes attachment between parent and child possible and helps us learn self-regulation. Learning to self-soothe is based in the experience of being soothed. In an ideal world, caregivers nurture and comfort their children with cues of safety, including gestures, touch, facial expressions, proximity, and vocal sounds. Ideally, caregivers help their children feel safe and teach them how to navigate feelings and sensations.

Unfortunately, we do not live in an ideal world, and this ideal situation does not happen for many of our clients. Lack of coregulation in childhood leads to poor affect regulation skills and impaired social skills in adulthood (Cozolino, 2017; Dana, 2018; van der Kolk, 2014; Porges, 2011). Coregulation teaches us how to exercise the vagal brake, which promotes the development of a resilient nervous system. Without safety and coregulation in childhood, the nervous system misses important developmental milestones that contribute to health and wellness throughout the life span. If we show up to our relationships in a constant state of defensiveness, have trouble neurocepting someone's cues of danger or safety, or struggle to manage our vagal brake, our lives and our relationships will suffer. It's that simple.

Coregulation in childhood is necessary for healthy neurological development (Porges, 2011). Therefore, it is vital that the therapist assess early attachment patterns and inquire about the quality of coregulation the client experienced in childhood. The therapist may learn that coregulation was inconsistent, unhealthy, or nonexistent. As a result, your client is more likely to struggle with interpersonal skills and have limited abilities to self-soothe. The therapeutic relationship must fill a developmental gap for these clients, teaching skills to self-soothe through the experience of coregulation. With enough coregulation, we learn the skills of self-regulation, which benefits our relationships.

Therapists must learn to harness neuroception and the social engagement system as allies in treatment. We can use these biological superpowers for good. We will explore how to do this in greater detail in the chapters to come. For now, invite curiosity into your sessions and remain reflective about your cues and body markers of safety and connection. How are you communicating safety to your client? How does your body express connection? How can you use the social engagement system more intentionally? Your own nervous system is your best study guide in this work.

Chapter 5

THE THERAPEUTIC RELATIONSHIP

The therapeutic relationship is a unique relationship, unlike any other. Sixteen meta-analyses by the American Psychological Association in 2019 concluded that the therapeutic relationship is just as important as, if not more than, the treatment provided (DeAngelis, 2019). Therapy is not merely the application of clinical interventions but rather the intentional use of a safe and supportive relationship to foster clinical growth. The quality of the client-therapist relationship is more important than the interventions provided as the relationship provides structure, consistency, safety, and regulation. For some clients, the therapy hour may be the only time they feel safe and emotionally nurtured in their week. As such, considerable attention must be given to the therapeutic relationship and establishing an attuned, shame-free, nurturing environment for the client. This principle is a cornerstone of every therapeutic modality, and EMDR is no exception.

THERAPEUTIC PRESENCE

The client does not have to feel safe or be safe everywhere in their life for healing to be possible. They must, however, feel safe with you (Porges, 2020). The therapeutic relationship is the most crucial variable in psychotherapy, for therapy can be effective only when the client feels secure and safe in the counseling relationship. Many of us learn this in our graduate studies, though we may not have realized the neurophysiological correlates that contribute to therapeutic rapport. So how does the clinician cultivate a nurturing relationship that supports the clinical work, and why exactly does it matter so much?

Therapeutic presence explains this process and is a demonstrated contributor to therapeutic rapport (Geller et al., 2010; Geller & Greenberg, 2012). As defined by Geller and Greenberg (2012), "therapeutic presence is the state of having one's whole self in the encounter with a client by being completely in the moment on a multiplicity of levels—physically, emotionally, cognitively, and spiritually" (p. 7). Therapeutic presence requires the clinician to be attentive and attuned to their own neurophysiological processes alongside the client's. Your client's nervous system is understandably of great significance in the counseling process; but yours is too. Your nervous system must be anchored in ventral and safety, allowing connection to be possible. Presence requires a multilevel, conscientious, and mindful approach to the profession and craft of counseling. Presence makes rapport possible.

Therapy is not simply a service, nor is it defined by the sum of clinical interventions provided. Rather, therapy is the skillful recruitment of the social engagement system to facilitate healing and integration. Counseling requires hard and soft skills and, above all else, a particular way of being with people. Presence is a critical contributor to the therapeutic process that is only possible when the clinician is fully in the moment with their entire embodied, regulated self. Presence cannot be faked. It can only be embodied.

The nervous system is a relational system wired for connection. The counseling process recruits the power of relational neurobiology as the synergist for growth and change. When the therapist is fully present, their ventral vagal circuit offers a pathway for the client's nervous system to experience safety and connection. Only then can we expect clients to have the courage to venture into new depths of self-discovery and vulnerability. Safety and connection are fundamentals for therapeutic presence, rooted in the therapist's neurobiology.

Developing presence requires active skills. Geller and Greenberg (2012) outline three categories of skill set in their model of therapeutic presence: (1) *preparation* (what therapists do to cultivate presence); (2) *process* (how therapists foster presence in the session with clients); and (3) *experience* (how therapists experience their own neurophysiological processes when with clients). Recognize that presence develops through a multilayered approach. To develop therapeutic presence, one must be actively involved in health and wellness activities and practices on and off the job. Presence isn't something that happens solely when you're in your therapist seat. It is an outcome of your well-being.

Presence is a physiological process of the ventral circuit. You must have enough access to ventral for presence to be possible. Presence requires the clinician to regularly care for their personal neurobiology, establishing a sufficiently regulated nervous system capable of holding space for someone else's dysregulation. The health and wellness of your nervous system has immense implications in this field of work. As the therapist, showing up to sessions in autonomic defensive states of dysregulation is not therapeutic and will negatively impact the counseling process. The client's nervous system will perceive your dysregulation. No matter how good you believe you are at putting on a mask, the autonomic nervous system communicates without conscious awareness, influencing the client's neuroception (Geller & Porges, 2014). Cues of safety come from the safe and connected circuit of ventral. If you show up regressed in dorsal, the client may experience flatness in your tone of voice and diminished eye contact. This could communicate disinterest and disconnection. If you're overloaded with sympathetic activation, it may be difficult to concentrate and track. You may be extra fidgety, jumping from one thought to the next, talking faster than usual. The client may perceive those cues as signs of anxiety, distraction, or disinterest. A dysregulated therapist cannot regulate a client and is limited in their capacity to send cues of safety.

Imagine you are having a conversation with someone. They pick up their phone and start scrolling through social media while you are in midsentence. What is your automatic internal process when this happens? For most people that's a "shut it down!" kind of moment, and you feel a visceral wave of distress and disconnection. Regardless of how you respond behaviorally, we can all resonate with what this is like inside. It's incredibly frustrating, can be hurtful, and is a violation of connection. It's an example of what Porges (2017) calls biological rudeness.

Within social interactions, moments of disconnection can cause a violation of neural expectancy (Porges, 2017). Porges coined the term "biological rudeness," which describes the visceral experience of shutting down and disengaging when someone conveys disconnection in social interaction. Because we are social creatures, and neuroception is constantly scanning, cues of disconnection can elicit immediate, physiological responses to disengage. Poor eye contact, flat vocal tone, interrupting someone, and breaking concentration are all ways that we commit biological rudeness. These small nuances happen regularly in our day-to-day conversations because we are human and tend to get distracted. However, biological rudeness can be quite harmful if it occurs regularly and without repair. It is easy to recognize that biological rudeness can be especially damaging if committed by the therapist. Biological rudeness is more likely to occur in times of autonomic dysregulation, highlighting with even greater importance the need for the therapist to be regulated.

How do we cultivate therapeutic presence? Considering that presence is a ventral process, presence is cultivated alongside increased capacity to connect with ventral. Therapeutic presence begins with self-care and is sustained by regularly exercising the vagal brake. If presence comes from ventral connection, then the way to create presence is to increase your capacity to connect to the ventral circuit.

Self-care is a messy concept in society today. Corporations have turned self-care into a billion-dollar industry, and the term can trigger images of elitism and privilege. If we strip away the commercialized ideals of self-care, we can reframe self-care as the intentional practice of self-regulation. Self-care activities are those that exercise the vagal brake and increase connection to ventral. Self-care time is merely self-regulation time. It is structured time to find rest and reprieve in ventral, which offers our physiology the nourishment to sustain us in the counseling space. The more regulated our autonomic nervous system is, the more helpful we are to others. The health and wellness of your autonomic nervous system directly influence the health and wellness of your client's.

Self-care is the intentional, daily practice of self-regulation using techniques that build resiliency. Research suggests that therapist well-being is positively correlated with effective treatment outcomes (Beutler et al., 2004; Delgadillo et al., 2018; Geller & Greenberg, 2012; Henry et al., 1990; Simionato et al., 2019; Shapiro et al., 2007). That is, when the therapist's nervous system is healthy and well-nourished, clients benefit. It is truly that simple. As therapists, we must recognize that our health and wellness directly contribute to our clients' therapeutic successes. Self-care is not just a massage, a vacation, or a trip to the salon. Pampering and self-care are not always one and the same. Self-care is a daily activity and an active practice of self-nourishment and regulation. Yes, your self-regulation time might include pampering with a vacation or a massage. But self-care might also be doing things that you don't necessarily want to do but that ultimately support your health and wellness. Getting yourself to the gym when you don't want to go, eating nourishing food when you just want ice cream for dinner, and getting to bed early when you'd rather keep mindlessly scrolling through social media are all acts of self-care. Think about self-care similarly to taking a daily vitamin. Taking it once or sporadically does not produce the same outcomes or benefits as regular, daily dosing.

Undoubtedly, it is an intense time to be a human and a very challenging time to be on the front lines of suffering. Our culture and world are not conducive to living consistently in the ventral circuit, and serving as a helper is often not a ventral vagal experience. These are stressful, scary, dysregulating times. Every member of the human race is experiencing autonomic responses to the many existential cues of danger and threat. Therefore, cultivating a solid self-care/self-regulating practice is more important than ever if we hope to remain resilient through crises and unprecedented change.

Trauma is an epidemic. With the additional political and social discord, climate crises, and COVID-19, everyone now shares in the experience of frequently dealing with toxic stress. Therapists are at heightened risk for vicarious trauma and burnout, considering the many risk factors of the profession. Large caseloads, immense need and demand, unprecedented change, an unpredictable world, multiple existential crises, immense death and loss, increasing resource disparity for low-income and marginalized clients, a volatile political climate, personal life demands such as childcare and sickness, and climate change challenge us personally and professionally. Given these risks and challenges, we must intentionally and mindfully create moments of regulation to remain resilient. If we therapists are not well resourced in our autonomic nervous system, we cannot communicate safety, cannot be present, and cannot be effective agents of change. You cannot be a healing force when you are acutely wounded and overwhelmed with stress. To expect anything else is fantasy based in denial of our true nature and human biology.

Regulating Resets

Establishing a consistent self-regulation routine to support your clinical work is not easy, nor is it any sort of guaranteed protection from burnout or compassion fatigue, though with regular self-care those experiences will be less distressing and will resolve more quickly. Even though self-care can sometimes feel like a challenge, recognize it's not only a requirement of this profession but also far easier than the alternative. Recovery can become a full-time job if we get too far down the burnout or vicarious trauma vortex.

I invite you to reframe self-care from this point forward as regulating reset time. Rather than thinking broadly, think more specifically about how you can find moments to reset throughout the day. Think about how you dose yourself with ventral energy on a consistent basis. Finding moments to exercise the vagal brake intentionally are more impactful long-term than a few vacations sprinkled here and there. Regulating resets can be any act or skill that increases connection to the ventral circuit. For inspiration, I share a few of my regulating resets here:

- Movement: Every day I find time for movement, whether that's a walk, a workout, yoga, wandering around my yard, or 10 minutes of mindful movement.
- Tea: For me there is something so comforting and soothing about a warm cup of tea. I will take a tea break when I need a reset, and it helps keep me connected throughout my workday.
- Hold blank space in my calendar: If I see a day of back-to-back appointments, my nervous system perceives a cue of danger and I quickly feel overwhelmed. I keep blank space in my calendar and keep that time sacred. Blank space isn't the same as being available.
- Playtime with pets: I have two dogs and two cats. Playing or snuggling with them gives me an instant reset.
- Dance and sing: When I feel the qualities of dorsal, I turn on a song and dance and sing. It is a guaranteed quick path for me to get out of shutdown and back to ventral.
- Clean up my workspace: If my workspace looks scattered and disorganized, I get anxious. At the end of the workday, I clean up my desk and organize, giving my nervous system the visual cue that it's time to wind down from work.
- Breath: In client sessions when I feel my autonomic nervous system getting activated alongside or in reaction to my client's process, I anchor my awareness to my breath. I slow down my breathing and try to breathe in a little deeper and out a little longer. Keeping my awareness on my breath and my client helps me to reduce flooding in sessions.

I invite you to take some time to self-reflect on what your regulation resets are. What do you already practice throughout the day, and what could you add to take better care of your neurobiology? Consider anything and everything that helps get you connected and regulated. This may include boundaries, work hours, supervision, your own therapy, personal self-care like massage and acupuncture, food, or mindfulness activities. Create this list and continue to add to it as you become more aware of what you need in times of dysregulation. The more you practice noticing your states and the impact these ventral resets have on you, the more you will embody presence.

CUES OF PRESENCE

We communicate presence with physiological cues. To understand what those cues are, it can be helpful to study your own lived experience. Recall a time in which you felt seen, heard, and connected to another person. Allow this memory to manifest in awareness. Bring neuroception into active awareness by appraising what you were perceiving that allowed you to feel that connection. What were the facial expressions, vocal tones, and physical gestures that provided you with cues of safety and connection in that experience? Perhaps it was their attuned eye contact, their facial expression of empathy or interest, or the soothing tone of their voice. Maybe it was a sense of calm they exuded or something about them that conveyed genuine interest and curiosity. Get as specific as possible about what this person's physiology did to foster that connection.

The specifics you identified are expressions of the social engagement system and examples of cues of presence. Cues of presence are the specific physiological gestures that foster connection and safety. They are communicated through facial expressions, eye contact, tone of voice, body posture, and breath. Cues of presence help us feel safe with one another and support the formation of social bonds. Feeling safe is a necessary ingredient for healthy and close relationships, as it is hard to impossible to meaningfully bond with someone who sends us cues of danger or threat.

Cues of presence are subtle but powerful physiological markers of the social engagement system, communicating active listening and empathic engagement. They are essential for healthy relationships, connection, and reducing vulnerability in counseling. Cues of presence are only safe and foster connection when they are authentic and come from ventral. That is, presence is only possible when one is present. Therefore, the therapist's biology must be regulated in the here and now for cues of presence to be possible. Applying the wisdom of neurobiology, you can use cues to build connection and safety. Some ways to do this include these:

- Use eye contact intentionally. Be mindful of how much eye contact you have, for how long, and how often you look away.
- Use facial expressions that express empathy, compassion, and positive regard.
- Use head tilts to communicate curiosity and tracking.
- Use breath to signal presence and compassion.
- Use body posture to communicate interest, openness, and attentiveness.

It's important to be cognizant that while sometimes predictable, cues of safety and danger vary from one client to the next. Biology, culture, and personal experience shape individual cues of danger and safety. Cues can vary from person to person significantly based on these factors, and therefore be careful not to make assumptions. Build an awareness of the current cues you use in counseling and consider how you can use them with greater intentionality and cultural sensitivity.

Cues of presence are critical in all therapies and especially EMDR, though therapists sometimes forget this when reading a script and following specific EMDR steps in reprocessing phases. It is important to remember that the therapist's cues of presence and safety are more important than getting the script right. EMDR reprocessing is not an invitation for your nervous system to disconnect and go offline. It is key that you remain present and engaged throughout all phases of EMDR, especially memory reprocessing. We will explore these concepts in greater depth in later chapters of this book. For now, know that no matter what phase you are in with your client, being present and communicating presence is vital for achieving positive treatment outcomes.

THE THREE Cs

The therapeutic relationship must be neurocepted as safe to the client. Awareness of the Three Cs in counseling, as described by Dana, supports this objective. The Three Cs contribute to establishing a reliable experience of safety in the therapeutic relationship. They are *context*, *choice*, and *connection* (Dana, 2018). The Three Cs are trauma-informed, neuro-informed, polyvagal-informed objectives that must be continuously present at every therapeutic juncture. Each of the three defines specific cues the autonomic nervous system scans for through neuroception (Dana, 2018). They are not interventions, worksheets, or checkboxes. The Three Cs are processes that must be continuously present in the client-therapist relationship. Every point of contact we have with a client, from our voice mail greeting to assessment, to the structure of each session, to the actual intervention provided, must be scaffolded by the Three Cs.

Context offers the client information and education about the why, how, when, where, and expectations of the work. Context provides the autonomic nervous system cues of safety with expectations and information. As in the saying "knowledge is power," the nervous system wants to know why and how something is happening. Without context, we are more likely to feel confused and unclear about boundaries. We may fill in the missing bits of information with inaccurate appraisals. A lack of context could negatively influence the therapeutic process. Therefore, we must always be mindful of creating and providing context, wherever and whenever possible. We create context by reviewing informed consent to treatment, explaining our attendance policy, and reviewing treatment options, to name a few. Explaining EMDR, the therapeutic process, and the boundaries of the therapeutic relationship also provide context. Context lets the client's nervous system know what to predict and sets boundaries and expectations. As a result, clients are more likely to feel supported and safe to engage in the therapeutic process.

Any intervention that takes power away from the client is not trauma-informed (Herman, 2015). Choice empowers the client and is a requirement of any good therapy. Being choiceless or powerless diminishes self-efficacy and leaves a client feeling trapped and helpless. The absence of choice is a hallmark of trauma, and therapists must avoid creating experiences of powerlessness or "choicelessness" as much as possible. Because a power differential exists in the therapeutic relationship, choice is also a way to keep this differential in check. Without choice, the therapeutic relationship risks exploiting the client's self-autonomy. We can offer choice to our clients in many ways, from scheduling to therapeutic interventions to selecting the focus for the day's session. Although there are situations when choicelessness is a reality of the therapeutic relationship (e.g., working with inmates, court-ordered clients, involuntary hospitalization), the therapist can look for ways to offer choice where possible.

Finally, the autonomic nervous system needs connection to the therapist. Clients must feel connected in counseling for it to be a therapeutic resource. No one heals alone. Polyvagal Theory teaches that human connection supports healing and recovery. As trauma is often an experience in disconnection, the healing antidote has to be safety and connection (Dana, 2018). Connection is maintained through therapeutic presence and the therapist being anchored in ventral. Safe connection can only happen with access to ventral. The qualities of ventral allow you to track, notice changes, and express genuine cues of presence to your clients. Connection is established in large and small ways, with consistency and reliability being key factors. When clients feel safe and secure with you, they can roll in the deep, confront the skeletons in the closet, and free themselves from the burdens of trauma and adversity.

THE THERAPEUTIC SOIL

Soil is the foundation for every living thing, providing structure and nutrients to support life on earth. Good soil upholds sturdy homes and buildings and nourishes living organisms. Bad soil leads to collapse, death, disease, and famine. "Feed the soil, not the plant" is a mantra of gardening culture. This wisdom can be applied to psychotherapy as we recognize how important the quality of the therapeutic relationship is for client outcomes. Perhaps a version for the practice of psychotherapy could be "relationship over intervention." The quality of the counseling relationship can be considered the therapeutic soil that nurtures growth and contributes to wellness. "Therapeutic soil" is a term I use to describe the therapeutic environment the clinician creates and maintains. A well-cared-for environment is like fertile soil, providing a sturdy foundation and nourishing the client's process.

Therapeutic presence is the most critical ingredient for good, healthy, rich therapeutic soil. It is enriched with cues of presence and the Three Cs. Without good soil, interventions will have little to no effect; change will be slow and minimal. "Bad therapy" may offer some support, but it fails to provide the client's nervous system the nutrients it needs to heal and transform. It's like bad soil; it provides some structure but fails to nourish the plants.

It is an exceptional thing to be invited into a client's inner world. The role of a therapist is unique, unlike any other role in our life. Clinicians are trusted with their clients' most significant vulnerabilities and most deeply kept secrets. It is an honor and a privilege to support someone on their personal and unique life journey. It is important that we take this role seriously and respect the influence we have in someone's life. If I do not take care of my health and wellness, I am limited in my ability to help others with their health and wellness. The real magic in therapy does not come from the interventions we provide or what we do. It comes from how we are with clients. How present or not we are with clients begins with caring for our minds and bodies.

Chapter 6

POLYVAGAL-INFORMED EMDR

I begin this section by inviting a moment of remembrance and respect for Dr. Francine Shapiro, who passed away in 2019. Unfortunately, I never had the privilege of meeting Dr. Shapiro, though I wish I had. I am in awe of her legacy and her relentless advocacy for a therapy that was initially considered pseudo-science and highly controversial. I can't imagine what it must have been like as a woman in the 1990s to stand in front of professional groups of mostly male academics and advocate for EMDR. Yet Dr. Shapiro remained determined to legitimize EMDR by researching its efficacy. Because of her steadfast perseverance, EMDR is now an internationally recognized evidence-based therapy that has positively impacted thousands and thousands of lives worldwide. Without Shapiro's dedication to her work, EMDR would not be here today.

EMDR is most notably known and researched with trauma and PTSD. The benefits of EMDR have also been explored with other common clinical presentations such as phobias, depression, and addictions (Gauhar, 2016; Shapiro, 2018). EMDR is not a diagnosis-based therapy. It is a memory-based therapy. Memory storage is the primary focus of treatment and hypothesized to be a primary contributor to symptoms and pathology. The EMDR protocol is designed to access, stimulate, and reprocess a maladaptively stored memory to the point of adaptive resolution. When this is accomplished, clients experience changes in symptoms and overall improved day-to-day functioning. One of my greatest privileges as a therapist has been to witness the incredible power of EMDR in the clinical setting, as clients report awe-inspiring insights, significant changes in symptoms, and overall greater well-being following EMDR therapy.

PV-EMDR focuses on the autonomic processes associated with the storage of memory, and how those processes relate to clinical presentations and trauma. To begin conceptualizing the link between memory and the autonomic nervous system, I invite you to practice this experiential exercise. First, bring to mind a happy, joyful memory, free of any grief, loss, or sadness. Allow yourself to recall that memory for 30 seconds or so, noticing how you experience this memory in your mind, body, and heart. Pause here to practice.

What happens inside when you think of that memory? What do you notice in your physiology? What physical sensations do you experience? Do any of your senses come alive? What emotions come up for you? Does your physiology change as you think about the memory? How do you know it is a happy memory?

Now call to mind a mildly distressing memory. Nothing too traumatic, but something that evokes mild discomfort or annoyance. Allow your awareness to rest there for a moment, and notice what happens to your mind, body, and heart. How do you know this memory is distressing or painful? What in your physiology tells you? What happens to your senses? What emotions do you notice? Where do you feel this memory in your body? How do you know it is a distressing memory?

Memories are not just thought; they are felt. A memory recalled in the brain is felt through the autonomic nervous system. Connecting to the emotional aspects of our memories is possible because of the autonomic nervous system. Recalling memories produces thoughts, feelings, sensations, smells, tastes, and images. A narrative or a story may unfold, told through the experience of the autonomic nervous system. These represent various components of the memory, felt here and now through a bidirectional relationship between the central and autonomic nervous system. Some memories elicit pleasant responses, some neutral, and others distressing. For those with histories of adversity and unresolved trauma, the nervous system becomes a complex landscape of miscalibrated neural networks that have developed in response to this interaction of unresolved memories and autonomic responses. Present-day triggers activate memory networks and autonomic defenses. Therefore, we can understand most clinical symptoms as manifestations of distressed neural networks triggering memories and autonomic states.

EMDR is a memory-based therapy, focusing on the storage of memory and how memory storage contributes to health and wellness or dis-ease and pathology (Shapiro, 2018). Adaptively stored memories are experiences that have integrated to the point of adaptive resolution. These memories contribute to resilience and self-efficacy. Maladaptively stored memories are relived in state-specific form in the here and now, expressed through chronic patterns of emotion dysregulation, poor interpersonal skills, diminished self-esteem, and physical illness amongst other symptom clusters. As Shapiro (2018) described, maladaptively stored memories are the basis of symptoms and pathology of a nonorganic nature and pose a risk for developing psychological disorders and diagnoses.

Adaptive and maladaptive memory storage can be further understood and conceptualized through Polyvagal Theory and the responses elicited by the autonomic nervous system. Memories that have adaptively integrated are experienced through the ventral vagal circuit when recalled. Maladaptively stored memories trigger defense responses of the sympathetic or dorsal vagal circuits. Maladaptively stored memories are held in state-specific form, meaning these memories elicit physiological responses in the present similar to those experienced in the past (Shapiro, 2018). These memories hold the feelings, thoughts, and sensations of the experience and cue danger or alarm in the autonomic nervous system when activated in the here and now.

THE ADAPTIVE INFORMATION PROCESSING MODEL

Shapiro developed the adaptive information processing model, or AIP, to describe and predict EMDR clinical phenomena (Shapiro, 2018). AIP is the theoretical model of EMDR, upon which clinicians build case conceptualization, navigate treatment plans, and reevaluate clinical work. Dr. Shapiro (2018) developed the AIP model following empirical observations along with researched methods of EMDR therapy. AIP "explains clinical phenomena, predicts successful treatment effects, and guides clinical practice" (Shapiro, 2007, p. 70). In simple terms, AIP is a function of the nervous system that processes and integrates information. AIP (i.e., the nervous system) is physical, intrinsic, and adaptive. The system is a physical part of human biology and is oriented toward health and survival. The AIP model describes the impact of memory storage on present-day symptoms and emphasizes that memories are the basis of health and wellness. The system continuously integrates internal and external information, assimilating this information into physically stored memories. Memories may be adaptively or maladaptively stored. Adaptively stored memories contribute to health and resiliency. In contrast, maladaptively stored memories lead to the emergence of nonorganic symptoms such as anxiety, hypervigilance, depression, sleep disturbances, and more.

Human beings are narrative creatures with a unique ability to create stories and narratives based on our experiences. The ability to create stories can certainly be entertaining and contributes to the richness of our lives. However, this storytelling quality can also be problematic and may be at the root of suffering if narratives are inspired by trauma, adversity, and toxic stress. We create narratives about ourselves, others, and the world based on experiences stored as physical memories (Shapiro, 2018). We are all biased by our experiences and memories. Toxic stress and maladaptively stored memories can manifest as narratives, perceptions, attitudes, and behaviors that contribute to dis-ease and despair. For example, clients who have experienced danger in their community and relationships may form narratives and perceptions that the world is unsafe, and people cannot be trusted. This narrative may manifest as behaviors and traits that align with this perception, such as isolation, hypervigilance, and interpersonal challenges stemming from the belief that they "can't trust anyone." In contrast, a client with adaptive experiences of safety and security will likely hold a very different narrative. Adaptive memory networks may inspire a narrative that says the world can be unsafe, but it is mostly safe and people are mostly trustworthy. This narrative would support behaviors and attitudes that align with this belief. These examples highlight how memories inform the human experience and their influence on our day-to-day lives.

AIP asserts that stored memories form memory networks based on similar components of memory, which can include thoughts, beliefs, feelings, sensations, or sensory data such as images, smells, tastes, and sounds. Memory networks activate in response to present-day cues that trigger a memory network and elicit responses of the autonomic nervous system. The more frequently a memory network is activated, the more its neural connections are reinforced and strengthened (Shapiro, 2018). Memory networks can therefore quickly trigger powerful autonomic responses.

To better conceptualize this process, consider Stickgold's (2002) forest analogy. Imagine a forest of trees with trails running throughout it. The trees represent memories, and the trails through the forest represent memory networks. Trails traveled frequently are well defined and quick to access, while trails seldom traveled are less defined and more challenging to identify and access. Building new trails is possible but requires tools and effort. This process takes time and patience because a new path has to be carved out, tended to, and frequently traveled before transforming into a well-defined trail.

In comparison, the more frequently a memory network is activated, the stronger the neural pathway becomes, just like the well-traveled trail in the forest. When clients share how out-of-control, reactive, and powerless they feel to triggers, they are describing the power of these well-defined memory networks. This is the physiological process unfolding when clients describe how rapidly a smell or sound triggers a flashback, or when a client explains how overwhelmed they feel by the belief that they are unworthy or unlovable. This is the constant battle for those held hostage to cravings and urges, struggling to maintain sobriety or manage disordered eating habits. These automatic states are expressions of neural pathways traveled time and time again, becoming superhighway neural networks. Thankfully, the nervous system is resilient and adaptive. Thanks to neuroplasticity, humans can create new trails and rewire memory networks. But just as building a trail takes time, building new neural networks takes time, patience, and practice. Integrating Polyvagal Theory and EMDR provides the therapist with a robust toolkit of neuro-informed tools to build new neural pathways and integrate memories to the point of adaptive resolution. The result is new adaptive pathways that contribute to health and wellness.

Another core premise of AIP is that the nervous system is oriented toward health and always working in your favor (Shapiro, 2018). The body has the incredible power to self-heal, and the nervous system is no exception. When you get a cut on your skin, you likely expect your body to heal the wound without formal intervention. Sometimes, however, we experience significant wounds, such as a broken bone or a major surgery, and medical intervention is needed to support the body to heal and recover.

Similarly, the nervous system also has the power to self-heal and move toward health and resiliency following adversity and trauma. Many adversities heal on their own, just like a small cut on the skin. However, some experiences overwhelm the system's capacity, just like major physical trauma or illness, preventing the system from resolving the experience independently. These experiences form maladaptive memory networks, which influence present-day experiences and symptoms.

I often use the metaphor of digestion when explaining this self-healing process and the significance of symptoms when I'm educating clients. What happens to the digestive system when we overeat? The system becomes overwhelmed and can't do its job of digesting because there is too much to process. This leads to symptoms such as nausea, bloating, and heartburn. Your digestive system wants to digest your food, but sometimes the system gets overloaded.

Similarly, the nervous system wants to integrate experiences but sometimes gets overloaded. Adversity and stress can overwhelm the system, preventing it from completing its task. When life experiences get stuck, they manifest as psychological symptoms such as nightmares, flashbacks, anxiety, depression, and so forth. These symptoms are manifestations of an overwhelmed nervous system that gets stuck in autonomic defensive states because the experience could not integrate. I use the language "what's stuck and causing yuck" when explaining these concepts to trainees and clients, inviting an opportunity to be curious about the maladaptively linked memories leading to the "yucky," or distressing, present-day symptoms.

The better you grasp the AIP model, the more advanced you will be in treatment planning, case conceptualization, and PV-EMDR therapy. AIP offers a framework to understand the significance of present-day symptoms through the lens of memory storage. Integrating Polyvagal Theory into the AIP model provides EMDR therapists with an additional framework to track the autonomic nervous system as it informs and guides the treatment planning process. Memories and the autonomic nervous system are interrelated, as memories elicit responses of autonomic circuits. Maladaptively stored memories trigger sympathetic or dorsal vagal circuits, while adaptive memories allow access to the ventral vagal circuit. Autonomic responses serve as a method for assessing memory storage and, in doing so, illuminate specific memories to target in EMDR reprocessing.

ADAPTIVE MEMORY NETWORKS AND AUTONOMIC RESILIENCY

The resiliency of the nervous system is an outcome of and contributor to adaptive memory networks. Understanding the resiliency of the nervous system is essential for understanding the factors that contribute to maladaptive memory storage. Without resiliency in the autonomic nervous system, we lack consistent, reliable access to the ventral vagal circuit. Resiliency is the ability to flexibly move between autonomic states and is a sign of well-being (Dana, 2021). Without the ability to flex between autonomic states, clients can become stuck in rigid and chronic states of dysregulation. Not only is the ventral vagus where psychological well-being resides, but the body can also rest and restore when connected to ventral. If clients lack autonomic resiliency and flexibility, they become stuck in chronic autonomic dysregulation, increasing the risk of maladaptive memory storage and the development of complex symptoms.

Resiliency is the capacity to cope with adversity (Connor & Davidson, 2003) and represents an ability to bounce back from and resist stress (Smith et al., 2008). Quantifying resiliency can be accomplished by measuring vagal tone (Pereira et al., 2017). Vagal tone (see Chapter 3) is a physiological marker of resiliency and is indicative of a flexible vagal brake (Kok & Fredrickson, 2010). Vagal tone is built through skills that moderate cardiac output by exercising the vagal brake (Souza et al., 2007, 2013). Kok and Fredrickson (2010) report that high vagal tone is associated with positive emotions and a strong sense of connectedness to others. High vagal tone is therefore synonymous with resiliency.

Resiliency is both the outcome of memory integration and a protective variable against the maladaptive storage of memory. Clients stuck in chronically dysregulated states are more susceptible to maladaptive memory storage because an overwhelmed system will impede the processes of memory storage and integration. A taxed nervous system is susceptible to developing a plethora of complex biopsychosocial problems. High vagal tone and a resilient nervous system contribute to growth and indicate skillful use of coping tools to manage autonomic states of stress, via flexible manipulation of the vagal brake. In sum, a resilient autonomic nervous system contributes to the adaptive integration of memory.

BILATERAL STIMULATION AND NEUROCEPTION

EMDR was considered controversial for many years. It is now one of the most-researched evidence-based therapies, partially because of the previously held belief that bilateral stimulation (BLS) was pseudoscience. There are a handful of researched hypotheses of BLS investigating its physiological mechanism of action. While researchers cannot say with certainty how BLS works, the scientific community cannot say with certainty how any therapy really works. Nevertheless, research has led to a few strongly supported hypotheses. Evidence suggests a mixture of neurophysiological processes that produce the positive clinical effects of BLS alongside the EMDR protocol. Supported hypotheses include the orienting response (OR), mechanisms similar to those produced in phasic REM sleep, and the taxing of working memory (Kuiken et al., 2001; Shapiro, 2018; Vojtova & Hastro, 2009). We will briefly explore the OR as it relates to Polyvagal Theory and overlaps with the process of neuroception.

Pavlov first described the OR in 1927 in his classical conditioning experiments (Zernicki, 1987). The OR was later systematically studied by the Russian scientist Sokolov in the 1950s. The OR (also referred to as the orienting reflex) is elicited when a new stimulus enters perceptual awareness, causing the organism to reflexively orient toward that stimulus to assess for threat and danger (Söndergaard & Elofsson, 2008; Sokolov, 1963). In simple terms, when you become aware of something in your environment, you turn your attention toward it to check it out. For example, imagine there was an unexpected noise behind you. What would you do? You would instinctively turn to face toward the noise and assess safety. That instinct to orient to the stimulus is the orienting reflex.

The OR, also dubbed the "what's that" reflex, is a function of the autonomic nervous system to rapidly assess a stimulus, followed by habituation and a relaxation response upon resolve. The reflex triggers movement with the head, eyes, and ears toward a stimulus to quickly appraise safety or danger. The OR is often an unconscious process and is an evolutionary gift to keep you safe. In Polyvagal Theory, this process of quick appraisal is called neuroception. Neuroception is the unconscious process of the nervous system to appraise cues of danger or safety and produce an autonomic response. Neuroception is, therefore, the autonomic process taking place behind the OR.

MacCulloch and Feldman (1996) proposed that the OR is an investigatory behavior and an "evolutionary development enabling organisms to assess their environment for both opportunities and threats." This description is synonymous with Porges's description of neuroception. Furthermore, MacCulloch and Feldman propose that actively engaging the OR results in the removal of distressing or negative affect from disturbing memories. Could it be that BLS is stimulating neuroception via the OR, allowing the nervous system to reappraise the memory?

Let's break these concepts down further and explore Polyvagal Theory as it relates to BLS. Bilateral stimulation is hypothesized to stimulate the OR and parasympathetic response (Shapiro, 2018; Stickgold, 2002). Another way to frame this may be that BLS activates neuroception within the context of the EMDR protocol. Phase 3 of EMDR activates a target memory via use of the scripted protocol, eliciting the stored experience and autonomic responses. In Phase 4, the clinician administers rounds of BLS while the client focuses on the memory and emergent associated channels. By activating the memory and the autonomic responses, BLS stimulates neuroception, which then reappraises the memory, asking "What's this?" from the present-day state of safety.

Phase 4 also includes a "reflexive pause, followed by reflexive exploration," as the clinician asks the client to pause and briefly report back on their experience (Kuiken, et al., 2001). This pause and exploration allow neuroception to investigate the experience in the here and now as it inquires, "What is this memory? What is this experience? What is this feeling? What is this story?" The check-in is also a way to maintain connection to ventral, which is necessary to prevent full activation of defensive autonomic circuits. As Kuiken et al. (2001) report, pausing and reflecting, as we do when we check in with our clients in reprocessing and ask "What do you notice?" are neurophysiological processes "incompatible with fear and avoidance." Reflecting and naming one's experience are processes only made possible with enough connection to ventral, for when defensive circuits are fully recruited, the ability to notice and name is lost.

When neuroception orients to safety, cardiac output decreases and autonomic defenses subside. In simplified terms, heart rate slows, which produces a state of calm. This change in physiology can be observed in therapy sessions, as clients often report feeling calmer after only a few rounds of BLS. Heart rate deceleration is a function of the vagal brake, which supports the autonomic nervous system move away from defensive states of mobilization or collapse while reprocessing the memory. As defenses diminish and safety increases, cognitive restructuring takes place and adaptive information assimilates into the network, allowing the memory to integrate to the point of adaptive resolution.

A review of these concepts offers an integrated framework for the potential mechanism of BLS as it relates to EMDR effects. BLS could be a method for orienting neuroception to present safety by actively engaging the reflex of the orienting response. When the memory is activated with the standard protocol and BLS is applied, neuroception reappraises the experience. We could consider the protocol and BLS to be a way to actively engage the nervous system in reevaluation of the experience and to reexamine the meaning it has made of the memory.

Though the orienting response is positively correlated with increased vagal tone, enough cues of safety must be present for the autonomic nervous system to maintain the vagal brake and integrate safety into the reconsolidated memory. Additionally, increased vagal tone and deceleration of heart rate are not guaranteed if the autonomic nervous system lacks resiliency. If a defensive state is necessary due to present-day danger, or if the autonomic nervous system does not have enough flexibility to support reprocessing, this reappraisal will not yield the desired clinical results.

The client's nervous system must be capable of maintaining connection to ventral and perceiving enough cues of safety for a memory to successfully integrate to a point of adaptive resolution. Connection to the ventral vagus may come through the client's physiology but is also sustained through the therapist's presence and use of coregulation skills. With enough cues of safety alongside active engagement of neuroception in the reprocessing phases, the memory reconsolidates with neuroception's reappraisal of safety. Successful memory integration produces autonomic shifts toward safety and connection and a new adaptive story about self, others, and the world. Successful adaptive memory integration results in changes to the memory itself, cognitive restructuring, emotional resolution, and enhanced self-efficacy.

The OR is not the only supported hypothesis for BLS. Two additional well-known and researched hypotheses include those of REM sleep and the taxation of working memory are two additional hypotheses of mechanism supported in the EMDR research (Shapiro, 2018). The REM sleep hypothesis posits that BLS stimulates similar processes as experienced in REM sleep, a phase of sleep important for memory consolidation and integration of experiences. Shapiro first suggested this hypothesis in 1989, suspecting that similar processes involved in REM may contribute to the outcomes observed in EMDR, and produced by BLS. The working memory hypotheses posits that by asking a client to think about the memory, while adding a dual attention stimulus (BLS), that working memory is taxed. That is asking someone to focus on two tasks at once is demanding of one's attentional capacity, which impairs the vividness and intensity of the memory, allowing it to adaptively integrate. These hypotheses may also have overlaps with principles of Polyvagal Theory and functions of the autonomic nervous system. This is a recommended area of further exploration and study. Research indicates that it is not simply one or the other, and

EMDR treatment effects are likely produced by multiple physiological mechanisms happening at once.

FUNDAMENTAL PRINCIPLES OF PV-EMDR

There are many points of intersection between Polyvagal Theory and AIP. Understanding the role of the autonomic nervous system as it influences memory storage and the impact of memory storage on the autonomic nervous system sets the stage for case conceptualization and treatment. These two branches of the nervous system maintain an interdependent, bidirectional feedback loop that influences present-day health and wellness and the storage of memory. The autonomic nervous system and AIP are always working and processing information, with the shared goals of surviving and thriving . To integrate these models is what I call polyvagal-informed EMDR, or PV-EMDR, which integrates the wisdom of Polyvagal Theory into EMDR clinical practice and aligns the phases of EMDR with the processes of the autonomic nervous system.

The fundamental principles of PV-EMDR are as follows:

- Memory storage and the functioning of the autonomic nervous system are the focus of polyvagal-informed EMDR therapy.
- The nervous system is the mechanism of assessment, intervention, and outcome of psychotherapy.
- Polyvagal Theory describes the functioning of the autonomic nervous system and the role of the vagus nerve as it mediates autonomic processes.
- The AIP model of EMDR describes the storage of memory.
- Memories are not just thought; they are felt through autonomic processes.
- The autonomic nervous system influences the storage of memory.
- The autonomic and central nervous systems have a bidirectional, interdependent relationship. The state of one system directly influences the state of the other.
- Autonomic resiliency is a means to an end and an end itself.

With these additional insights into AIP and Polyvagal Theory, the EMDR clinician can practice therapy with a sense of curiosity and deep respect for the nervous system. With knowledge of the neurophysiological processes influencing memory integration, the clinician can intervene with the nervous system as the focus of assessment and intervention. Clinicians sometimes share with me that EMDR therapy and the scripted protocol can feel rigid, strict, and unnatural. Yes, reading a script and following phases can feel confining compared to many of our talk therapy approaches. When we can better understand how the protocol works and how each phase engages with the nervous system, we have an opportunity to feel less scripted and bound by protocol in our EMDR practice. Therapy shifts from a rigid process to a fluid process that ebbs and flows alongside the client's neurobiology.

THE EIGHT PHASES OF PV-EMDR

EMDR is not a tool in your toolkit or simply an intervention. EMDR is an entire therapeutic orientation. Because EMDR offers a framework for conceptualization and eight phases of therapy, it is a comprehensive therapeutic model. While many people consider EMDR to mean, "Think about what hurts and follow my fingers," this is only one phase of EMDR. Though EMDR began as an intervention, Shapiro's dedication to research resulted in a comprehensive, phase-oriented therapy. You are not only practicing EMDR when you take clients through desensitization of a target. You are always an EMDR therapist, no matter which phase or clinical intervention you are using.

Shapiro developed the eight phases of EMDR to outline a therapeutic path. She notes that the length of time for any phase can greatly vary from client to client (Shapiro, 2018). Some clients move through the phases rapidly, and others take months or years. Healing is not a race, and we must remember that healing takes time. The length of treatment depends on the state of the autonomic nervous system and the storage of memory, along with a multitude of other biopsychosocial factors.

The eight phases of EMDR have traditionally been outlined as these:

Phase 1: History taking and treatment planning
Phase 2: Preparation
Phase 3: Assessment
Phase 4: Desensitization
Phase 5: Installation
Phase 6: Body scan
Phase 7: Closure
Phase 8: Reevaluation

The eight phases of PV-EMDR are slightly adapted to embrace the wisdom of Polyvagal Theory within the EMDR model. The majority of Shapiro's model is untouched in my outline of PV-EMDR, with only a few minor recommended adjustments. These modifications allow the phases to align with the research and best practices of Polyvagal Theory, while maintaining EMDR fidelity. The adaptations outlined here do not threaten the legitimacy of EMDR, fidelity to it, or the core objectives of each respective phase. The modifications incorporate the needs and the role of the autonomic nervous system throughout the therapeutic process.

As therapists, we must always consider the necessary ingredients the autonomic nervous system requires to heal, its role in readiness and preparation for memory reprocessing, and its vital contributions to the integration of memories. Integrating Polyvagal Theory into the eight phases of EMDR adds merit and validity to each phase and offers you, the EMDR therapist, a neuro-informed framework for facilitating change.

The eight phases of PV-EMDR are as follows and are reviewed in detail in the following chapters:

Chapter 7, Phase 1: Safety and case conceptualization
Chapter 8: Phase 2: Preparation
Chapter 9, Phase 3: Assessment
Chapter 10, Phase 4: Desensitization
Chapter 11, Phase 5: Installation
Chapter 11, Phase 6: Body scan
Chapter 12, Phase 7: Closure
Chapter 13, Phase 8: Reevaluation

Chapter 7

PHASE 1: SAFETY AND CASE CONCEPTUALIZATION

Safety provides the sustenance and possibility for transformative healing. Safety *is* the intervention (Badenoch, 2008; Herman, 2015; Porges, 2011). Porges emphasizes the importance of safety time and again in his teachings, as Polyvagal Theory articulates the undeniable power of safety for health, wellness, and resiliency (Porges, 2022). When the autonomic nervous system neurocepts safety, our biology allows us to thrive and form bonds with others. Conversely, when the autonomic nervous system neurocepts danger, defensive responses move us toward disconnection and survival. Safety is the most vital and fundamental factor for successful therapy and should therefore be the explicit foundational phase of PV-EMDR therapy.

Phase 1 of EMDR therapy is traditionally known as history taking and treatment planning, as outlined by Shapiro. This phase focuses on gathering history and assessing client readiness for memory reprocessing (Shapiro, 2018). Phase 1 also focuses on therapeutic rapport, client safety, and developing an EMDR treatment plan. Each of these objectives remain relevant in Phase 1 of PV-EMDR. However, integrating Polyvagal Theory into the eight phases illuminates the need to slightly shift priorities and the order of treatment objectives. The PV-EMDR therapist begins with safety at the forefront of awareness, recognizing that safety is the primary pathway of intervention. While building safety, case conceptualization is also developed, providing direction and intentionality for developing an EMDR target list, also known as an EMDR treatment plan.

Identifying client goals is always a part of initial work and a standard objective for any therapeutic relationship. Client goals should be discussed early on and revisited throughout the lifecycle of the professional relationship. The EMDR model also discusses, sometimes confusingly, "treatment planning" as it relates to developing a list of targets. An EMDR treatment plan identifies the specific targets for reprocessing. You might also consider this to be an EMDR target list. An EMDR treatment plan identifies targets for reprocessing, typically using floatbacks and affect bridges. This specific aspect of EMDR, or "treatment planning," does not always align with Phase work.

The PV-EMDR model offers a revised Phase 1, titled Safety and case conceptualization. This revision is based on the knowledge that safety is the fundamental cornerstone of healing and therefore should be explicitly outlined within Phase 1 as the first objective of therapy. Further, case conceptualization inspires treatment planning. You cannot move into EMDR treatment planning without first establishing safety and case conceptualization.

In this proposed PV-EMDR revision of the eight phases, treatment planning is reviewed in Phase 3 because it is an activating intervention and a precursor to the standard protocol assessment. Creating an EMDR treatment plan without enough safety in the therapeutic relationship or enough flexibility in the autonomic nervous system is contraindicated. The EMDR treatment planning process typically includes floatbacks or affect bridges. Floatbacks and affect bridges are commonly used techniques in EMDR, in which the clinician uses images, thoughts, feelings, or body sensations to identify memories from the past which need to be reprocessed. These treatment planning techniques can be triggering and distressing for some clients, and they are processes which potentially require dual awareness and skill to tolerate stress responses. Prematurely establishing an EMDR treatment plan poses a risk of flooding the client's autonomic nervous system, activating defensive states. EMDR treatment planning can also involve high levels of vulnerability as the client discloses the specific memories associated with the presenting issue. In the absence of safety, this process may leave the client with what I call a vulnerability hangover—the visceral experience of sharing too much, too fast, without enough safety and connection. Safety must be in place for treatment planning to be a trauma-informed process. For these reasons, I offer a revised Phase 1, which begins with safety and case conceptualization, with EMDR treatment planning taking place only when the nervous system is ready.

CUES OF SAFETY

Safety is a multilayered experience and requires a multilayered assessment and conceptual framework. When determining the pace of treatment and readiness for memory reprocessing, the therapist must consider cues of danger and safety on micro- and macrolevels as experienced by the client. There must be enough cues of safety for the nervous system to have the resources to successfully reprocess memories to the point of adaptive resolution. When defensive states are recruited, memory integration becomes impaired or impossible, because of the physiological processes that affect neurophysiological functioning and memory consolidation.

Imagine you are preparing to run a half marathon. You have just consumed a cheeseburger, a liter of soda, and a hot fudge sundae. Would you feel nourished and ready to attempt this incredible feat? Likely not. That's a recipe for disaster and absolute misery. Similarly, we cannot expect a client's nervous system to have the flexibility and capacity to integrate maladaptively stored memories if sympathetic or dorsal circuits are chronically activated in response to fear and danger. Trying to reprocess memories when a client's nervous system lacks safety and stability is like asking someone to run a half marathon on cheeseburgers and sugar.

Cues of safety and danger are important markers when determining the pacing of treatment and the right timing to begin work on memory reprocessing. Just as safety is important within the therapeutic relationship, the client must also have neuroception of enough cues of safety in their life for reprocessing to be possible. For example, if clients are at imminent risk because of an abusive relationship, a natural disaster, or a major medical event, reprocessing memories may be counterproductive and burdensome. The adaptive responses of the autonomic nervous system are serving a purpose in such circumstances, as the autonomic nervous system assesses legitimate cues of danger that require a response to survive.

Further, a client's nervous system can be stuck in chronic states of defensive activation due to faulty neuroception. That is, their system continuously misappraises cues as dangerous when they aren't, causing chronic activation of defensive states. In that case, their physiology will also present as consistently dysregulated and stuck in survival mode. In such circumstances, the therapist must start with the real or perceived cues of danger and build safety through appropriate interventions. Some of these interventions are reviewed in Chapter 8 (Phase 2, Preparation).

It is not uncommon that clients present for counseling with a lack of safety cues and an abundance of danger cues. Food insecurity, unhealthy relationships, incarceration, gang violence, a recent disaster, or ongoing poverty, among many other scenarios, all present actual cues of danger in the present moment. Note that it is not the specific situation that rules out reprocessing. It is the nervous system's response. The therapist needs to assess the client's current autonomic state and determine how much access the client has to the ventral vagal circuit (I discuss how to do this in the upcoming sections). When cues of danger override the nervous system's capacity to access ventral, memory reprocessing via the full EMDR protocol may be contraindicated. In some circumstances, constricted forms of EMDR may be supportive in reducing acute symptoms promoting stabilization, or even preventing the emergence of more complex clinical presentations. Knipe's (2014) CIPOS protocol, Manfield et al.'s (2017) flash technique, Shapiro's (2018) constricted intervention technique of "EMD," and the recent event protocols all represent constricted forms of processing that have the potential to be supportive and even stabilize those clients who are highly triggered, dissociative, or avoidant of feelings and sensations.

Cues of safety and danger can ebb and flow. There may be periods of safety and easy access to ventral, followed by increased crisis and risk along with heightened autonomic defenses. This ebb and flow is the energetic pulse of life, and very much the state of our world and society at the time I write this book. It is a normal, human thing to experience fluctuations in stress levels in response to life circumstances and is indicative of a functioning autonomic system. Some clients have had the privilege of experiencing consistent and dependable states of safety and stability. However, for many clients, safety and stability may be rare or inconsistent experiences. The PV-EMDR therapist recognizes the parallels between the pulse of the nervous system and the pulse of life, and embraces the dance of autonomic regulation and activation. In times of increased danger, support your client to find ways to increase safety and stabilization. In times of increased safety and stability, explore the potential to venture into memory reprocessing and greater clinical depths.

Therapy should never go faster than the nervous system can tolerate. Pacing is not determined by the client's urgency, a hasty parent, a court order, or the therapist's desire to fix things for the client. The nervous system sets the pace. EMDR therapists who overlook the functioning of the autonomic nervous system in case conceptualization may inadvertently try to bypass dysregulation that requires stabilization, with the misconception that target reprocessing is the ultimate goal. Moving faster than the nervous system can tolerate can lead to increased distress and overwhelm, impeding reprocessing and creating distrust in EMDR and perhaps even therapy itself. It is easy to forget that memory reprocessing is not necessarily the goal of therapy. Integrating and moving toward health and wellness is.

Urgency is contagious. Through countertransference, we can easily take on the imperative feelings and sensations of our client. You might feel a sense of urgency to hurry up and make things better because, of course, we naturally want to ease the suffering of others. Sometimes the reality is that the client's life is not safe enough to run the metaphorical marathon of memory reprocessing. In such cases, focus on creating reliable, dependable, and consistent safety through the counseling process and relationship. Never diminish the value of safety. It is, in fact, more important than reprocessing targets. Phases 1 and 2 of PV-EMDR focus on building safety and stabilization. The breadth of impact these phases can have on a client's life should not be devalued or dismissed. Learning to feel safe and stable is priceless.

CASE CONCEPTUALIZATION

Clinical interventions must align with intentionality, which emerges from case conceptualization. Case conceptualization is an opportunity to identify strengths and resiliencies and explore neurophysiological correlates of client complaints. From the integrated lens of PV-EMDR, recognize that many clinical presentations are the outcome of maladaptively stored adverse experiences eliciting defensive responses of the autonomic nervous system. Most if not all *DSM* diagnoses have a component of autonomic dysregulation as a core feature or outcome of the condition (Porges, 2011). As a PV-EMDR therapist, you will establish case conceptualization by assessing the functioning of the nervous system while also gathering information about life events. The client's biographical history is only a portion of the story, while the nervous system's response is the other. We must first conceptualize the autonomic patterns if we are to integrate aligned and intentional interventions based on the client's needs. Without case conceptualization to guide those interventions, you simply don't know what the nervous system needs. Skillful case conceptualization leads to skillfully planned interventions.

Case conceptualization requires a multifaceted assessment, examining historical experiences and present-day functioning. The nervous system shares its story in many ways, and we begin case conceptualizing from the first moment of interaction with our client, collecting hard and soft data points. Soft data points include observations of body posture, tone of voice, eye contact, social skills, and the client's narrative about self, others, and the world. Hard data points include closed-ended questions and formal assessments the clinician may use to ask about specific experiences, symptoms, and diagnostic sequelae. Both forms of information gathering are relevant and should be integrated into your case conceptualization.

Conceptualization is a constant, ongoing, evolving process because the nervous system is constantly evolving. With every interaction and intervention, new data becomes available, which fine-tunes clinical insight. Case conceptualization begins at the first client meeting and continues through to termination. Because clients are constantly changing, parallel to the nervous system, case conceptualization is also continuously evolving. The nervous system is always telling its story, and the more skilled the clinician becomes at tuning in to that story, the more helpful they can be. Conceptualization is a fundamental component of Phase 1. Without conceptualization, it is impossible to chart a treatment plan with much wisdom or insight. While it is an essential component of Phase 1 work, recognize that this process is ongoing throughout the course of therapy, and changes in conceptualization will naturally influence treatment recommendations and interventions.

ASSESSING AUTONOMIC FUNCTIONING

The state of the autonomic nervous system is expressed through physical and psychological symptoms and implicit narratives. The small and significant physical symptoms clients report are indicators of autonomic functioning. The client's psychological symptoms are also indicators of autonomic functioning as well as the implicit narrative the client expresses (e.g., I'm not lovable; the world is not safe; people can't be trusted; I'm all alone). Tracking these processes provides insight into the client's autonomic functioning. The Autonomic Nervous System Graphic (Figure 3.1) outlines physical and psychological correlates and can be helpful in learning to track and identify correlated responses. Let's review a few case examples to practice this skill of tuning into the autonomic processes.

Case Vignettes

> Lynn (she/her) reports nightmares, flashbacks, and panic attacks. She has a diminished appetite and has been losing weight over the last few months. She talks rapidly in session and has a hard time sitting still. Her breathing often appears shallow, and she takes quick, almost gasping breaths between sentences in a rushed manner. She struggles to get to sleep and wakes frequently at night. She describes herself as restless and says, "I'm just an anxious person. I think I have an anxious personality type." She is so verbose in session it's hard for you to focus or direct her, provide interventions, or even get a word in sometimes. When asked about coping skills, she says that yoga and exercise are helpful, and after a good yoga class or a good workout she tends to feel calmer and can feel hunger. She also reports concerning use of benzos, prescribed by her doctor, and often turns to benzos before using other regulating skills.

Lynn's symptoms are indicative of an overactive sympathetic circuit. Her symptoms are those of a nervous system stuck in mobilization and hyperarousal. The intrusive psychological symptoms and the digestive issues correlate with sympathetic activation. The therapist can observe the mobilizing energy in the rushed manner that Lynn speaks, with gasps for air between sentences, along with her observed and reported restless energy. She also stated her implicit autonomic narrative: "I'm an anxious person. I have an anxious personality." She describes some capacity to exercise the vagal brake, which she accomplishes through yoga and exercise. However, her use of benzos to manage anxiety demonstrates minimal flexibility and resiliency, which would need to be assessed before beginning EMDR reprocessing. This client could benefit from building skills to regulate and soothe sympathetic arousal.

> Alex (they/them) presents with chronic depression. They have loss of motivation, loss of energy, no future directed goals, and increased needs for sleep. Alex's lifestyle is sedentary, as they sleep more than 10 hours a day and upon waking mostly spend their time eating, watching TV, or playing video games. Alex has one close friend, though they have not connected for some time. Alex presents with flat affect, has a slow gait, and makes little eye contact. They cannot describe feelings or body sensations, and almost falls asleep in session. Alex is overweight and is regularly constipated, and their breathing is typically slow and slightly labored.

Alex presents with symptoms of dorsal shutdown. All of Alex's symptoms have qualities of immobilization and hypoarousal. It's almost like the life has been sucked out of Alex. The psychiatric symptoms of depression, loss of motivation, numbness, and no future-directed goals are clear dorsal correlates. The additional symptoms of increased need for sleep, trouble with bowel movements, and difficulties breathing are also symptoms of dorsal vagal collapse. Alex is not ready for memory reprocessing, and prep work will need to focus on moving Alex out of dorsal collapse.

> Joti (she/her) says she's worried all of the time and feels an intense pressure inside her heart and mind. She says she feels a mix of urgency to get things done and to get up and move, but she also feels stuck and unable to make decisions. "Sometimes, I feel like a wet blanket. Heavy and weighted down." Her husband gets frustrated with her about this, which leads to arguments and to Joti feeling unworthy and unlovable. You observe that Joti is petite and thin. She often fidgets with her hands or a tissue. Her neck muscles and jaw look tight and constricted. She reports she sometimes gets lost in chores and will lose track of hours of time. When you ask her about feelings and sensations, she cannot name them.

Joti presents with signs of a mixed state of freeze. There are clear indicators of both sympathetic and dorsal activation. Joti's symptoms of "pressure," urgency "to get up and move," fidgeting, and muscle tension are all sympathetic mobilization responses. Her symptoms of being "stuck," unable to make decisions, feeling like a "wet blanket," struggles to name feelings or sensations, and loss of time are all symptoms of dorsal withdrawal. The narrative she experiences of being "unworthy and unlovable" is also a dorsal narrative. Joti will need to spend time working with this mixed state and building flexibility to connect with ventral before she is ready to proceed to memory reprocessing. She may not need to spend extensive time building skills, but increasing her capacity to access the ventral circuit will be an important part of the early work in therapy.

> Trevor (he/him) reports mild anxiety and worry. He says that overall, he feels moderately happy with his life. He volunteers, tolerates his job, and has a close friend group. He is engaged and looking forward to marrying his partner, Tim. His home was recently broken into when he was away at work. He has been feeling an increase in anxiety, is hypervigilant, and gets anxious when he comes home. He wakes easily at night as he feels "on guard," and his appetite has suffered a bit, especially for meals he eats at home. He has future goals and reports he uses skills regularly to try to manage symptoms and wellness. These include meditation, long walks with his dog, reading spiritual books, and volunteering.

Trevor describes a strong connection to his ventral circuit, as indicated by feeling "happy and content" with his life, future-oriented goals, and skills to increase his connection to ventral. He presents without chronic, long-term autonomic dysregulation. He has suffered a recent adverse experience with a home break-in, following which he is reporting an increase in sympathetic activation. Sympathetic activation is evidenced by reduced appetite, disrupted sleep, anxiety, hypervigilance, and feeling anxious when he comes home. Based on this brief synopsis, Trevor is ready to move into memory reprocessing if that is his chosen path for treatment.

To conduct a thorough assessment and form a robust conceptualization, the clinician needs to filter through significantly more information than that provided here in these brief vignettes. However, these vignettes outline clear themes and patterns that indicate the client's level of readiness and ANS functioning. Even with a short description, you can get a read on the client's internal climate.

Clients who report feeling out of control, overwhelmed, chronically flooded, and afraid, are unable to name internal experiences, and lack coping skills require time and practice to build autonomic resiliency. On the other hand, a client who can reflect on their experiences while noticing and naming their internal process and has a few skills to regulate their internal processes likely has enough vagal tone and autonomic resiliency to support memory reprocessing. While perfect stability is not necessary for EMDR reprocessing, the client needs some flexibility and resiliency in their nervous system for the nervous system to tolerate reprocessing. Without flexibility, autonomic and limbic system responses can hijack the nervous system, and impeded the pathways necessary for adaptive memory integration (Drexler & Wolf, 2017).

As you build your case conceptualization, assess your client's autonomic state(s) and their ability to use adaptive skills to regulate. Clinical symptoms are correlated with autonomic functioning. It is helpful to tune in to themes of distress. In doing so, the patterns of dysfunction and dysregulation will become clear. Tune in to themes through direct questioning and observation that tell the autonomic story. Does your client describe correlates of ventral vagal functioning and a robust toolkit of regulation skills? Or does the client describe chronic correlates of sympathetic or dorsal activation? Does your client have skills to regulate their physiology, are these skills adaptive, and how well do they work? Further, what physical ailments does your client disclose, and what might they indicate about autonomic functioning?

DUAL AWARENESS

Dual awareness is a gold standard of many trauma therapies. Also sometimes called dual attention, this term describes the neurophysiological function commonly referred to as "one foot in the past, one foot in the present." Dual awareness is the client's capacity to maintain connection to ventral while reflecting on the past. To reframe dual awareness within Polyvagal Theory, we can understand dual awareness as a mixed media state involving one foot in the autonomic stress response and one foot connected to ventral vagal.

Dual awareness is a skill that clinicians must assess in their clients as a component of case conceptualization and readiness for target reprocessing. Clients without dual awareness can get swept away by autonomic survival responses when triggered. When they recall the memory and connect to the feelings and sensations, the autonomic nervous system moves into defense. Therefore, if the client does not have dual awareness, the clinician will need to spend extended time in Phase 2, Preparation, building skills and capacity for dual awareness before proceeding to memory reprocessing.

Conversely, clients who can flexibly exercise the vagal brake in response to triggers, stress, and day-to-day life demands demonstrate considerable autonomic resiliency and may quickly transition into reprocessing phases. These clients demonstrate the neural capacity to reflect on past memories or present-day triggers without becoming overwhelmed by sympathetic or dorsal activation. Though these clients may report feeling distress when they recall a memory, they can maintain a mixed state defined by sufficient connection to ventral.

You can assess for dual awareness in several ways. One is with a scale asking the client to appraise their level of autonomic disturbance subjectively. This is also known as the Subjective Units of Disturbance Scale (SUDS), a component of the standard EMDR protocol. For example, the clinician may ask, "On a scale of 0 to 10, with 0 being no disturbance and 10 being the most you can imagine, where are you now?" The clinician should also be mindful of dorsal responses, which create a numbing effect and may not be identified with a scale assessing disturbance. Therefore, it's important to also check for dorsal vagal activation when assessing dual awareness, by using a similar scale for numbness. That is, "On a scale of 0 to negative 10, with 0 being no numbness or disconnection, and negative 10 being completely numb and disconnected, where are you now?" If a client reports higher numbers on either scale, that is not a guarantee they have lost dual awareness. The clinician can cue a regulating exercise, and how quickly the client benefits from coregulation is an indicator of how strong the autonomic defense is and how far the trigger takes them away from ventral. Clients who are slow to connect to ventral, or who cannot connect to ventral, likely have limited dual awareness.

Additional techniques include checking in and asking the client what they notice and if they are present. For example, the clinician can ask, "Are you still with me? Can you feel your body? Does any part of you feel like you are reliving your past right now?" Clients who report heightened levels of autonomic arousal when reflecting on triggers or past traumas may need time and care to build dual awareness. Memory reprocessing without dual awareness will prove distressing to the client, and the memory will be unable to integrate to the point of adaptive resolution. Skills for building dual awareness are reviewed in Chapter 8 (Phase 2, Preparation).

Case Vignettes

Charla (she/her) is talking about her childhood trauma history. As she shares her story of abuse with you, you notice she stops making eye contact, her voice loses prosody, and she looks visibly weighted down.

You ask, "Charla, I want to pause you for just a moment here and check in. On a scale of 0 to 10, with 0 being no disturbance and 10 being the worst, where are you right now?"

"I don't know. A 2, maybe?" Charla responds.

"Thank you. How about this one? On a scale of 0 to negative 10, with 0 being totally here, and negative 10 being totally numb and disconnected, where are you now?"

"Oh, a negative 8," she says.

You use grounding techniques to increase Charla's connection to ventral. You ask her to look around the room and name what she sees out loud. You ask the scale questions again, and this time she reports a 2 on the disturbance scale and a negative 2 on the numbness and disconnection scale. This indicates Charla has some level of dual awareness, as she demonstrated the ability to flexibly increase her connection to ventral with coregulation.

Luke (he/him) is talking to you about his history of grief and loss. Several of his close family members and friends tragically died around the same time for different reasons. He appears visibly uncomfortable, fidgety, and red in the face. You pause him and ask, "How are you doing right now? Is any part of you feeling like you're reliving these experiences right now?"

"Yes. I don't feel good," he says.

You ask Luke to try a breathing technique with you, which seems to produce no effect. You then try to switch his focus and ask him about his dog, whom you know he adores and is a ventral experience for him. He still says he feels stuck in high levels of disturbance. You ask him if he'd like to take a walk, and he agrees. After a 10-minute walk outside, he reports feeling calmer.

Luke's dual awareness appears lacking, without enough access to ventral to move into reprocessing phases. This is evidenced by the amount of coregulation and time he needed to return to ventral. His access to ventral will need to be further explored for you to more fully conceptualize how much or how little dual awareness he has.

These vignettes are highly simplified and limited in their focus. As the clinician, you would have access to much more information and data to help guide this assessment. Just because a client doesn't respond to an intervention doesn't mean they don't have dual awareness. Additionally, just because the client experiences distress doesn't mean they aren't ready to reprocess memories. The keys are to look at the entire clinical picture, the client's themes of distress, their coping strategies, and how effective those strategies are. Clients who get stuck in autonomic states get stuck because they don't have the flexibility in their autonomic nervous system they need to regulate back to ventral. Many of our clients come to us with less than ideal autonomic resiliency and limited capacity for dual awareness. After all, that is a defining characteristic of trauma. Therapy will focus on increasing their capacity for dual awareness with skills that exercise the vagal brake. For some clients, that may take only a few sessions and for others that may take months or even years. You must get a baseline, however, to chart your course and plan interventions.

NEURO-INFORMED HISTORY TAKING

Neuro-informed approaches can be beneficial at every clinical juncture, and history taking is no exception. Phase 1 is rich with opportunities for integrating EMDR and polyvagal-informed approaches, setting a safe and supportive tone for therapy from there on out.

As Shapiro (2018) outlines, in Phase 1, history taking is necessary to determine your treatment course and develop case conceptualization. However, it is important to understand history taking as a process rather than a specific clinical task to complete. Some clients present with a resilient autonomic nervous system and can easily share their stories and experiences without evoking defensive autonomic responses. Others do not have this capacity. Given that the most important foundational element of the work rests with the experience of safety, the clinician must keep safety front and center when gathering history.

Many standard approaches for gathering client history involve asking the client to divulge detailed, vulnerable, sensitive information. Safely sharing history requires some capacity for dual awareness. Without dual awareness, the client may become triggered by their past or the vulnerability of sharing sensitive information. Some clients cannot share their pasts while remaining connected to the ventral vagal circuit. Some clients become flooded and overwhelmed. Some disconnect and dissociate, telling the story as a matter of fact. In either case, sharing history without enough safety is not good therapy. We must always pace the inquiry portion of history taking with the client's nervous system. You don't need the entire story to be helpful.

The skilled and attuned therapist anticipates history taking to be triggering and tracks the autonomic states as the ultimate pacesetter. Never move faster than the autonomic nervous system can tolerate. In the first few sessions I have with a new client, my focus is always on creating a welcoming therapeutic space and establishing safety in the relationship. I pay careful attention to how I welcome them, how my space feels to them, and how I provide context for our work together. We should be hyperfocused on the subtle, and sometimes not so subtle, indicators from the client's nervous system that clue us into the best treatment pace for the client. In essence, the clinician plays the role of Goldilocks, searching for the not-too-fast, not-too-slow, just-right zone in the client's nervous system. In cases where autonomic defenses are easily triggered, it is best to intentionally steer away from detailed questions about the past, focusing on the present and immediate stabilization. Asking clients about their past when they live in chronic states of dysregulation can do more harm than good. The present state is more important than the historical story. Safety and coregulation cannot be sacrificed in the name of history taking. Rather, history taking should be delayed in the name of safety and regulation.

When a client is sharing vulnerable or potentially triggering information, it's important that you check in periodically and ask for feedback to track autonomic arousal. Just because a client is telling their story and outwardly appears to be regulated does not mean they are. Clients sometimes believe they are supposed to be overly vulnerable and share all the details. Isn't that what you do in therapy? Intentionally inviting moments to pause and check in may seem insignificant, but this is an impactful multifaceted intervention. Pausing to check in establishes a safe feedback loop between you and the client. It also contributes to safety in the relationship as you explicitly ask for feedback, taking steps to attend to distress by increasing access to ventral when needed. Checking in is also a neural exercise that practices skills to notice and name. For some clients, noticing and naming their internal experience may be foreign, dissociated, or confusing. Therefore, pausing to notice and name paves the way for new skills and techniques. Finally, checking in allows you to track for dual awareness, which is a necessary ingredient for successful integration.

How do you stop and check in politely during a client's big, vulnerable share? We certainly need to be mindful of our technique as we pause and check in so we do not come off as rude or disinterested. Here are some of my go-to statements to gently insert a moment of pause and check-in:

- "I'm so appreciative of what you're willing to share with me. You can decide how much and how fast to share. I want to hear everything you want to share with me, but I also don't want you to walk out of here with a vulnerability hangover. So, how are you doing right now with this story? How's the pace?"
- "This information is very helpful, and I also recognize it's sensitive. I want to check in on how that's feeling in your nervous system. On a scale of 0 to 10, where 0 is no distress and 10 is the most distress you can imagine, where would you say you're at right now? What about a 0 to negative 10 scale, with 0 being connected and present and negative 10 being numb and checked out?"
- "Thank you for sharing your story with me. I'd like to take a quick moment to check in with you, as I recognize this might be tender or triggering stuff to share. How are you doing right now? Are you fully with me as you share this, or has any part of you left this space? Is any part of you reliving this experience right now?"

In each of these examples, I thank the client and acknowledge the information being shared in an effort to avoid what may feel like biological rudeness. I want the client to clearly understand why I'm asking the question and creating a break in their storytelling. I provide context, or a "why," for the check-in. As we reviewed with the Three Cs, context contributes to transparency and safety. Based on my client's report, I may pause our discussion and guide them through a regulation skill if their level of distress or dissociation is heightened. This intervention could be mindfulness, breathing, guided imagery, gentle movement, or even a brief distraction by shifting to a lighter topic such as talking about their pet, a show they like to watch, or something fun they've recently done. Titrating the level of arousal is a neural exercise, which builds new adaptive neural networks and helps to develop and maintain a connection to the ventral circuit. It relies on coregulation to exercise the vagal brake in the moment in response to increasing autonomic arousal (Porges, 2021a). These micromoments of pausing, reflecting, and choosing are examples of neural exercises, which we review in more detail in Phase 2. Neural exercises build resiliency of the autonomic nervous system and enhance self-efficacy by strengthening adaptive neural pathways and contributing to vagal tone. You might even think of this pause as a way to microdose connection to ventral as you gather history.

You may gather history through structured and nonstructured methods. Structured, reliable, and valid assessment tools can detect relevant symptoms that questioning skills miss. However, be mindful not to rely too much on structured assessments as a primary means of data gathering and conceptualization. People are multidimensional, and psychometric assessments are not. Moreover, psychometric tools have the potential to cue neuroception to danger. Formal assessments can make the client feel like they are taking a test, that there is a right or wrong answer, or that they are being judged and labeled. Additionally, recognize the trigger risk in asking a client to complete assessments independently outside of the session. Reflecting on personal history, symptoms, traumas, and all that's wrong can activate memory networks and autonomic defenses. Without you to serve as a coregulator, your client may experience significant distress and lack the means to regulate. Therefore, I recommend refraining from sending formal assessments home with clients, and creating time to complete these in session or while in your waiting room.

A standard assessment should include the following biopsychosocial domains in no particular order: mental health history, medical history, drug and alcohol history, disordered eating behaviors, physical wellness (sleep, diet, hydration, exercise), onset and duration of complaints, suicidal and homicidal history, history of acute mental health episodes, stress/trauma history, dissociation assessment, family history, attachment history, cultural assessment, primary supports and strengths, and adaptive and maladaptive coping strategies.

Depending on the individual client and the state of their nervous system, Phase 1 may take place over a handful of sessions, several months, or even years. Remember to follow the autonomic nervous system as the pacesetter. Going faster than the system can tolerate causes unnecessary distress and can do the client a disservice. You can offer your clients significant relief and support by attending to the state of their dysregulation, even when you're still in the dark about what happened that led to their distress. Attending to the state is more important than attending to the story.

ATTACHMENT HISTORY

Attachment sets the stage for neurodevelopment and the capacity for self-regulation (Cozolino, 2017; Puhlmann et al., 2021; Newman et al., 2015). The autonomic nervous system is a relational system and relies on connection for safety, comfort, and nurturing (Dana, 2018). Therefore, we can understand attachment's vital role in shaping the nervous system. Because attachment is necessary for survival and a biological imperative, our nervous systems can be positively or negatively impacted by the quality of our early childhood attachments, more so than any other stage of our human development (Porges, 2011).

The literature on early childhood development overwhelmingly outlines the consequences of unhealthy attachment or trauma in early formative years (Baylin & Hughes, 2016; Bowlby, 1988; Courtois & Ford, 2013; Cozolino, 2014; van der Kolk, 2014; Kain & Terrell, 2018; Porges, 2011; Shapiro, 2010). Children will learn defensive patterns for survival and self-protection if those developmental years are spent in traumatic and stressful environments, lacking a safe and secure attachment figure. The nervous system is prone to develop in a way that elicits chronic states of emotion dysregulation, diminished learning capacity, and social withdrawal.

Assessing a client's early attachment history examines what did and did not happen in early formative years and assesses the experiences that shaped the autonomic nervous system. Attachment figures serve as protectors and safe keepers for a child's physical health and safety. Attachment figures also care for the child's emotional needs. Children growing up with depressed caregivers, in substance-abusing homes, or without a sense of feeling loved present with complex layers of neural dysregulation and significant levels of autonomic distress. Clinicians often look for early childhood big-T trauma but may forget to assess the quality of early attachment figures and how much love and nurturing the client experienced. Just because a client says, "I had a good childhood" and denies early experiences of physical or sexual abuse does not mean they had healthy, nurturing attachments.

For these reasons, conceptualization must factor in the quality of early childhood attachments in the client's life. The PV-EMDR therapist tunes into clinical themes and what the client's autonomic nervous system learned early on. Did they have caregivers who modeled healthy coping skills, or were they taught to numb or explode in response to difficult emotions? Did the client learn that emotions are safe, or that emotions are scary, dangerous, or bad? Did the client learn to regulate through coregulation, or are they void of self-soothing skills because their caregivers did not coregulate them?

Attachment history can inform preparation techniques and potential targets to include on a treatment plan. For example, if an unhealthy attachment history is a primary focus of treatment, you may install specific allies (e.g., a nurturing figure or a parental figure) as resources as part of Phase 2, Preparation. Additionally, you might utilize preverbal target formation techniques to organize a treatment plan. Failing to assess the client's attachment history can also result in misinformed treatment plans and blocked processing.

Several attachment assessments are available to clinicians. The Adult Attachment Interview (George et al., 1985) and Solomon and Siegel's Attachment Questionnaire (2003 are two free assessments that can be found online. An attachment questionnaire that I have developed over the years is also included in the appendix for your use (see Attachment Interview in the appendix).

CULTURAL ASSESSMENT

Per the AIP model, memories and experiences inform present-day perceptions, attitudes, and behaviors (Shapiro, 2018). Culture and identity inform our perception of ourselves, others, and the world based on information and experiences stored in memory networks. Therefore, assessing a client's social identities and culture must be a part of case conceptualization. Exploring the client's cultural background invites an opportunity to identify internalized adaptive or oppressive messages stored in memory networks, experienced through the autonomic nervous system. Many cultural assessment tools are available to clinicians, and there is no specific assessment that I advocate for. Explore the resources available to you and choose one that is inclusive of the many dimensions of culture and identity.

Each of us has a number of social identities. Some of these may be outwardly identifiable, to some extent, and some may not. For example, age, gender, race, ethnicity, and physical ability are a few core identities that are often assumed based on outward appearances. Some identities are not outwardly identifiable, including mental health diagnoses, military status, socioeconomic status, religious beliefs, political affiliation, level of education, and sexual orientation, to name a few. Recognize that no matter how obvious or subtle an identity may be, it has played a role in the client's life, influencing the development of the autonomic nervous system and memory storage. The clinician must never assume a client's identities or experiences and should always include awareness and discussions about culture as a standard component of case conceptualization. Failing to ask about culture and social identities is a privileged thing, whereas inviting discussions about culture and identity into the session is antioppression work in the therapeutic process.

To be an ally in the fight for equality and justice for all, we each must reflect on our held biases and notice our autonomic responses as they intersect with antiracism and antioppression work. Self-reflecting is the doorway to self-correcting. We all have blind spots and biases, as we live in an unfair, biased, oppressive society. Assuming that you do not hold biases is like expecting to take a walk in the rain without getting wet. Regardless of what privileged or marginalized identities you may personally hold, self-assessment and reflection is necessary to remain a social justice advocate for all peoples.

Antioppression and antiracism work is hard, and we know it because of what it feels like in our nervous system. It can trigger our adaptive defenses, evoking fight, flight, freeze, or collapse responses. Track your autonomic responses as a guide in this work. Perhaps you notice an autonomic reaction when someone shares a story that reminds you too much of your own. Or perhaps asking clients about their identities and experiences of oppression elicits a freeze response within you. Or maybe you avoid asking about culture because it leads to feelings of anxiety and overwhelm. Perhaps there are certain client identities that trigger anger and rage in you, and others that trigger shame and shutdown. Feedback is a gift, and consider such experiences to be feedback gifts from your autonomic nervous system, pointing out your growth spots.

Learning a client's social and cultural identities will provide helpful information and insight. Our identities can inform emotional expression, self-regulation, and interpersonal relationships. Consider the differences between a client who grew up in a disciplined and stoic military family versus a client who grew up in a highly expressive and chaotic family. Consider the difference between a client who grew up in a large family with lots of aunties, uncles, and cousins around to help care for them versus a client who grew up in a single-parent household without extended family support. Consider the difference in a client who grew up in a poverty-stricken, segregated community versus a client who grew up with privilege and wealth. These variables shape the development of our nervous system and hold significance for case conceptualization and autonomic resiliency. If we fail to explore these factors and life experiences, we miss a significant amount of the client's history.

DISSOCIATION

Clinicians should always be assessing for dissociation because everyone does it. You have likely had little blips of dissociation while reading this text, such as spacing out, daydreaming, or losing awareness of your body in the present. This is normal. Dissociation is common and adaptive. Thank goodness we can dissociate when we sit through a boring lecture, go to the dentist, or survive a pandemic lockdown or overwhelming social discord. Dissociation is not bad, for it is adaptive in nature. Dissociation can become problematic or maladaptive when it happens repeatedly, involuntarily, or outside of necessity and disrupts day-to-day functioning. Dissociation can be very subtle and sometimes difficult to identify. This section does not serve as a comprehensive review of dissociation, though I review this concept briefly related to PV-EMDR Phase 1 work.

It can be helpful to conceptualize dissociation as occurring in two forms. One form is dorsal dissociation, which produces a numbing effect, disconnection, immobilization, collapse, and disorientation (Nijenhuis et al., 2010). Physiologically, dorsal dissociation slows heart rate, respiration, digestion, and metabolism. It is an adaptive autonomic response to disconnect and collapse in the name of survival.

A more clinically complex form of dissociation that results from repeated activation of defenses is known as structural dissociation. Structural dissociation is much more complex, as it is a fragmentation of the psyche. This form of dissociation is a way to describe a dissociated, fragmented, or splintered personality structure, as evidenced by the presence of multiple parts, alters, or ego states. The theory of structural dissociation (van der Hart et al., 2006) describes three levels of dissociation of the personality, each level having increasingly severe symptoms. Dissociation of the psyche results from repeated adversity, often occurring in early developmental years, stemming from trauma and dysfunctional attachment patterns. In these cases, parts of self or ego states develop to protect the core self from overwhelming memories, feelings, sensations, or thoughts. Parts can present as apparently normal, and others may present with high levels of emotional distress. Parts can exist in dorsal, ventral, sympathetic, or mixed states. Therefore, not all parts are dissociated due to dorsal vagal withdrawal.

Case conceptualization is critical for deciphering which flavor or form of dissociation your client may be experiencing. Determining if dissociation is present, in which form(s), and to what degree, is the starting point for planning aligned interventions. For example, a client may present with a relatively intact personality structure, though experiencing an overactivation of the dorsal vagal circuit and correlated physiological symptoms. You may identify interventions to move the client from dorsal toward ventral in such cases. On the other hand, the clinical focus is different for clients with fragmented personality structures, presenting with an array of autonomic defenses. Treatment guidelines for clients with complex dissociative presentations outline a phase oriented approach focusing on stabilization and coping, integration of experiences, and integration of the client's internal world (International Society for the Study of Trauma and Dissociation, 2011).

There are many valuable tools to assess for complex dissociative patterns. The Dissociative Experiences Scale (DES), the Dissociative Disorders Interview Schedule (DDIS), the Somatoform Dissociation Questionnaire (SDQ), and the Multidimensional Inventory of Dissociation (MID) are all well-known, respected, and commonly implemented assessment tools to screen. These can be located with a quick online search. Review the available assessments and choose those that align best with your practice. Screening tools can pick up on presentations that verbal history taking may miss. Clients presenting with high levels of structural dissociation typically require more time spent in Phases 1 and 2 of PV-EMDR, building autonomic resiliency and capacity to integrate parts. If we fail to identify complex dissociation due to a lack of assessment, we risk causing the client significant distress and destabilization by proceeding to reprocessing phases before the system is ready. Remember that dissociation is nothing to be afraid of, for it is an adaptive defense and has helped your client survive, as evidenced by the fact that they are still here.

DEFENSIVE ACCOMMODATION

Polyvagal Theory and AIP both highlight adaptation over pathology. Both theories emphasize the adaptive nature of the nervous system. When faced with challenges, the nervous system will search for ways to adapt and protect. This can lead to the development of chronic maladaptive coping strategies, which cascade into complex physiological and psychological symptoms. The tendency to develop maladaptive compensation strategies to manage overwhelm and chronic dysregulation is known as defensive accommodation (Kain & Terrell, 2018). Patterns of defensive accommodation include somatic, physical, psychological, or behavioral strategies to influence autonomic states. Examples include binge eating, drug and alcohol use, avoidance, isolation, overworking, and many, many more.

When clients lack dependable access to the ventral vagal circuit, they are likely to turn toward coping strategies, behaviors, and belief systems to substitute for genuine regulation (Kain & Terrell, 2018). Understandably, a distressed system will seek strategies to soothe, even if those strategies may produce a fake or "faux" ventral state. The faux window of tolerance describes a fake neurophysiological state that mirrors the ventral vagal circuit. The faux window is not a genuine ventral state, as it is not the outcome of a client's capacity to exercise the vagal brake. The faux window is accessed by behavioral or chemical interventions that dampen or mask hyper or hypoarousal. Common behaviors that elicit a faux window include the use of controlled substances such as benzodiazepines or stimulants, drugs and alcohol, self-harm, eating-disordered behaviors, sex, or numbing behaviors. The clinician should recognize that all behavior is an attempt to cope, and the brain and body will seek out clever strategies in pursuit of safety. These behaviors are attempts to defend and accommodate.

The problem is not the problem; it is a solution. Often, the initially identified problem behavior or symptom is not the real problem, but the nervous system's attempt at a solution. For example, the client who experiences psychosomatic pain may be unconsciously compensating for the chronic experience of numbness. Alternatively, a client who drinks to the point of blacking out at night may be attempting to numb out flashbacks. Or the client who experiences suicidal ideation is seeking a strategy to make the painful experiences of shame and despair stop. You can miss the elephant in the room if you get distracted, only focusing on the maladaptive solution. Instead, get curious about the actual problem behind the defensive strategy and explore the root of the issue.

Invite curiosity into the clinical space with your client to explore what the defensive accommodation strategy may be solving. Consider what the maladaptive coping strategy could be trying to solve. What would the client experience without that behavior or strategy? What happens before, during, and after the strategy is used? What is the nervous system trying to solve with this strategy? Is the strategy one that invites sympathetic or parasympathetic energy?

These are some of the questions to consider as you explore the intention behind defensive accommodation strategies. With a better understanding of the deeper problem, you can develop thoughtful and insightful interventions, and build resiliency and capacity for stability and reprocessing.

CLINICAL THEMES AND MALADAPTIVELY STORED MEMORIES

As you gather relevant history, you will start to pick up on the clinical themes. Shapiro (2018) outlines these clinical themes, or information processing plateaus, as safety, responsibility, and choice. Sometimes our clients present with a mixture of themes or informational plateaus, and in others, one theme is running the show. As you home in on patterns within the context of the client's life experiences, you will start to hear the underlying process and clinical theme. As you learn your client's history, taking as much time as indicated in the process, stay curious about the experiences that led to the manifestation of clinical symptoms and sequelae. PV-EMDR therapists should always, always stay curious about what happened to the client and their reaction to it, versus what's wrong with the client. As we learn about what did and did not happen in their lives, we can start to identify specific adversities, stressors, or traumas that are maladaptively stored and eliciting autonomic defenses.

In summary, a PV-EMDR therapist considers the state of the autonomic nervous system and paces treatment accordingly. They conceptualize the level of autonomic dysregulation and whether that dysregulation is mild, moderate, or severe. Based on history taking and assessments, flavors of distress and themes of autonomic functioning will emerge. Those with mild levels of dysregulation can quickly transition to memory reprocessing as compared to those clients with severe levels of dysregulation, requiring ample time spent in preparation.

Additionally, consider the contributions of memory storage to the presenting problem. Are the contributions of maladaptively stored memories seemingly mild, moderate, or severe? This question also highlights interventions and treatment planning. For example, a client may present with moderate levels of autonomic dysregulation due to a current stressor, while simultaneously presenting with seemingly few maladaptively stored memories contributing to the distress. Conversely, a client may present with moderate levels of autonomic dysregulation and a plethora of maladaptively stored memories. Treatment will look different for clients depending on the mixture of autonomic functioning and memory storage.

Assessing both the autonomic nervous system and the contributions of stored memories is imperative for skillful conceptualization. Forming a working conceptual framework for the functioning of these two branches of the nervous system informs treatment recommendations. More often than not, clients seek out therapy due to a mixture of autonomic complaints and moderate to severe levels of contributing maladaptively stored memories. Clients with mild levels of dysregulation and minimal maladaptively stored memories rarely come to counseling. Why? Because they aren't suffering from distressing symptoms that motivate people to seek help. A well-resourced and resilient autonomic nervous system with few maladaptively stored memories is an indicator of integration, health, and wellness.

Chapter 8

PHASE 2: PREPARATION

Phase 2 focuses on client stability and setting the stage for EMDR (Shapiro, 2018). In this phase, we take time to educate our client about treatment options, including the process of EMDR therapy, and the initial preparation work begins as the client learns regulating resources such as safe/calm place, light stream, and containment as indicated. This phase is rich in opportunities to integrate Polyvagal Theory, as the autonomic nervous system becomes a primary focus of stabilization in preparation for memory reprocessing. This phase resources the autonomic nervous system and builds vagal tone, via aligned and thoughtful interventions.

There are critical autonomic resiliencies that must be present for the work to progress past Phase 2. Figure 8.1 outlines the preparation hierarchy, which I developed to highlight the specific skills a client needs to transition to memory reprocessing with the full EMDR protocol and a comprehensive treatment plan. The preparation hierarchy represents four autonomic capacities that support memory reprocessing and integration. These essential functions represent specific neurophysiological skills that build on each other and collectively support a resilient autonomic nervous system. They are the skills that contribute to a wide window of tolerance and a flexible vagal brake.

Neural exercises are the key to developing these autonomic capacities, provided in the form of clinical interventions. Neural exercises are skills that exer-

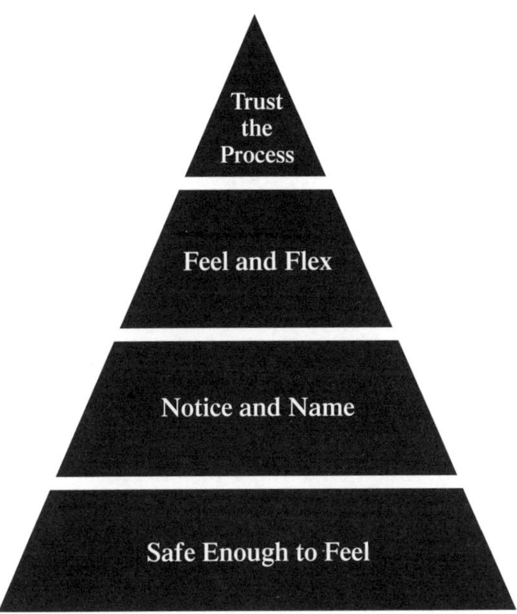

Figure 8.1: Preparation Hierarchy Graphic. Porges, S. (2000). Clinical Applications of the Polyvagal Theory. Lecture presented at PESI in Https://catalog.pesi.com.

cise the autonomic nervous system, building capacity to accurately appraise cues of danger or safety, and inhibiting or mobilizing states (Porges, 2021b). Neural exercises focus on building the specific skills of being safe enough to feel, notice and name, feel and flex, and trust the process.

THE EMDR THERAPIST MYTH

Myth: Reprocessing targets is the ultimate goal of EMDR and the thing that makes clients better.
Fact: Helping someone learn to regulate their nervous system is priceless.

Many EMDR clinicians believe the myth that the goal of an EMDR therapist is to move clients into reprocessing targets. This belief puts memory reprocessing on a pedestal, believing it to be the ultimate healing intervention. Many of us have learned that memory reprocessing is the goal. This is not completely accurate. The intention of all therapy is to help people feel better and live more functional lives. Reprocessing targets is one intervention that can support this, but it is not necessarily the most important. Never diminish the power of the Phase 2 work of preparation. Supporting a client to learn to feel safe in their physiology and develop skills to manage autonomic responses is significant because knowing how to navigate your internal world is invaluable. Phases 1 and 2 of EMDR are crucial for the client to live a more meaningful and less distressing life.

If you have been practicing under this myth, I give you permission to let it go. When we practice with this belief, we can get stuck and lose sight of the fact that healing is a journey and a process. We may believe that we're a terrible EMDR therapist if our client, after months or years, still isn't ready to reprocess memories. Or we may feel like we need to talk clients into reprocessing, even if they say, "I don't feel like doing EMDR this week." Or we might come to think of EMDR as an intervention rather than an entire therapy. We can lose sight of where some of the most important work lies. While yes, reprocessing memories via the EMDR protocol can be highly impactful, it is only one part of the work. Learning to feel safe in your nervous system, learning skills to manage dysregulation and distress, and learning to trust that you can feel and not spontaneously combust is much more impactful than processing memories. Learning to trust your nervous system is a gift that benefits every part of your life.

Of course, we can argue that unresolved and maladaptively stored memories trigger autonomic distress (de Jough et al., 2016). Without reprocessing memories, the autonomic nervous system will continue to be hijacked when triggered, resulting in continued struggles with regulation and stability. Yes, this is also true. Because the autonomic nervous system and memory networks have an interdependent relationship, dysfunction in one will produce dysfunction in the other. However, without autonomic flexibility, memories simply will not reprocess. Therefore, the clinician must remain mindful of the pitfalls of moving too slow and fostering avoidance, or moving too fast and producing flooding. These dynamics are parallels of trauma; avoidance and flooding. You do not have a crystal ball or a litmus test that can 100% guarantee when your client is ready to begin reprocessing. But remaining mindful of the role of the autonomic nervous system, getting skillful in conceptualizing readiness through the lens the of the preparation hierarchy, and engaging your client in such careful decisions is key.

For many clients, Phases 1 and 2 take considerable time. Clients often present for therapy with significant distress held in their nervous system, poor vagal tone, and minimal capacity to exercise the vagal brake. However, don't forget that their nervous system is resilient, always changing, and continuously integrating. Healing and developing vagal tone don't happen overnight. (I know, bummer.) This process takes time, practice, repetition, and consistency. If we rush through Phase 2 and proceed to reprocessing when a client truly isn't ready, we will create more work for ourselves and the client. Healing takes as long as it takes, and in many cases the slower you go, the faster you go.

THE WINDOW OF TOLERANCE

The window of tolerance is a concept originally proposed by Dan Siegel (1999) that is widely embraced in the clinical field. Siegel (2020) defines the window of tolerance as "a band of optimal functioning that flows between chaos on one side, and rigidity on the other. This flow emerges from integrative processes and has the features of FACES: being flexible, adaptive, coherent, energized, and stable" (p. 511).

This concept is typically defined as a needed optimal zone of arousal that is necessary to support trauma processing and overall health and wellness (Corrigan et al., 2010; Ogden, 2006). Outside of the window lies hyper- and hypoarousal, zones in which autonomic defenses activate survival strategies and impede processing. Within the window is the ideal zone for clinical work to take place.

How can we understand the window of tolerance as it relates to Polyvagal Theory? Is the window of tolerance defined by ventral? Can a mixed state exist in the window? Is the window only defined by the autonomic nervous system?

The window of tolerance is a construct of ventral functioning, vagal tone, and the vagal brake. The window is not purely defined by connection solely to ventral. Rather, we can still be in our window with a little sympathetic energy or dorsal energy. The key is in understanding the client's flexibility to maintain connection to the window and return to the window with skill.

Some clients have a very narrow window of tolerance. This means that they struggle with skills to effectively exercise the vagal brake and may have limited ability to connect to ventral. These clients likely also have low vagal tone. A narrow window of tolerance does not rule out EMDR reprocessing. But it may be an indicator that you need to modify your protocol with constricted approaches such as constricted EMD (Shapiro, 2018) or the Flash Technique (Manfield et al., 2017). Starting with constricted protocols can help to expand the window while refraining from going faster than the client can tolerate.

Conversely, clients with a large window of tolerance have a strong connection to ventral, high vagal tone, and a flexible vagal brake. When autonomic states of defense get triggered, the client has ways to increase their access to ventral. They may even be able to access skills to use during the stressor. These clients have high levels of resiliency that will benefit their counseling process and their lives.

We must assess the client's window of tolerance and use this information to inform the clinical work (Shapiro, 2010). Without access to the window of tolerance, clients typically experience overwhelming physical and sensory activation that impedes the capacity to feel safe and connected. Good therapy happens inside, not outside, of the window. The window of tolerance is an important concept in psychotherapy and when assessing level of preparation for EMDR reprocessing. Recognize that the window is a function of the vagal brake, the ventral circuit, and vagal tone and can therefore be built and expanded with practice and neural exercises. The window of tolerance is not defined by a client living in ventral 24/7. No one does. But a solid window of tolerance is defined by reliable connection to ventral, and skills to flexibly work the vagal brake in response to stressors and increased activation.

THE PREPARATION HIERARCHY

Clinicians often ask me, "How do I know when my client is ready to reprocess targets?" While there is no guaranteed test or assessment to answer this question, there are a few key readiness indicators. I have organized these indicators into a hierarchical skill set informed by AIP and Polyvagal Principles. The autonomic nervous system must be capable of certain skills to support memory reprocessing, which include being safe enough to feel, notice and name, feel and flex, and trust the process. These four foundational skills can be conceptualized as the preparation hierarchy (Figure 8.1). Collectively, these skills support memory reprocessing. When the client demonstrates the capacity to practice these skills in the therapy office and to some level on their own, you and the client can progress to reprocessing EMDR targets. These skills, or neurophysiological capacities, develop by practicing neural exercises, which build autonomic flexibility by exercising the vagal brake.

Pretend you have set a physical goal for yourself to bench press 100 pounds.

This is something you aren't currently capable of; therefore, you can't expect to go to the gym, set up your weights, and ta-da, you did it! No, of course not. You need to exercise and train to work up to this goal. So you set up a schedule and get to training. How long and how much you must train depends on your current level of physical fitness and how heavy the lift is. Training may take a while if you're in poor physical health and can barely bench press 5 pounds. If you are in excellent physical health and can already lift 50 pounds, you are well on your way and will likely reach your goal in less time. We can apply this metaphor to EMDR therapy and Phase 2. The length of time in preparation depends on the nervous system's fitness, or autonomic resiliency, and how heavy the lift is, or how extensive and charged the memories for reprocessing are. As at the gym, if you try to lift too much too quickly, you can cause injury. Similarly, if we attempt to process targets before the nervous system is ready, we can do harm. Additionally, even if you never reach your goal, getting in shape and exercising will still have a positive impact on your life. This analogy is the same for clients who spend extended time in Phase 2 but never proceed to memory reprocessing for whatever reason.

The vagal brake allows the autonomic nervous system to mobilize or inhibit defense responses (Porges, 2011; Porges, 2021a). Developing this flexibility contributes to vagal tone. In healthy development, we learn to exercise the brake through neural exercises with caregivers. Neural exercises are activities that practice "transitory disruptions and repairs of the physiological state through social interactions employing cues of safety and that promote greater resilience" (Porges & Dana, 2018, p. 62). Neural exercises train neural networks through the practice of engaging or inhibiting defensive states. Play, peekaboo, hide and seek, and soothing through coregulation are all examples of neural exercises. Therapy serves as a surrogate experience for neural exercises, as the clinical work focuses on building capacity to shift autonomic states through clinical interventions and the use of the social engagement system (Porges, 2021b). As clients experience the benefits of coregulation and safety, the autonomic defense states begin to shift and resolve, allowing self-regulation skills to emerge and develop.

Many clients present for therapy with limited abilities to self-regulate due to a lack of healthy and secure attachments in childhood, which negatively impacts neurophysiological development. A lack of safety and coregulation in childhood translates into a lack of opportunities to practice these neural exercises and develop autonomic resiliency. No one enters this world knowing how to self-soothe and self-regulate. As children, we look to our caregivers to teach us how to do this. If our caregivers do not teach us these skills, our nervous systems get stuck in chronic states of dysregulation and distress. The therapeutic space fills this deficit by offering neural exercises through safety, coregulation, and clinical intervention.

All therapies trigger clients to some degree. No matter one's orientation or chosen intervention, therapy by nature asks clients to think about or talk about distressing thoughts, feelings, and experiences. We ask this of clients while weaving in techniques that support the nervous system to stretch and grow, careful to avoid burdening the nervous system with too much stress. Supporting clients' moderate states of arousal is the purpose of neural exercises. No matter your orientation or specific intervention, all good therapy uses neural exercises. Opportunities to practice skills in the presence of safety is, in essence, the mechanism of psychotherapy. Neural exercises are therefore already alive and well in the counseling space. This chapter will teach you to conceptualize and integrate neural exercises with intentionality alongside the preparation hierarchy. These neural exercises support the nervous system to establish the foundational skills needed for successful memory reprocessing.

FOUNDATIONAL SKILLS OF THE PREPARATION HIERARCHY

The preparation hierarchy is organized into four skill sets. These skills are developed from neural exercises practiced through clinical intervention within the safe container of therapeutic presence. The skills are organized hierarchically, as skills at the bottom of the hierarchy must be achieved to support skills at the top of the hierarchy. Neural exercises target the development of these four skills and build autonomic resiliency as the client learns to exercise the vagal brake. There is no specific set of clinical interventions to apply to each skill. Rather, consider how interventions align with these categories and use intentionality to plan interventions among the hierarchy model. Most importantly, think about these skill sets as you assess your client's readiness. Does your client have the capacity to be safe enough to feel, notice and name, feel and flex, and trust the process? If the answer is no to any of those, more preparation work is likely needed.

1. Safe Enough to Feel

First and foremost is the fundamental need for safety; therefore the first exercise is to support the client to learn to be safe enough to feel. Safety is a prerequisite for healing. Because safety is the most important intervention, every intervention is a neural exercise in this foundational skill of being safe enough to feel. This neural exercise begins from the first interaction with the client and carries through every step of the way. As trauma is an experience of extreme disconnection, trauma healing must offer a reparative experience of connection (Dana, 2018). Connectedness is required for health and wellness, and healing cannot happen if a client does not feel safe and connected in therapy. The experience of being safe enough to feel is the foundation for psychotherapy. Safe enough to feel is established in therapeutic presence and rapport. As Porges (2011) teaches us, opportunities to coregulate are the basis of thriving. Therefore, it is vital that the therapist be well regulated and anchored in their ventral vagal circuit when engaged in this clinical work. The therapist being safe enough in their physiology allows safe connection to be possible.

Being safe enough to feel allows clients to explore feelings and sensations with curiosity in a titrated and safe manner. As you remain a reliable coregulator and a safe anchor, the client can approach what has otherwise been unapproachable. Just as children with secure attachment use a secure base to explore and gain mastery, the client uses the therapist as a secure base to explore and gain mastery over their inner world (Applegate & Shapiro, 2005). With consistent safety and reliable coregulation, the client can be curious about their internal world, thoughts, feelings, sensations, and physiological processes. The experience of coregulation allows the client to begin to explore their experience, with the therapist providing reliable coregulation along the way.

Case Vignette

Laura (she/her) is a 46-year-old, Latinx, heterosexual client with complex PTSD. She is a veteran who served in the army and experienced sexual, physical, and emotional abuse as a child. This is our first session. Laura is transferring from another therapist who retired. I meet Laura in the waiting room and invite her into my office.

As soon as Laura sits down, I can see that she is anxious and experiencing heightened sympathetic arousal. She sits down, grabs a magazine, and starts fanning herself, saying she's "really hot." She shares, "I'm anxious to be here. I really liked my last therapist and it's hard to start over." I don't know much about Laura at this point. But I do know the most important thing for me to know right now, which is that Laura doesn't feel safe here.

"I'm so sorry that your last therapist is leaving. That would be so hard. You two had worked together for some time, is that right?" I ask to validate and offer compassion.

"A year. I feel like I made progress with her. I haven't with the other therapists I've worked with," she replies.

"That would be really hard. And probably kind of scary. I am glad you're here, but I recognize this feels uncomfortable and anxiety producing. Let's just take our time and ease in. I tend to slow things down to help your nervous system feel more comfortable. I wonder if it would be helpful to just take a moment and explore my office. You're welcome to touch anything or get up and look at anything you want. But take as long as you want to really look around. You've never been here before, and it can feel good to look around this new space." I offer this to Laura to slow the process down and help her neuroception take in my space.

Laura looks around the room with curiosity, and I notice she takes a bit of a deeper breath. I look around the office too so as not to sit there awkwardly staring at her. It's also orienting and soothing to my nervous system to take a moment to look around my environment, even though I know it well.

After a minute or two, I ask, "What's this space like for you as you look around? Anything you can't stand? Anything that you like? You can be honest. I will not be offended at all."

"That picture is really nice," she says about a picture that's hung behind me. It's a picture of a forest and purple flowers. Most clients remark that it's soothing, so I have it strategically placed right behind me, in a client's direct line of sight.

"Oh yeah." I turn to look at the picture with her. "Yeah, I really like that one too. What do you like about it?" I ask to invite curiosity and encourage her to focus more on what she finds pleasant or appealing. This has the potential to increase her connection to ventral.

"I like the way the light looks in the trees. And those purple flowers," Laura shares.

"Mmmmmmhm. Yeah. Me too. I really like the light and the flowers too. What do you notice right now inside as you're taking that picture in? How's that anxiety and the heat you were feeling?" I ask to check in and assess how she's settling and to track her.

"It's a little better. But my heart is still beating fast," she responds and continues to fan herself.

"I wonder how it might feel to just rest your gaze on this picture for a few moments and take three deep, slow breaths. Would you be open to trying that?" I ask. I'm trying to invite in connection to ventral with breathing as a mechanism to engage the vagal brake, while neuroception simultaneously rests on the cues of safety she shared from the picture.

Laura nods in agreement.

"Great. I'm going to take a few deep breaths with you. Just gaze at the stuff you like in that picture, and let's just take some time to breathe."

I take three breaths with Laura, tracking her breath and making my breath audible to help her slow down her inhale and exhale. At the end of the last breath, Laura's shoulders drop a little, and I notice her facial muscles soften just a bit.

"What's that like now?" I ask.

"That's a lot better actually," she responds.

We continue exploring my office. Laura notes that she likes the light coming in the window and that she can see the door. She said there wasn't anything that she strongly disliked, except the parking lot, which was too busy for her comfort

We then proceed to complete a few pieces of administrative paperwork. I review my disclosure statement, consent to treatment, privacy rights, and fee agreement with her. I take time to answer her questions. After we've completed this, I check in again to assess where to go from here.

"How are you doing right now?" I ask.

"I feel hot again," she says and picks up the magazine and starts fanning herself.

"Are these hot flushes normal for you? Do they happen a lot?" I ask to check in on the symptom. I'm curious if this is sympathetic arousal in distress or if there may be something medically related happening.

"It's anxiety. When I get anxious, I get hot and start sweating a lot," she responds.

"Sounds like you know yourself. That is a very normal response to feeling anxious. You can always pick up a magazine to cool down in here, and I'll take that as a sign to slow it down. How would it be to take your attention back to that picture, and how about we take five breaths together and slow things down?" I ask.

Laura nods, rests her gaze on the picture, and starts to breathe.

"Nice. Just rest your focus on what feels appealing in that picture and notice your breath." We take five breaths together, and I can visibly see Laura calm. She sets the magazine down, and her body relaxes.

"How is all that now?" I ask.

"Better. I feel a lot calmer," she responds.

I continue to return to the picture and the breath in our session a few more times, as I track her autonomic activation. The picture and the breathing are serving as an anchor point to increase connection to ventral in this first session. This is a *pendulation* technique, a method of moving back and forth between activation and the ventral window of tolerance. It is a skill that creates safety, helps a client learn to notice and name, and builds autonomic flexibility.

While I do not know much about Laura, I was able to quickly find a way to increase her safety and connection to ventral by asking her to scan my office. You can do this with your clients too when you're still getting to know them and there are clear indicators that they quickly need more connection to safety. As Laura and I work together over the next few weeks, we develop additional ways to anchor her to safety. We install her ventral state as a resource (see the PV-EMDR exercise of Resourcing Ventral), and I teach her breathing techniques. We return to the picture regularly in the beginning of our relationship when she feels a flare of sympathetic energy in our sessions. Eventually we shift to anchoring back to her resourced state of ventral. Laura's resourced state is a waterfall, and she quickly begins using it outside of session.

A month later Laura comes in for her session, and I start by checking in on how we're doing. "I wanted to take a moment to check in with you and see how our relationship is doing. I like to check in regularly to ensure I'm being helpful and meeting your needs. How is our work together going for you?"

"I wasn't sure how I felt when we first met. I was so sad that I had to change therapists because Sam closed her practice. I wasn't sure about this at first. But you feel really different to me than other therapists. You've given me tools already that help. I feel comfortable with you."

This excerpt highlights how safety is the focus from the very beginning of the relationship. I intervene as soon as I notice she's experiencing significant sympathetic activation and set the stage for therapy to be a coregulating experience. I consistently track her autonomic response and increase connection to ventral through basic clinical interventions when needed, to keep her connected to safety. Tracking her responses and cueing interventions is the art of coregulation. With consistency and repetition, I become a safe base for Laura, which allows Laura to be safe enough to feel in our clinical work.

2. Notice and Name

The second skill, notice and name, supports the client to learn to observe, notice, and explicitly describe internal experiences. Another name for this is interoception. Interoception is the internal aspect of neuroception and is the ability to perceive sensation within the body. Interoception is necessary for reprocessing, as the client must be able to notice and name their internal world to adaptively integrate a memory (Payne et al., 2015).

When autonomic defensive states are recruited, activity in the prefrontal cortex diminishes, which is also the area of the brain needed to notice and describe feelings, sensations, thoughts, and memories. You may observe this process with your clients when they struggle to put words to their experience. Being able to notice one's physiology and put words to it requires enough cues of safety to access the prefrontal cortex and Broca's area, the area responsible for speech (van der Kolk, 2014). This skill is developed by inhibiting defense responses through coregulation, increasing safety, moving slowly, and inviting the client to practice observing their experience.

Learning to notice is one component of this work, while learning to name is the other. To put words to your internal experience, one must have the vocabulary to do so. That is, clients need to have some vocabulary to describe feelings and sensations. While clients need not have an advanced vocabulary to describe their internal world (though it is a great asset if they do), they need to have some language to express their experience. Learning words to describe feelings and somatic sensations is important for autonomic resiliency and may be a focus of the work to build this skill. Learning feeling words and somatic vocabulary can help clients begin to shift the implicit to the explicit.

Learning to notice and name shifts the client's attention from an otherwise unconscious experience to one of conscious, explicit awareness (Gibson,

2019). With the ability to notice and name comes the gift of discernment. We must discern our physiological state to intentionally use regulation strategies when needed. For example, the client must become aware of feeling anxious to discern if that anxiety is because of a trigger or because they had too much caffeine. Discerning the cue for that increase of sympathetic energy then offers one the opportunity to cue a behavior to manage the distress. One must be able to notice the internal experience of dysregulation and the specific type of dysregulation to employ coping strategies, which notice and name sets the foundational capacity for.

Scanning neuroception, surfing imagery, and mapping circuits all help build the capacity to notice and name. These interventions are outlined in the following pages. I also like to teach my clients feeling words, and we spend time describing what they feel like with sensory descriptor words. The client may identify sensations such as hot, cold, tight, loose, hard, soft, shooting, stabbing, pulsing, and so forth. "Pretend I've never felt anger. How would you describe it?" is a question I ask to get them curious. This is great to practice between sessions and focus on in sessions as well, to help the client grow their emotional and somatic vocabulary.

3. Feel and Flex

The third skill of the preparation hierarchy is feel and flex, which begins with learning to feel feelings. This skill is different from notice and name, as learning to feel can require some tolerance and patience. It takes practice to learn to sit with feelings versus numbing or desperately trying to escape the feeling. Mindfulness is an excellent tool to develop this skill. Additionally, it can be helpful to explore a client's relationship to feelings. Do they flee from their feelings as if they are a threat? Do they turn to substances to numb out and avoid? Did they learn that feelings are unsafe and dangerous? Unpacking these defenses while learning to tolerate feelings, in tolerable doses, is the neural exercise that supports the skill of learning to feel.

Learning to feel autonomic states also requires the development of skills to regulate, or flexibly maneuver autonomic states. A key contributor to vagal tone is the ability to accurately appraise safety and inhibit or mobilize defenses (Porges, 2011). Without the ability to assess and inhibit or mobilize defensive states, the nervous system lives in states of chronic stress (Porges, 2003; Porges, 2021a; Porges, 2021b). With a safe therapeutic relationship, you can use coregulation to help your client learn to inhibit defense responses when they are not needed. With repeated practice, these skills can transpose to the client, as they learn to self-regulate. Coregulation paves the way to self-regulation, as safe coregulators teach us how to exercise the vagal brake and maneuver autonomic states.

Without the capacity to feel and flex, reprocessing phases will be challenging. A client's defensive strategies against feeling may thwart reprocessing. Or if a client is unable to accurately appraise safety and inhibit an autonomic defenses, the client may get stuck in states of distress. Learning to flex and feel not only supports EMDR reprocessing but also empowers the client to exert some control over their internal world. To reclaim one's mind, body, and heart is the antithesis of the powerless experience of trauma and toxic stress.

Feel and flex can be a neural exercise of focus in Phase 2 work, although constricted symptom-focused protocols can also be of aid. The clinician may employ strategies of Shapiro's (2018) EMD or Manfield's Flash Technique (Manfield et al., 2017) to diminish strong abreactions of mobilized autonomic defenses. These protocols may be called upon when the preliminary exercises of being safe enough to feel and notice and name have been established, but the capacity to feel and flex is stunted or limited in scope. However, these protocols cannot be implemented without some level of autonomic stability and must be used with intentionality.

4. Trust the Process

The fourth skill of the preparation hierarchy, trust the process, should be conceptualized as an outcome of learning the first three skills rather than a skill in and of itself. This skill is a byproduct of vagal flexibility and autonomic resiliency. "Trust the process" is a commonly used EMDR mantra. The saying reminds us EMDR clinicians to trust the nervous system's innate capacity to heal and integrate experiences. We also ask that our clients trust the process and EMDR therapy. However, trust is not given. Trust is earned. Just as it took you some time and experience to trust EMDR, clients need time and experience to trust the therapeutic process and their own nervous system.

Think about when you were a brand-new therapist. Do you remember how scary it felt to sit with your first clients? The experience of sitting in the chair of the therapist with minimal training and just getting your feet wet is uncomfortable at first. But then you find your flow, you learn how to practice therapy with ease, and you trust your skills to be a clinician. Getting to a place where you can trust yourself as a therapist took time, practice, and experience. Trust requires these three ingredients: time, practice, experience. With enough time, practice, and experience working the first three skills of the hierarchy, the client learns to trust the therapeutic process, the therapist as a coregulator, and their own ability to regulate their states. Trust may come quickly for those with autonomic resiliency, though it may take time for those who need to build the foundational skills of preparation.

BLS AND NEURAL EXERCISES

The term "resource" is a commonly referenced intervention of EMDR therapy, specific to Phase 2. Korn and Leeds (2002), created the Basic EMDR Resource Development and Installation protocol (RDI), which is a staple of Phase 2 work well known amongst EMDR clinicians. The RDI protocol is one example of a resource, though there are many resources clinicians can integrate into Phase 2, Preparation. Resources can be thought of as any skill the client learns that enhances their connection to the window of tolerance or the ventral circuit. All resources are neural exercises as they all influence autonomic arousal with the intention of creating flexible capacity to access ventral. The well-known EMDR-based interventions of a safe/calm place, light stream, and resource development and installation are all examples of resources you have likely learned in your EMDR training.

EMDR clinicians learn that pairing bilateral stimulation (BLS) with a resource can enhance the client's adaptive experience. Shapiro (2018) and Korn and Leeds (2002) instruct us to apply short and slow rounds of bilateral movement in combination with a resource. Adding passes of BLS while a client is connected to a resource has the potential to expand the client's experience and deepen their connection (Korn & Leeds, 2002; Stickgold, 2002). One way to conceptualize the use of BLS in relation to resourcing exercises is that it gives the client time to pause, notice, and marinate in ventral, which deepens their connection through exercising the vagal brake.

With this in mind, you can cue short and slow passes of BLS (approximately four to eight passes) with any intervention that connects the client to the ventral circuit. I typically use tapping or swaying from side to side rather than eye movements or tones when resourcing, however, it is ultimately the client's choice. Clients often prefer these forms of BLS, and I find them to be more versatile for Phase 2 work. Swaying or self-tapping are often experienced as soothing, and they allow me to be quick on the draw, or rather, quick to cue BLS in a moment of opportunity. Using tapping or swaying is easily accessible in a spontaneous moment, versus eye movements or tones, which require some initiative to set up prior to utilization. If my client is reporting that they are feeling more connection to ventral after an intervention like resourcing ventral (see below), guided breathing, orienting to the room, or mindfulness, I can seize the moment and quickly cue BLS with swaying or tapping. After each set of BLS, pause and check in with your client to track activation. Asking, "What do you notice? What are you aware of? What is coming up?" are all ways you can check in with your client between rounds. If the client's report is adaptive and indicative of increasing ventral energy, you can continue to add rounds of short and slow BLS to further enhance the experience. If the client loses connection with the resource or gets triggered, you may attempt to redirect them to the resource. If they are unable to reconnect to the resource, move on to another intervention.

If BLS is not available for any reason, you can alternatively ask the client to take three slow, deep, intentional breaths. For example, you may say, "Notice all of those feelings and sensations, and take three long, deep breaths as you do." Doing so can achieve a calming effect similar to BLS, given the breath's innate connection to the vagal brake (Dana, 2020). Because the exhale engages the vagal brake, breath can be used to lean into moments of ventral connection.

Case Vignette

I am working with Ryan (he/him) today. I just guided him through a simple breathing exercise I like to use. It involves asking the client to focus on their breath while saying "breathe in" on a long inhale, and "breathe out" on the exhale. I generally go through a few rounds with a client where I say these words out loud, and then invite them to repeat them inside. I may have them practice for 10–15 rounds on their own. Ryan has gotten very still and quiet following this practice. This is a shift from his baseline presentation, which is restless with sympathetic activation and chronic pain from injuries sustained in the navy.

"What do you notice now?" I ask.

"I'm so calm. My back doesn't hurt anymore. Super relaxed," he says with his eyes closed. His voice has softened and deepened a bit, a sign of his increased connection to ventral.

"How would it be to add some tapping with those feelings of calm and super relaxed?" I ask. I have used other resourcing techniques with Ryan before, and I know he likes to tap on his shoulders.

He nods, crosses his arms across his chest, and taps slowly from right to left.

"Good. Just pause when you're ready," I say after about four passes.

Ryan pauses and lets out a big sigh.

"Nice breath. What's that like for you?" I ask.

"Good. I feel really good," he replies.

"Amazing. How about another round of taps?" I encourage him.

He nods and taps again. I let him go a little longer now, as I can tell by the expression on his face and the stillness in his body that he is having a deep connection to ventral in this moment. After about eight passes, I cue him: "Just pause when you want." He taps a little longer and pauses around after about 12 rounds.

Suddenly, Ryan's phone goes off. The ringer is turned up, and it startles us both. Ryan opens his eyes and rushes to grab his phone from his pocket. "Sorry," he says, and I can hear frustration in his voice. He fumbles for a moment to turn it off, and then puts it on silent. "Damn," he says, along with a big sigh. "I lost it. I'm sorry—I thought I turned that off. What were we doing?" he asks, a bit rattled.

"That's okay. Things happen. We were just adding some taps to your experience of feeling calm and relaxed. Do you think we can we get back there?" At this point, I could have moved on to something else. But I want to help Ryan build flexibility in his nervous system and this could be a great opportunity to practice exercising the vagal brake. He nods, and I take him back to the exercise.

"Last you said was that you were feeling calm and relaxed. Can you try to connect back to those feelings again?"

Ryan closes his eyes, and his brow furrows. He tries to think about that experience. "A little," he says.

"Let's take a few breaths, and I invite you to think about what 'relaxed' and 'calm' feel like." I cue a recall of our exercise again, noting "you might notice your breath again and go back to those words breathe in, breathe out. I offer these instructions to help Ryan focus and engage the vagal brake. "Take your time. Let your body remember what that experience feels like." After a few breaths, I see Ryan's physical body soften a bit as he connects with those feelings and sensations. "What are you noticing right now?"

"Yeah, I can feel them again," he responds.

"Where do you feel them in your body?" I ask to increase his connection.

"I feel it in my legs and my arms. They are light but heavy," he shares.

"Good job. How about a few taps noticing those sensations?" I ask. We continue with a few additional rounds of BLS as his connection builds. I invite him to slowly start to become aware of his environment again before opening his eyes. "Notice the temperature, the smell. Notice any sounds. And very slowly, as you're ready, come back to the room and open your eyes."

In this excerpt I outline the use of a simple breathing technique as a resource. I cue BLS once the client is connected to the resource, or their ventral circuit, which is evidenced by their report at check-in. I also demonstrate in this excerpt how to return to a resource if your client loses connection. Finally, I share my technique for transitioning away from a resource. I like to bring my client back slowly and mindfully, as transitioning too quickly can be jarring.

RESOURCING NEURAL EXERCISES FOR PHASE 2

You likely have a plethora of EMDR and non-EMDR resources you utilize in your clinical work. Recognize that it's not about the specific intervention, but rather what these skills exercise in the nervous system that's important. Resourcing interventions build skills that contribute to the preparation hierarchy, and all of them support a client to be safe enough to feel, to notice and name, to feel and flex, and trust the process.

Phase 2 can include any skill that builds flexibility and resiliency of the autonomic nervous system. If a client doesn't find the safe/calm place exercise appealing, the therapist can shift to another intervention with a similar intention. The PV-EMDR therapist recognizes that Phase 2 is focused on developing vagal tone and autonomic resiliency using neural exercises. The clinician can be creative and integrative in this phase, as they find skills that are appealing to the client's nervous system and align with the clinician's own areas of specialty. Techniques that are wonderful to integrate into Phase 2 work include ego states, internal family systems, mindfulness-based stress reduction, dialectical behavioral therapy, somatic therapies, yoga therapy, art therapy, sand tray, trauma-focused cognitive-behavioral therapy, and more. It's not about the specific intervention. It's about the neural exercise.

Below are some of my favorite go-to techniques for PV-EMDR and Phase 2 work. Some of these techniques are my own, and others are inspired by the work of the brilliant Deb Dana. These techniques may be practiced in one session or over several sessions. The best way to learn about the autonomic nervous system is through your own direct experience, and I encourage you to practice each exercise on your own before practicing with clients. Your best teacher is your own nervous system.

CLINICAL INTERVENTIONS AND SCRIPTS FOR PHASE 2, PREPARATION

Building Connection to Ventral

From the get-go, we must always be exploring ways to assist clients to increase their connection to ventral. While methods for achieving this will ultimately be built throughout the course of therapy, identifying skills is a high priority when stabilizing clients. What does building connection to ventral mean? It means learning skills that exercise the vagal brake. Luckily, you already do this in therapy. The reframe to take away from this book is how to do so with greater intentionality. When we offer our clients ways to soothe themselves in session, or when we ask our clients to practice coping skills outside of session, we are essentially building their connection to ventral. I imagine you already do this through teaching grounding exercises, mindfulness, breathing exercises, distress tolerance skills, and emotion regulation strategies. These are all neural exercises that increase connection to ventral.

For some clients, building connection to ventral may rely heavily on your coregulation. Clients with more resiliency in their nervous systems may have skills already in place. Asking your client, "How do you cope or deal with distress?" will give you insight into their capacity to connect to ventral. If your client responds with a list of adaptive and effective coping skills, this indicates that this client probably has the capacity to feel and flex and engage their vagal brake. For clients with limited coping skills, time will need to be spent exercising the vagal brake and building resources.

Therapists regularly support clients to build connection to ventral. It's kind of at the heart of our job. Explore skills that work for your client and build a list of go-to's. You may find that Sara responds well to safe/calm place, while Hector does well with his ventral resource, Sam likes guided mindfulness techniques, and Kris lights up when they talk about their dog. Learn what feels appealing to your client.

Here are some of my clients' go-to's to increase connection to ventral in sessions:

- Pausing to take three to five slow breaths together.
- Taking a break from heavy material by talking about someone or something that brings the client joy, such as a pet, a loved one, or a hobby. For example, "Let's shift for a moment and regulate. How's your garden going? Have you gotten any yummy veggies yet?"
- Scanning the room for things that feel comfortable or pleasant to look at, then resting the gaze there for a few breaths.
- Taking a break in safe/calm place or other supportive resource.
- Mindfulness.
- 5-4-3-2-1 Grounding: Asking the client to notice five things they see, four things they can touch, three things they can hear, two things they can smell, one thing they can taste.
- Progressive muscle relaxation (see script in appendix).

Building connection to ventral serves as a way to anchor the client to safety. Skills that increase your client's connection to ventral can be used to titrate the level of autonomic activation in a session. Their preferred skills can also be used to close sessions and ensure they leave anchored in ventral.

I invite you to take a moment and reflect on some of your go-to interventions that increase a client's connection to ventral. What interventions do you find to be most effective? What are your favorites? What's most effective for each client? Developing awareness of the skills you use to accomplish this will allow you to grow your list and use skills with more intentionality and fluidity in session.

Scanning Neuroception Exercise

Adapted from POLYVAGAL EXERCISES FOR SAFETY AND CONNECTION: 50 CLIENT-CENTERED PRACTICES by Deb Dana. Copyright © 2020 by Deborah A. Dana. Used by permission of W. W. Norton & Company, Inc.

Scanning neuroception is an exercise that can be practiced individually or in a group setting. The exercise teaches the client about neuroception and explores cues within, without, and in between. The intervention targets the neural exercises of safe enough to feel and notice and name, and has the potential to incorporate feeling and flexing. Safe enough to feel is targeted through the client scanning for cues, while notice and name is incorporated as the client notices and names cues of danger or safety. The practice of feeling and flexing may be incorporated if the client identifies any cues of danger or discomfort. At this point, the clinician can empower the client to make choices and change their experience.

1. Create context and choice for this intervention, and begin by offering education on neuroception. Here is a sample script I encourage you to modify to fit with your style:

   "I'd like to teach you about a concept called neuroception. Learning about this can help you better understand your nervous system. Imagine a home security system. You turn it on, and it scans your home for cues of danger. The luxury of a home security system is that it monitors your environment without you having to be involved. You can trust it will sound an alarm if it senses any danger, allowing you to focus on other things. You have a system like this in your nervous system, called neuroception. Neuroception is like your own personal, internal home surveillance system. It is always scanning for threats, and if it senses anything potentially dangerous or distressing, it sounds the alarm. It sounds the alarm by triggering anxiety, or hypervigilance, or racing thoughts [you may state your client's specific symptoms to make this more relevant to them]. Or it may sound an alarm by causing you to go numb, making you spacey or dissociative. Just like the home surveillance system, sometimes it sounds a false alarm. This exercise will help you learn what your internal home surveillance system, or neuroception, is perceiving and whether the alarm is accurate or false.

"To practice, we are going to explore the three environments that neuroception scans. These are within, without, and in between. That's within your physical body, without in the external environment, and in between you and those you come into contact with. What do you think about trying this out together?"

2. Scan the three environments:

   Have the client scan cues within, without, and in between, one at a time [instructions below]. As your client scans, offer choice and opportunities to make changes to anything they identify as a cue of danger. Offer choice every step of the way and empower the client to interact with their experience, increasing cues of safety where needed.

   "Let's start by becoming aware of the space around you in your external environment. Look around your environment and scan for cues of danger or discomfort, or safety and comfort. You might notice the light, where the exit is, pictures, smells, temperature, and sound. Are there any cues of danger or distress here? What about cues of safety and comfort?

   "Turn your awareness inside your body. Take a moment and scan for any internal feelings and sensations. As you tune in, scan for cues of danger or distress, as well as cues of safety and comfort. You might consider things like energy level, the absence or presence of pain or tension, how rested you are, hunger, thirst, emotions, and so forth. Are there any cues of danger or distress? What about cues of safety and comfort?

   "Finally, scan the space in between you and me for cues. You might get curious about my tone of voice, my facial expressions, my physical posture, our proximity to one another, and so forth. Are there any cues of danger or distress here? How about cues of safety or comfort?"

3. Debrief the experience. Some potential questions include:

   "What stood out to you? Was anything surprising? Was it hard or easy to find cues of safety? Was it hard or easy to find cues of danger? Was there anything that you became aware of that you weren't aware of before? How might this apply to your day-to-day life? Are there specific places or people that trigger your nervous system to feel safe or unsafe? If you examine the accuracy of those appraisals in this moment, what are you aware of?

4. End by offering coregulation and connection to ventral if needed. The client should leave anchored to their ventral circuit, or window of tolerance.

5. Invitation to practice. Encourage the client to practice scanning neuro-

ception throughout their day. Remind them to make choices to increase their cues of safety when needed and possible. The therapist and client can explore themes in cues that may inform an EMDR treatment plan.

Surfing Imagery

Imagery is a powerful sense that can elicit feelings and sensations in the body. This exercise can be useful to help clients learn to notice and name and develop interoception. Using nature images, you will ask the client to bring the image to mind and notice feelings and sensations in their body. You can change the imagery as appropriate for your client, sticking with pleasant or neutral imagery. Nature images are used for this exercise as they pose minimal risk to trigger the client, and the autonomic nervous system resonates with nature images.

Note that some clients struggle with imagery because they lack interoception, others because they aren't wired to picture imagery. For those who lack interoception, you may need to start with only a few images (e.g., one to three) and work your way up as the client builds skills. For clients with aphantasia, a condition in which an individual cannot create mental images in their mind, you may still explore if they experience a somatic response to the images you cue. The somatic experience is more important than the image itself. This intervention may not be appealing to all clients.

1. Start by providing context, explaining the intention of this intervention, and offering a choice to participate. For example, "Surfing imagery is a process in which I'll name a pleasant or neutral image from nature, and your role is to just surf it. Just notice what comes up as you think about it. You might notice imagery, or a sound, feelings, or sensations. It's a helpful, nondistressing way to learn to notice your experience and name it. Would you be willing to try?"
2. Begin by inviting your client to "take a moment to get comfortable. Allow the eyes to close or find a soft focal point to rest the gaze. Take a few breaths and feel yourself sitting here right now."
3. Inform your client, "I will name a scene or image from nature. As I do, allow yourself to picture the image. Observe what happens to your emotions and body as you think of the image. Just notice what happens inside with each image. I will pause on each image briefly and then move on to a new one. Are you ready to try?"

4. Here is a sample list of images to ask your client to picture. You may pause for 5 to 10 seconds after naming each image, giving your client time to connect and notice the internal experience. If your client has limited tolerance for this, you may shorten the list.

   Feather in the wind
   Sandy beach
   Starry night
   Autumn leaves
   Colorful sunset
   Meadow of flowers
   Glisten of snow
   Puffy clouds
   Open field

5. Debrief the experience together. Some potential questions include:
   "What was this like to do? Did different images evoke different feelings or sensations? Was anything comfortable or uncomfortable? Was it hard or easy to connect to the internal process?"
6. Explore how the client might practice noticing feelings and sensations throughout the week.

   Modified version: This exercise can be elaborated on by pausing and asking the client to share what they notice as each image is called to mind. This can be an opportunity for clients to practice noticing and naming feelings and sensations that arise with each image (e.g., feeling warmth in the chest, a smile on the face, hearing the sound of the wind, feeling the warmth of the sun).

Mapping Circuits

This intervention is inspired by Deb Dana's Personal Profile Map (Dana, 2018). Mapping autonomic circuits builds safety and self-awareness, and supports the capacity to notice and name.

This exercise should only take place once safety and rapport are established. The safety net of coregulation serves as an anchor, as this exercise can activate some of the autonomic disturbance associated with the sympathetic and dorsal circuits. Additionally, this exercise may make the client feel quite vulnerable without enough therapeutic rapport.

1. Begin with context for the intervention and offer a choice to participate. Start by providing psychoeducation on the autonomic nervous system, using the Autonomic Circuits Graphic (Figure 3.1) in this process. You may share this visual in the therapy office or screen share in telehealth. Note the adaptive survival functions of each circuit as you provide psychoeducation. "It can be helpful to create your own map so you better know your internal world and your specific symptoms. Would you be open to trying that?"
2. Use the Map of Circuits worksheet (Figure 8.2) to support the client's map of their nervous system. Note that for clients with complex symptoms and strong autonomic defenses, this exercise may need to be visited over a series of sessions. Some clients may not be able to tolerate exploring all three circuits in one session.
   a. Focus on one circuit at a time.
   b. Ask the client to name the circuit in their own words.
   c. Ask the client to identify physical and psychological symptoms they experience with each circuit. Be sure to explore the following for each circuit: appetite cravings, substance use, sleep, energy, exercise, mood, sexual desire, work or school, self-esteem, relationships, and spirituality.
   d. Are there any images, symbols, people, animals, or figures they associated with each circuit?
3. Debrief the experience together. Some potential questions to review:
   "What stood out to you? Which circuits do you know well? Which circuit is your preference? Which circuit is least comfortable for you? What is your relationship to each circuit? How easy or difficult is it to identify which circuit is activated? How have these circuits helped you survive? "
4. End by offering coregulation and connection to ventral with a resourcing strategy. The client should leave anchored to their ventral circuit, or window of tolerance.

Name This State	Window of Tolerance Safe & Connected
Psychological Responses	Physiological Responses
Name This State	**Hyper-Arousal Mobilize/Fight Or Flight**
Psychological Responses	Physiological Responses
Name This State	**Hypo-Arousal Immobilize/Collapse**
Psychological Responses	Physiological Responses

Figure 8.2: Map of Circuits. Adapted from THE POLYVAGAL THEORY IN THERAPY: ENGAGING THE RHYTHM OF REGULATION by Deb Dana. Copyright © 2018 by Deb Dana. Used by permission of W. W. Norton & Company, Inc.

Study the Map

Simply mapping circuits is not sufficient to create change. With knowledge comes necessity to practice and develop skill. Without practice and reflection, mapping circuits will have little impact.

Imagine you are going on a long adventure, hiking through the wilderness. You get a map to help guide your journey. Would you just put the map in your pack, or would you take time to look it over and study it? If you're going about your adventure with thoughtfulness, you probably take time to study your map, learning the route and geography of the land. This analogy applies to the client learning their nervous system after having completed the map of circuits exercise.

Studying the map is best practiced through reflection and introspection. This can be achieved by reflecting on states in session with you, and independently between sessions. Reflecting on the map in sessions is a great place to start. You can do this by periodically pausing the client and asking them to reflect on their map. This may be explored at the beginning and end of sessions, as a mindful way to begin and end the work. Some ways to do this include asking the client questions such as these: "As we start our session today, where are you on your map? Where are you on your map as you tell me that story? What is your map telling you about your experience right now? What state or states are you aware of right now? Where are you on your map? How do you know? What is your map telling you?"

The client can also journal and reflect on their map between sessions. This is a helpful practice for them to translate the work from session to daily living. Ask your client to keep a copy of their map accessible every day and find moments to pause and reflect throughout the week, as much as possible, on their map. This invitation for reflection asks clients to become the experts on their own nervous systems through self-study.

Here are some helpful journaling or reflection questions to provide to a client to study their map:

- Where am I on my map?
- What are the physical and mental things I notice that put me at that point on my map?
- What is contributing to this state? It's okay if I don't know, but if I were to guess, what might it be?
- Is there somewhere else I want to be on my map?

- What is a helpful strategy I can use to get me closer to my desired destination?

Resourcing Ventral

Once the client has developed awareness of their ventral circuit, you can resource and install their connection to ventral by adding rounds of BLS. This intervention supports the client to develop the skills of being safe enough to feel, notice and name, and feel and flex.

1. Establish context by explaining the intention of this intervention and offering a choice to participate. Explain that this exercise builds on mapping and includes BLS. Be sure to explain BLS to the client and select a chosen form for resourcing.
2. Resourcing script:

   "I invite you to connect to your [repeat client's chosen name for ventral]. Think about what that feels like. Allow yourself to travel there. [Pause and offer time to connect.] What do you notice as you bring this to mind?"

   Ask for the client's feedback and support the client to access their ventral state. If they struggle to connect, you might repeat some of the symptoms they associate with ventral, which they listed on their map. Or you can ask them to name out loud some of the words they associate with ventral.

   "As you think about this state, is there an image that goes along with it? What picture represents this state to you?

   "What feelings do you notice?

   "What do you notice in your body?

   "Now hold the image, along with those feelings and sensations, and add BLS."

   Pause and check in after four to eight passes and ask the client, "What do you notice?"

   Repeat short and slow passes of BLS to enhance the ventral state. Complete three or more rounds. If the client loses focus or connection, try to refocus them. Some clients may only be able to tolerate brief moments of ventral connection. Start where the client is and build capacity over time.
3. Cue with distress (practice this if the client was able to successfully connect to and maintain connection to ventral). Note that *no* BLS is

provided while the client thinks of the disturbance. BLS is only paired with the ventral state.

"I'd like for you to think of something mildly distressing. On a scale of 0 to 10, perhaps a 2. What do you think of?

"As you think of that distress, become aware of how your body changes. Notice any changes in feelings, sensations, or thoughts.

"Now say those words [insert name of ventral state] and allow yourself to get back there. You may use your breath to help you settle. Recall all of the feelings and sensations of that space, along with the image.

"What do you notice?"

If the client can return to ventral, add passes of BLS as they notice the connection to ventral. If they cannot, the therapist may offer coregulation to support them connect, or this may be the end of the work for the day.

4. Debrief the experience together. Some potential questions include:

   "What did you notice and what stood out to you? What was your experience like? How and when can you practice this exercise from day to day?"
5. Invitation to practice. Encourage the client to practice this exercise on their own.

The Narrative

Adapted from POLYVAGAL FLIP CHART: UNDERSTANDING THE SCIENCE OF SAFETY by Deb Dana. Copyright © 2020 by Deborah A. Dana. Used by permission of W. W. Norton & Company, Inc.

The narratives we hold about ourselves, others, and the world are shaped by the autonomic state leading the way (Dana, 2018). These narratives can be understood as the cognitive expression of the autonomic story. When connected to ventral, our narratives may take on one flavor, which can change when we are mobilized in sympathetic, and change even more when we are immobilized in dorsal vagal. This exercise builds awareness of the common narratives told through the client's autonomic states.

This exercise builds on the previous exercise of the Map of Circuits (Figure 8.2). Exploring the narrative integrates the neural exercises of being safe enough to feel and noticing and naming. As the client builds this awareness, the opportunity to feel and flex naturally comes.

State Name	Window of Tolerance Safe & Connected
I am People are The world is	

State Name	Hyper-Arousal Mobilize/Fight Or Flight
I am People are The world is	

State Name	Hypo-Arousal Immobilize/Collapse
I am People are The world is	

Figure 8.3: The Narrative. Adapted from THE POLYVAGAL THEORY IN THERAPY: ENGAGING THE RHYTHM OF REGULATION by Deb Dana. Copyright © 2018 by Deb Dana. Used by permission of W. W. Norton & Company, Inc.

1. Establish context by explaining the intention of this intervention and offer a choice to participate. Explain that this exercise builds on the map of circuits and explores how the story about the self, others, and the world can be affected by our nervous system.
2. Review the Narrative worksheet (Figure 8.3), working through one circuit at a time.

   Ask the client to connect to each circuit on their map, one at a time. As they connect with each circuit, ask them to complete the sentences:

   "I am . . . "

   "People are . . . "

   "The world is . . . "

   Move through each circuit and ask them to write down their statements.
3. Debrief the experience together. Some potential debrief questions:

   "What stood out to you? What are your takeaways from this exercise? Which stories seem to dominate your world? How do these narratives influence your self-esteem, relationships, view of the world, day-to-day functioning? Are there any lessons from this exercise? Are there unhelpful narratives that you get stuck in? What do you prefer the narrative to be, and which state would you need more of to get there? How can you use this day to day?"
4. End by offering coregulation and connection to ventral with a resourcing strategy if needed. The client should leave anchored to their ventral circuit, or window of tolerance.
5. Invite the client to practice this work by observing their narrative throughout the day.

Pathways of Regulation

Adapted from THE POLYVAGAL THEORY IN THERAPY: ENGAGING THE RHYTHM OF REGULATION by Deb Dana. Copyright © 2018 by Deb Dana. Used by permission of W. W. Norton & Company, Inc.

This exercise builds on psychoeducation about the nervous system and the map of circuits exercise. It is inspired by Deb Dana's Regulating Resources exercise (2018). Once the client has learned their circuits and corresponding symptoms, they can begin to explore techniques to work with their autonomic responses.

State Name	Window of Tolerance Safe & Connected
Maintaining this state requires . . .	
State Name	**Hyper-Arousal Mobilize/Fight Or Flight**
Maintaining this state requires . . .	
State Name	**Hypo-Arousal Immobilize/Collapse**
Maintaining this state requires . . .	

Figure 8.4: Pathways of Regulation. Adapted from THE POLYVAGAL THEORY IN THERAPY: ENGAGING THE RHYTHM OF REGULATION by Deb Dana. Copyright © 2018 by Deb Dana. Used by permission of W. W. Norton & Company, Inc.

This exercise supports the client to identify skills and strategies to navigate their autonomic circuits with intentionality. This is an ongoing exercise and one that should be revisited periodically. As the client develops reliable coping techniques, they begin to trust the process and their internal world. Learning that they can influence their internal environment and use skills to feel better is an empowering experience.

1. Establish context by explaining the intention of this intervention and offer choice to participate. Explain that this exercise builds on the map of circuits and explores coping skills or strategies to navigate their nervous system. The list of strategies will naturally grow and change with time.
2. Review the Pathways of Regulation worksheet (Figure 8.4), working through one state at a time. Ask the client to connect to each circuit on their map, one at a time. As they do so, explore techniques that help to maintain ventral vagal and techniques to navigate through sympathetic and dorsal circuits back toward ventral. Note that some skills may be listed in more than one circuit.
3. Debrief the experience together. Some potential questions include:

   "What was this like for you? Which circuit is easy to interact with, and which is most challenging? Where are your strengths, and what are your areas that need additional attention and skill building for each circuit? How can you start practicing this on a day-to-day basis? Are there any common sore spots in your life where you need to implement some of these skills? Which circuit do we need to work on building up more?"
4. End by offering coregulation and connection to ventral with a resourcing strategy if needed. The client should leave anchored to their ventral circuit or window of tolerance.
5. Invite the client to practice using skills throughout the day as they notice themselves traveling states of the nervous system. You can also encourage them to continue to add new skills as they find what's appealing and helpful to their nervous system.

Chapter 9
PHASE 3: ASSESSMENT

You and your client embark on Phase 3, having achieved a number of impressive milestones. This is something to celebrate. Progression to Phase 3 is a marker of client resiliency, as they are prepared for the next chapter of work, which lies in memory reprocessing. The client must feel safe enough with the clinician and the process to share information in this phase and transition to Phase 4 (Shapiro, 2018). Phase 3 activates the memory and the client's nervous system, then immediately transitions to reprocessing the experience in Phase 4.

There is truth and wisdom in the old psychotherapy saying, "You have to feel to heal." Avoidance is a hallmark of trauma and a normal protective defense. Although avoidance is protective in nature, it also has its limitations, ultimately contributing to an exacerbation and compounding of symptoms. To grow, heal, and evolve, clients must feel their feelings and sensations so that experiences can integrate to a point of adaptive resolution. The intention of Phase 3 is to feel it so that Phase 4 can heal it.

Shapiro uses "treatment planning" for two different clinical objectives. She refers to "treatment planning" as the standard clinical process of identifying client goals, a part of any therapy. Identifying client goals should happen early in the work and be revisited throughout the lifecycle of the counseling relationship. She also uses "treatment planning" to refer to the process of identifying specific targets to reprocess. Creating an EMDR target treatment plan is a specific step of EMDR that I will review here.

Before you can begin to reprocess a target, you must first identify your EMDR treatment plan, or sequence of targets. We'll review that process in synchronicity with Assessment to create a fluid picture outlining how early phase work prepares the client for the activating steps of EMDR treatment planning, the standard protocol, and reprocessing.

Though Shapiro outlines Phase 1 to include EMDR treatment planning, this objective has been shifted to our review of Phase 3 in PV-EMDR therapy for a few key reasons. The most important of these reasons is autonomic stability and timing. Clinical interventions must pace alongside autonomic capacity. EMDR treatment planning for EMDR can tax a stressed nervous system for clients who live in chronic states of fight, flight, freeze, or collapse. Clinical interventions should bolster the nervous system rather than burden it. Therefore, the EMDR treatment plan should be developed when Phase 1 and 2 work is well established or completed, and the client is prepared to reprocess targets.

The three-pronged protocol of EMDR therapy identifies past experiences to reprocess, present day triggers, and future anticipatory events and desired outcomes (Shapiro, 2018). The three-pronged protocol is commonly referred to as "past, present, future." EMDR treatment planning with the three-pronged protocol often includes floatbacks or affect bridges which require some baseline level of autonomic flexibility. Therefore, if the client's nervous system is chronically flooded, treatment planning can be burdensome and cause unnecessary stress. Remember, floating back to the past prong requires dual attention. Although many clients can tolerate EMDR treatment planning techniques at an early stage, it is important to remain mindful of the neurobiological correlates that are involved in treatment planning, and to consider the effect of too much too fast for complex trauma presentations.

For those clients who require considerable time in Phases 1 and 2, creating an EMDR treatment plan too early may prove to have little use when it comes time to begin reprocessing memories. EMDR treatment plans over six months old should be reviewed and rewritten, given that memories have likely reconsolidated in that time frame and the memory network has changed. It is best for the therapist to conduct treatment planning immediately before reprocessing. After all, why create a list of targets if the client is not ready to reprocess them?

Case conceptualization, client goals, and flexibility of the autonomic nervous system inform the focus of the treatment plan. The EMDR treatment plan specifically outlines the target or targets for desensitization. The clinician uses the three-pronged protocol to guide treatment planning, identifying (1) past experiences, (2) present triggers, and (3) future anticipatory events and desired outcomes. Once the treatment plan is established, the clinician can flow into Phase 3, Assessment. This phase links the target memory held in the central nervous system with the stored autonomic state. The assessment phase serves as a bridge between the memory and the stored autonomic experience.

EMDR TREATMENT PLANNING

An EMDR treatment plan may be comprehensive or symptom focused. Perhaps a helpful analogy is that comprehensive treatment affects the climate (i.e., the overall clinical picture), while symptom-focused treatment affects the weather (i.e., symptoms). A comprehensive treatment plan will produce generalized changes and shifts in several symptoms and clinical themes. A symptom-focused treatment plan will have a narrow focus, typically influencing a few symptoms related to the target.

Comprehensive treatment planning is traditionally taught in EMDR basic training and focuses on the three-pronged protocol (past, present, future). Comprehensive treatment plans utilize floatbacks, affect bridges, or direct questioning to locate targets on the past prong. The clinician identifies present-day triggers, future anticipatory events, and desired future outcomes. Comprehensive treatment plans can focus on various issues, from the very specific to the more generalized. They often require significant stability and may take some time to work through, depending on the memory network and autonomic flexibility. Because AIP teaches us that past experiences inform present day symptoms, comprehensive treatment planning is the recommended path whenever possible. However, there are many times when unique clinical factors contraindicate a comprehensive treatment approach. This includes clients with limited autonomic flexibility, urgency, limited sessions, and client goals, to name a few. In such cases, a symptom-focused treatment plan may be most supportive.

Symptom-focused treatment plans are typically time limited, focusing on only one prong at a time versus a three-pronged treatment plan. The symptom-focused approach can support stabilization and improve day-to-day functioning. Symptom-focused treatment plans increase autonomic flexibility and titrate activation as clinically indicated by neurophysiological capacity. Examples of a symptom-focused treatment plan include targeting present-day triggers one by one, targeting a specific intrusive flashback or nightmare, or targeting distress about an upcoming event such as an exam or court appearance. They may even include targeting a specific aspect of a memory instead of the memory as a whole.

Using a symptom-focused treatment plan, it's important to remain cognizant of the potential impact of the past prong on present-day and future symptoms. Comprehensive treatment begins with the past prong, as memories from the past contribute to present-day symptoms. While targeting present and future triggers may lead to significant relief and stabilization, it is unlikely that the client will experience a complete resolution of associated symptoms without processing the past prong. Comprehensive treatment plans get to the heart of the wound, typically located in the past. On the other hand, symptom-focused treatment plans take the sting out of the wound but don't necessarily heal it at its core. If the past prong is not explored or reprocessed, symptoms may reduce but not resolve, and the potential for feeder memories and blocking beliefs can impact progress. Without integrating past memories, the clinician should remain mindful of expectations, assessing for small but meaningful shifts versus broad and generalized changes. Or in other words, you and your client may notice changes in the weather, but not the climate.

Treatment planning should align with what is tolerable for the client's nervous system. It is common with complex presentations to need to titrate the work as the client's resiliency expands along with the window of tolerance. As symptoms lessen or resolve, the client may experience greater autonomic flexibility and capacity to tackle more complex material. I often think of taking an approach in which I piece the treatment plan together like a puzzle. You can start with a constricted treatment plan to increase stability, working up to a comprehensive approach. Let's explore how you may puzzle-piece treatment plans together in the following case.

Case Vignette

Joseph (he/him) is a 33-year-old, white and Hispanic, heterosexual male seeking relief from PTSD. He is an army veteran who served two deployments in Iraq and faced combat. He lives with his fiancé and is attending college full time. His childhood was traumatic as both parents struggled with mental illness and heavy substance abuse. In addition, he experienced physical abuse and witnessed violence between his parents. His father died of a heart attack when he was 10, and his mother died from liver failure when he was 25.

Presenting symptoms include irritability, hypervigilance, anxiety, nightmares, flashbacks, and chronic tension in the body. Joseph reports that when he and his partner argue, he feels rage followed by collapse and shutdown. He drinks at night, having four drinks per night on average. He has no history of suicidal or homicidal ideation or psychosis. He initially presented to therapy with hesitancy and guardedness due to messages throughout his life that men shouldn't feel emotions, and that feelings are a sign of weakness. Dissociation screening indicated that Joseph experiences disconnection from his body and feelings of numbness. He presented with minimal flexibility in his autonomic nervous system and few coping skills.

Joseph and I spent six months in Phases 1 and 2. He learned to be safe enough to feel and how to notice and name. Preparation work established a container, a safe/calm place, and installed a nurturing and protective resource, which was his late *abuela*. We explored Joseph's cultural heritage. Joseph's cultural strengths included being hardworking and dedicated to achieving his goals. He asked for therapy homework, which he usually did, and consistently came prepared for sessions. We explored blocks to feeling feelings, which he identified as being informed by machismo and military culture. Exploring beliefs about feelings invited Joseph to get curious about his internal process, and he began to establish a new narrative about feelings: "Feelings are human." This allowed him to open up to new depths in therapy as he learned to be safe enough to feel.

We developed a strong therapeutic relationship, which served as a reliable source of safety and coregulation. Joseph started to learn to flex and feel in and out of sessions. He began to trust the therapeutic process and his ability to use skills effectively on his own. Yet even with all this growth, his nervous system was still frequently hijacked by nightmares and flashbacks. He struggled to find skills to manage these intrusive symptoms. Sleep hygiene, coping skills, and medication had limited effects. Though Joseph had some skills for managing autonomic responses, his nervous system was not prepared to reprocess his childhood traumas or combat. "I can't go there yet," he said as we discussed potential focus areas for EMDR treatment.

We began with a symptom-focused treatment plan targeting nightmares. These nightmares were incredibly distressing for Joseph, and he would wake up disoriented and overwhelmed with terror. He regularly used alcohol in attempts to suppress these dreams. There were two specific nightmares Joseph reported as especially disturbing. Each of these was individually targeted using Shapiro's (2018) technique of EMD. The use of EMD was chosen to titrate the amount of activation and constrict the memory network. This is an example of a symptom-focused approach, with the goal of stabilization and pacing treatment alongside the client. He reported fewer nightmares and significant reduction in his level of distress when he did have them. His sleep was not ideal, but it was greatly improving. He also reported a reduction in urges to drink, as he felt less fearful about his dreams.

We reevaluated progress and treatment goals, Joseph shared that he wanted to move on to combat memories. His sleep was continuing to improve, as was his relationship to alcohol. He reported an increased ability to feel and flex, as evidenced by enhanced capacities to tolerate feelings and sensations and use coping skills to self-regulate. We progressed to a treatment plan focused on combat trauma based on these factors and his goals. Four targets were identified via direct questioning. I asked Joseph, "What are the most disturbing memories from combat that haunt you still?" Each experience was fully reprocessed, minus the last. The final combat target led to a feeder memory from childhood.

The feeder memory emerged first as stuck body sensations. I tried a few simple techniques and two interweaves (see Chapter 10), and the distressing somatic sensation remained stuck. I then conducted a somatic floatback by asking Joseph to focus on the stuck body sensation and float back to the earliest memory he could recall with a similar sense. He shared, "I can't believe this is coming up. I am thinking about a memory from when I was about six years old. My parents are fighting in the school parking lot, and I'm sitting in the car crying." Joseph experienced a flood of sympathetic and dorsal energy when he brought this memory to conscious awareness, and he lost dual awareness. He reported feeling frozen, overwhelmed, and unable to find his words. I could also visibly observe this flood of activation in Joseph's physical appearance, as his neck muscles constricted, his jaw became tight, his posture stiffened, and his breathing became shallow and still. I supported Joseph with coregulation by inviting in containment, a breathing technique, and safe/calm place. We ended the session with him reconnected to ventral.

In the following session, Joseph and I explored the events of the prior session. I educated Joseph on feeder memories and how memories can fire and wire together. "So my brain is telling me I have to work on that to feel better about the memory from my deployment?" he asked. "It appears to be that way," I responded. Joseph said he felt ready to work on his childhood past. He shared that he felt nervous and scared, though at the same time hopeful and excited to be free of all that "darkness." This statement alone was an indicator of Joseph's capacity for dual awareness as he reflected on the fear he felt for that memory while remaining connected to the hopeful state of ventral.

With Joseph's consent, we targeted the feeder memory from childhood. This memory reprocessed completely. We returned to the combat trauma memory that had elicited the feeder memory, and this memory was fully integrated as well in just a few minutes. A present-day trigger related to loud noises was targeted, and the anticipatory anxiety he felt about the upcoming fourth of July was also targeted on the future prong.

Joseph took a month off from therapy at this time due to exams and wanting a break. I fully supported his choice and encouraged him to enjoy the outcome of the hard work he'd done. He returned to therapy, ready to work on his childhood memories.

The next treatment plan focused on childhood experiences of feeling out of control. This phase of work took several months. Some sessions were spent in talk therapy, as Joseph had days when he did not want to reprocess and had present-day stressors he needed support with. I tracked his pacing and allowed him choice in directing our sessions.

After three months, we completed the treatment plan on childhood trauma and reexamined the two remaining present-day triggers were

> targeted and cleared, and a future template was installed for a specific anniversary date. We reevaluated the work to date and the client's goals. Joseph felt he had met his goals and was ready to live his life. He stepped down to meet once a month for maintenance and eventually terminated therapy, with PTSD in complete remission.

This case outlines the integration of case conceptualization and treatment planning as I puzzle-pieced the treatment plan together. Preparation work supported Joseph to learn to be safe enough to feel, established therapeutic rapport, and taught Joseph how to notice and name, along with strategies to feel and flex. As Joseph developed more stability and resiliency in his nervous system, we then progressed to a constricted, symptom-focused treatment plan that targeted nightmares. I used the EMD technique to constrict the memory network, preventing the activation of significant past traumas, and in doing so creating a tolerable experience for the client, which led to improved sleep. With better sleep and trust for EMDR, Joseph was ready to address combat trauma memories. The next puzzle piece was transitioning to combat trauma and reprocessing the memories and experiences that continued to haunt him. It was no surprise that a feeder memory emerged that blocked reprocessing of the final combat trauma target. This was expected given the theme of the work and that we did not start in Joseph's childhood. The block proved to be helpful though, as it informed Joseph's decision to start working on his childhood trauma. Joseph insightfully identified that he felt ready for this big piece of work, which he had not been prepared for before. He trusted that he could handle it now. With each puzzle piece, Joseph's autonomic nervous system became more resilient and flexible.

ASSESSMENT

The intention of Phase 3, Assessment, is to identify, assess, and measure (Shapiro, 2001). Assessment of the target uses the scripted protocol to quickly activate the memory, moving the client from thinking about the memory to feeling the memory. I think of assessment as the phase that "pokes the hornets' nest." This phase triggers and activates the memory for reprocessing with intention. During this phase, "the clinician determines the components of the target memory and establishes baseline measures" for reprocessing (Shapiro, 2018, p. 124). Assessment of the target activates the memory as it is stored. The scripted protocol creates a bridge between brain and body, body and brain, and skillfully stimulates the memory for reprocessing. The EMDR protocol serves as a tried and tested bridge between these two branches of the nervous system and opens a neural pathway for memory integration.

I believe that Polyvagal Theory is already embedded in the scripted protocol. Exploring the integration points can provide depth to the script and insights into why and how the protocol works. This phase serves as a link between the brain and the autonomic nervous system and activates the stored responses held in the body.

Dr. Shapiro (2018) teaches us that the order of the assessment questions is intentional, as it activates cortical structures necessary for reprocessing and memory integration. The protocol questions are top-down and bottom-up as they elicit responses of the brain and autonomic nervous system. A slight modification to the order of the questions is proposed for PV-EMDR based on the key tenets of Polyvagal Theory and neuro-informed approaches to counseling. Let's review the components of the PV-EMDR assessment.

Image/Sense

The first question on the standard protocol is, "What image represents the worst part of the experience to you now?" Shapiro states that selecting a picture is necessary to access the memory network and shifts the focus from an abstract thought to a specific memory. The image also serves as "a link to the neurologically stored information" (Shapiro, 2018, p. 125). The image may be symbolic or metaphorical, or it may be a specific image from the actual event.

Many clients describe a clear picture or image when asked this question. However, a small portion of the population cannot visualize imagery, a condition known as aphantasia. In some cases, a client may say that the worst part of the experience is represented by another sense, such as a smell, sound, or even taste. In such circumstances, you can shift the focus to another sense by asking, "What picture, sound, smell, taste, or texture represents the worst part of the experience as you think of it now?"

This first step of the standard protocol connects the body to brain and brain to body experience through the senses. The autonomic nervous system is 80% sensing due to the makeup of afferent nerves, and sensory components of memories can quickly connect to the autonomic defenses. There are times when a client may even describe the memory with a number of their senses. For example, "I see the explosion, hear the ringing in my ears, and smell the dirt." Such sensory-rich targets can establish a strong connection to the stored experience.

Negative Cognition

The second question in the protocol is, "What words go best with that experience that express your negative belief about yourself now?" Shapiro (2018) outlines that the negative cognition (NC) should be self-referencing, stated in the present tense, and expressed as a belief rather than a thought or a description of affect. She notes that "pinpointing the appropriate negative cognition seems to allow the stratum of dysfunctional material to be more fully accessed" (Shapiro, 2018, p. 126).

The negative cognition is a cognitive expression of the autonomic narrative. Because our internal narratives are shaped by our autonomic process, the NC is the verbalization of the autonomic state. The client's narrative about themselves, others, and the world shifts and changes based on the autonomic state leading the way. Therefore, the NC is a verbalization of the stored experience as relived in the nervous system. This question asks the client to put words to their implicit, unconscious experience locked in the body.

Finding the most accurate negative cognition can ignite the nervous system like a spark on dry tinder. The client can experience an influx of emotions and sensations as the autonomic nervous system explicitly expresses its story. I teach clinicians to look for the "zinger" cognition, which elicits affect and somatic responses. The NC evokes strong responses of the nervous system, allowing the client to more deeply connect to the feelings and sensations.

Sometimes the client offers a statement of affect, such as, "I'm afraid" or "It's scary." Such instances are not examples of NCs, and you should ask the client, "What does that say about you if you're afraid?" or "What does that mean about you that it's scary?" There may also be times when a client says that there is no NC. In these circumstances, I have found it helpful to first clarify that the client is thinking of the specific memory and not an NC that relates to their entire life. Second, you can rely on the autonomic nervous system to identify the NC by moving on to feelings and body sensations, then looping back to the NC. I often find that when the client connects to the feelings and sensations and I ask for the NC again, it is now clear and evident to them because they are connected to the autonomic experience.

Positive Cognition

Following identification of the NC, you and your client identify the positive cognition (PC) (Shapiro, 2018). "When you bring up that experience, what would you prefer to believe about yourself now?" This question offers an opportunity for curiosity by exploring the potential narrative of the ventral circuit. That is, if this memory were processed and did not activate autonomic defenses, what would the narrative be? Identifying the PC is challenging for many clients, which indicates how distant that ventral narrative may be from the stored experience. It may be that the client can't find a PC because the narrative of ventral hasn't been a reality for them. In such cases, I'll ask, "Let's pretend this no longer troubled you. What might you believe if this were resolved?" Or you may pull upon preparation work with the client and ask, "If this memory were only experienced from your ventral state, what would you believe about yourself then?"

Finding the PC is an important component to activating adaptive memory networks that support successful reprocessing. It can also instill a sense of hope or possibility about the future. The PC is an expression of the desired state and asks the client to self-assess their experience and future goals as related to the target. The PC should be stated in the positive, self-referencing, generalizable, related to the same theme as the NC, and feel somewhat true to the client (Shapiro, 2018).

A challenge of this phase of assessment is that this question can sometimes stall assessment. Clients may look at you dumbfounded as they try to consider what their PC may be, because they can't even begin to imagine it. My approach is not to overwhelm clients with finding the PC when a little support and curiosity won't flush one out. Getting stuck here can become distracting to the process and the nervous system. In addition, the client's system may start to experience frustration or anxiety because they can't answer the question, taking them away from the memory. In these situations, I will skip the PC and the validity of cognition scale and move to emotions on the standard protocol. Doing so is not abandoning the PC, as it is revisited and installed in Phase 5, Installation. This choice can be made when the PC proves to be distracting and blocks the assessment phase from moving forward.

Validity of Cognition

With an identified PC, you now check the strength of the positive cognition with the validity of cognition scale. "When you think of the memory, how true do the words [repeat PC] feel to you now on a scale of 1 to 7, where 1 feels completely false, and 7 feels completely true?" (Shapiro, 2018). This question invites an opportunity to make the implicit explicit by taking a baseline measure. When the client reports the VOC is very low and therefore highly unbelievable, I consider this a potential indication of how far this memory may be from the ventral circuit. Higher VOC ratings can indicate autonomic resiliency and flexibility, and strong adaptive networks.

It's important to note that it's not the specific 1–7 scale that's relevant, but rather the opportunity for the nervous system to quantify its subjective experience. Any explicit scale can be used when assessing VOC. Many times, clients find the 1–7 scale confusing. "What? Can you read that again?" I sometimes ask my clients, "On a 0 to 100% scale, how true do those words feel to you now when you think of the memory?" You can also use a ruler, the size of the room, or any scale that feels clear to the client.

Emotions

The next assessment question asks about emotions. "When you think of the memory and the words [repeat NC], what emotions do you feel now?" (Shapiro, 2018). This question focuses on the emotions elicited by the stored autonomic response and asks the client to be explicit about the implicit experience. The emotions are the feeling narrative, or the emotional story automatically told when the memory is activated. This question is supported by the client's ability to notice and name.

Body Sensations

Shapiro's standard protocol inquires about body sensations last, after the client has identified the subjective units of disturbance (SUD) (Shapiro, 2018). The PV-EMDR protocol moves this question about the body second to last in the assessment. The SUDS rating must include the body because the body holds the autonomic response. Eighty percent of the autonomic nervous system is afferent, sending signals from the body to the brain (Porges, 2017). Therefore, the body must be included in the explicit scaling of the internal experience. The body isn't an afterthought; it is the primary focus of intervention and healing. When you ask, "Where do you feel it in your body?" the client names and identifies the somatic experience, which is inseparable from the autonomic defensive response.

Subjective Units of Disturbance Scale

The final question of the PV-EMDR assessment asks for the SUDS. As previously stated, the SUDS score is the last question of the PV-EMDR Assessment as it must include the body sensations along with the other components of the target. The clinician checks the SUDS by asking, "On a scale of 0 to 10, where 0 is no disturbance or neutral and 10 is the greatest disturbance you can imagine, how disturbing does it feel to you now?" (Shapiro, 2018).

As a common theme with all the assessment elements, this phase is another opportunity to make the implicit explicit, by quantifying the experience using the SUDS. Scaling provides a baseline measurement of the memory as the client experiences it in the present moment. The SUDS is not specific to any one portion of the memory but rather encompasses the entire cognitive, emotional, and physical experience of the memory network. The SUDS is revisited at various points throughout reprocessing to track progress and resolution of adaptive defenses.

COMPLETING PHASE 3

As we've reviewed in this chapter, Phase 3 of PV-EMDR holds two objectives. The first is to develop a treatment plan informed by case conceptualization. A symptom-focused approach builds autonomic flexibility and reduces acute symptoms. A comprehensive treatment approach addresses a larger picture over the three prongs and often requires stability and autonomic flexibility. The second objective of Phase 3 of PV-EMDR is assessing the memory through the scripted protocol. At this point, the client is feeling distress, and you should transition directly into Phase 4, Desensitization.

Phase 3 should be relatively brief. Treatment planning can take anywhere from a few minutes to a full session. On the other hand, target assessment should be conducted in one session quickly (sometimes it takes less than five minutes!) and only if there is enough time to transition to Desensitization. Assessing the target should be focused and succinct, as this process is not intended to drift into talk therapy. Limit your process-oriented questions and stay focused on the intention of the script. Stimulating the memory and autonomic response is the primary goal of this phase, which cannot be achieved through verbal processing and talk therapy. While this process can feel uncomfortable and different to those used to talk therapy as their go-to modality, the discomfort of doing something different shouldn't be a reason to slide into old habits. Remember that EMDR is an evidence-based protocol, and trust the process.

Some clients may share and tell stories in this phase. Remain mindful of individual client differences. Storytelling is a central theme of communication, healing, and relating among many nonwhite cultures. Additionally, some clients may tell stories because their system needs someone to bear witness to their story. Assessing the target may be a rare moment in which they feel seen and heard, which is a powerful component of healing and therapy. If your client tends to tell stories, don't be too quick to cut them off or shut that down. Track if the client is storytelling in a way that keeps them connected to the memory and process, or if storytelling is becoming a distraction, taking them away from feelings and sensations. Storytelling is a process of human connection and turns the implicit into the explicit. Therefore, it's not necessarily something to squash. But refrain from talk therapy and process-oriented questions, which could quickly divert the focus of the work away from Phase 3. Validate and offer compassion, but don't slide down the slippery slope and make storytelling the focus of the session if the intention is to get to reprocessing.

Treatment planning and completing the script are areas in which clinicians typically express some initial discomfort in their ability to attune. "I want to ask more questions." "I want to talk about what they just told me." "I feel like I'm being a jerk." These are typical worries I hear about this phase. Just because the wording of Phase 3 is scripted doesn't mean therapeutic presence isn't part of the process. By remaining present with the client, your physiology can convey incredible depths of compassion and support via your tone of voice, simple statements of encouragement and attunement, facial expressions, breath, and posture. We cannot attune the same way we do in talk therapy in Phase 3 of PV-EMDR, but that doesn't mean we don't attune at all. While we shouldn't say, "Oh gosh, tell me more about what happened when you were 10," nor say, "Let's challenge that negative cognition of I'm not worthy with CBT," we can say, "I know this is tender. Can you keep going?" offer a facial expression and a big sigh to convey we are imagining what that must have felt like, or provide a timely deep breath to resonate with the heaviness the client is feeling. Polyvagal Theory teaches that feeling safe, seen, and heard are felt experiences conveyed through presence and physiological cues, rather than eloquently formed open-ended questions and cognitive interventions. Don't let your talk therapist get in the way of Phase 3 and stifle your client's opportunities to connect to the felt sense. Remember, if talking about it were enough, you wouldn't be reading this book.

THE PV-EMDR ASSESSMENT PROTOCOL

Used with permission of Guilford Publications, Inc., from Eye Movement Desensitization and Reprocessing (EMDR) Therapy: Basic Principles, Protocols, and Procedures, Francine Shapiro, Third Edition, 2017; permission conveyed through Copyright Clearance Center, Inc.

Image/Sense

"What image represents the worst part of the experience as you think of it now?"

If there is no clear image, you may ask, "What picture, sound, smell, taste, or texture represents the worst part of the experience as you think of it now?"

Negative Cognition

"What words go best with that experience that express your negative belief about yourself now?"

Positive Cognition

"When you bring up that experience, what would you prefer to believe about yourself now?"

If the client struggles with the PC, you may ask, "Let's pretend this no longer troubles you. What might you believe if this were resolved?"

VOC

"When you think of the memory, how true do the words [repeat PC] feel to you now on a scale of 1 to 7, where 1 feels completely false and 7 feels completely true?"

Emotions

"When you think of the memory and the words [repeat NC], what emotions do you feel now?"

Body

"Where do you feel it in your body?"

SUDS

"On a scale of 0 to 10, where 0 is no disturbance or neutral and 10 is the greatest disturbance you can imagine, how disturbing does it feel to you now?"

Chapter 10
PHASE 4: DESENSITIZATION

Phase 4, Desensitization, is perhaps the most powerful and seemingly magical phase of EMDR. Witnessing the spontaneous insights and transformation clients experience in desensitization is humbling and inspiring. This phase requires the clinician to let go of control, recognizing that even a highly degreed, trained, and educated brain can't hold a candle to the healing authority of the nervous system. This revelation can be terrifying for some and freeing for others. Not knowing what might come up, where the memory could travel, or how to be present and hold space without talk therapy can be anxiety provoking. But trusting in the nervous system's innate capacity to heal, staying curious, and relying on you own ventral circuit as the most important tool of intervention can also unburden you from intellectual and cognitive intervention models.

The specific objective of Phase 4 is to desensitize the target assessed in Phase 3 with dual-attention bilateral stimulation. Desensitization may require one session or multiple sessions and is accomplished when the target is reported at a SUDS of 0 or "ecological level." While many targets will desensitize to a SUDS of 0, some targets may not and may retain a slight charge, hovering around a SUDS of 1 or even 2. Some possible examples may include those associated with death and loss, or present-day targets. A SUDS of 0 indicates that when the experience is recalled, it does not cause distress in the present. Some experiences, no matter how much they're desensitized, just don't get to a 0.

Such targets should be carefully considered before prematurely moving on from desensitization, to determine their ecological appropriateness.

Phase 4 metabolizes the memory through the central and autonomic nervous systems and reappraisal of the experience via neuroception. Autonomic defenses of fight, flight, freeze, and collapse resolve, and the client eventually experiences the memory from the safe and connected state of ventral.

This chapter begins with a brief review of the specific steps and techniques for integrating Polyvagal Theory into desensitization of a target. I also explore the integration of Polyvagal Theory within Phase 4 as I review the role of therapeutic presence, how to track autonomic responses, and polyvagal-inspired interweaves for stuck points.

TARGET DESENSITIZATION

Before beginning desensitization, it's important to provide an outline of instructions and expectations. This is a component of informed consent and is an opportunity to integrate the Three Cs of context, choice, and connection into Phase 4. I often say something like the following.

> As we begin the BLS, I invite you to just notice what happens inside. You might notice thoughts, other memories, other parts of this memory, feelings, or sensations. There's no right or wrong. Try to remain an observer and watch the process unfold. We can stop at any time for any reason.
>
> I'll give a cue to pause every 30-ish seconds or so and check in. When I ask what you're noticing, I just need a few words to describe your experience. This is a little different from therapy as you're used to, as I won't be asking you many questions, and we won't be talking so much. Talking too much in EMDR can sometimes distract you from the experience inside, but please know you can share whatever you need and as much as you need with me. If you need to stop, just let me know or wave a hand at me. I'm right here with you. You got this. Do you have any questions right now? Are you ready to start?

Beginning with these instructions or some similar version gives the autonomic nervous system context. The client is told what to expect and how the process works. The instructions give some direction or context on what to do as a client in EMDR and encourages the client to remain an observer to their process. Connection between client and therapist is also made explicit as the therapist reminds the client "I'm right here with you" and offers some encouragement. Finally, the clinician offers choice by asking if the client has any questions and consents to start.

How we set up Phase 4 matters. Using the Three Cs of context, choice, and connection can provide the client's autonomic nervous system with cues of safety and sets the stage for success. Some clients may need more concrete instructions, while others require less. Add more context and clarification as needed, though you should refrain from overwhelming the client with details and delaying the work. Without context, the client may begin reprocessing feeling distracted and anxious, unsure of what they're supposed to do or experience. If your client says, "I don't understand what I'm supposed to do" or "What do you mean, what do I notice?" at check-in, you might need to firm up your instructions. However, there are also times in which confusion on the client's part may be a form of avoidance that is activated in the memory network and a defense of the autonomic nervous system. The sense of not knowing what to do may be part of the stored experience. In such cases, the clinician may ask the client to "notice the confusion" or say, "Can you be curious about the part of you that's unsure of this process?" and start passes of BLS. This choice point would be based on your knowledge of the client, clinical intuition, and the client's overall case presentation.

To start this phase, we ask the client to bring the memory to mind and then begin passes of BLS. "Bring up the picture and the words [repeat the NC]. Notice all the feelings and sensations and just notice" is how I start this phase. The recommended starting range of BLS is 24–30 passes per set, though the length depends on the client (Shapiro, 2018). I gauge BLS length and speed by tracking my client's autonomic nervous system. Clients often have tells or cues that indicate it's time to check in. Cues can include a deep breath, a change in posture, a reduction of strong affect, or a facial expression. If there are no cues, I generally guesstimate, checking in after 20–30 seconds have passed. I do not watch the clock or keep a timer, as those will distract me from my client's process.

You may let the client choose the check-in point, as opposed to choosing the check-in point yourself, a technique to further integrate Polyvagal Theory into this phase. Typically, the clinician decides the check-in point, or where to pause the BLS. To empower the client, avoid assumptions, and increase choice, the PV-EMDR approach allows the client to be involved in identifying that point. I often cue my clients by saying, "Pause when you're ready" or "Find the point that feels right to pause." If clients are tapping, they can stop tapping when ready. If using eye movements, the client can stop tracking or wave a hand. They can wave a hand or open their eyes if receiving auditory tones. Cuing check-in gives the client permission to select the point that feels right but doesn't put the responsibility for tracking time on them. Meaning, the client isn't told, "Start BLS and stop when you want." Placing this responsibility on the client asks them to be subjective and objective at the same time, which can be distracting and confusing. Instead, cueing check-in keeps you in the timekeeper role but lets the client choose when exactly to pause. As I've used this in my practice, I have found that many clients go considerably longer than when I would have otherwise paused the BLS.

At check-in, the clinician asks a brief, nondirective question: "What do you notice? What comes up? What are you experiencing? Where's all that now? What are you aware of in your mind, body, and heart?" These are some of my go-to phrases. You should avoid asking distracting or leading questions, for example, "What's the image like now? How are you feeling? How does that remind you of the issues with your ex?" Shapiro (2018) explains the importance of letting the nervous system guide the process, requiring you to remain a neutral observer. Checking in allows the client to notice, name, and connect to the present, which promotes sustained connection to ventral.

Shapiro's protocol includes client instructions to "take a deep breath" at each check-in. A deep breath can certainly be a way to maintain connection to the ventral circuit and dual awareness. However, we should also be mindful of the teachings of Polyvagal Theory. The autonomic nervous system desires choice. Therefore, best practice is to refrain from directing clients to do something with their bodies even if it's as seemingly simple as taking a breath. Instead, you can give an option to breathe by stating, "Take a breath if you like" or asking, "Take a deep breath?" or "If it feels appealing, you might take a breath here." In these examples, breath is an option rather than a directive.

Additionally, a deep breath will engage the vagal brake and increase parasympathetic energy. The result may be a lessening of distressing affect that the client is tolerating and needs to reprocess. Breath is a beautiful way to support autonomic arousal and therapeutic work. I incorporate a great deal of breath work into my practice. However, the important takeaway is to be mindful of the power of breath, its effect on autonomic processes, and the importance of choice. Sometimes your client may not need to take a breath, and asking them to do so can be disruptive or distracting. "My therapist is always telling me to breathe. It's so annoying." That is not the dynamic you want to create here.

This is a process of rinse, wash, repeat as you continue providing passes of BLS, checking in, and returning to processing by saying, "Go with that; notice that." In reprocessing, the clinician has two roles: (1) remain connected as a coregulator, and (2) track the process. The client's brief check-in provides a means to track integration and autonomic arousal. For example, you may hear signs of sympathetic arousal, dorsal shutdown, or ventral integration. Shapiro's instructions are to track for "positive, neutral, or negative" material at check-in. I use the terms "adaptive, neutral, or distressing," which are slight modifications that refrain from placing value on the neurophysiological process.

Continue adding rounds of BLS for any remaining distress, as the client continues to reprocess associations and associated channels. Processing might include various aspects of the target memory or other memories. Some channels of processing include broad shifts in awareness and perspective, and others are more focused and detailed. Clients may experience various images, alternative points of view, other memories, other aspects of the same memory, internal dialogue, thoughts and beliefs, feelings, and sensations. Remember, there is no right or wrong, as it's all a product of the nervous system working through the memory network and the autonomic response, as it moves toward integration.

After two to three consecutive rounds of adaptive or neutral material, you will return to the target by asking, "As you bring up the original experience now, what do you notice?" Note that you do not ask the client to return to the image or the negative cognition. The reason is that the image and negative cognition were only components of the memory and not representative of the entire experience. Returning to the "memory" or "original experience" keeps you out of the way and allows the client to focus on what's most relevant to them.

Once the client returns to the target and the target remains clear, you will check SUDS. "As you think of the original experience now, on a scale of 0 to 10, with 0 being no disturbance and 10 being the greatest disturbance you can imagine, where is it now?" The question invites an opportunity to notice, name, and make the implicit explicit. Checking SUDS also focuses the work on the remaining distress or disturbance. If the SUDS is above 0, the clinician directs the client back to reprocessing.

Desensitization is complete when the SUDS reaches 0 and remains 0 after two to three additional rounds of BLS. Some targets will not resolve to a 0. Examples might be targets related to grief and loss, chronic pain, moral injury, present-day or future targets. If a target remains at 1 or 2, you may ask your client, "What keeps it from being a 0?" The client may identify a relevant reason that the target will not diminish to 0, or this question may help home in and resolve the remaining disturbance. Do not prematurely accept a SUDS above 0, as most targets can resolve to a point of 0.

As desensitization completes, the client will experience a shift in aspects of the target that no longer serve them. They may see the target from the perspective of their most grown self rather than through the eyes of their child self. The image may be hard or impossible to recall. Their perspective may change along with insights and meaning made. As the maladaptive material held in the memory network resolves, so too does the stored autonomic response, resulting in the client experiencing the memory from a state of ventral.

DON'T LEAVE THE ROOM

When I was a newly trained EMDR clinician, a coworker and I would practice EMDR together to learn the protocol and improve our skills. It was my turn to be the client, and I chose a present-day unhealthy coping strategy I wanted to change as the issue to work on. I chose tappers for BLS, and during passes I closed my eyes to connect with the process. I was in the middle of a set and felt ready to check in. My colleague didn't stop the BLS, so I waited. I waited and waited for the pause. When it never came, I opened my eyes and looked at her. She was focused on her phone and didn't even notice I had stopped. She had completely disconnected and left me to do the work on my own. A visceral wave of shutdown and withdrawal flooded my system, as I experienced the visceral effects of what Porges (2011) terms biological rudeness. I felt hurt, small, unimportant, and silly. Was I not interesting enough? Was I doing something wrong? Did she not want to practice with me? Old wounds of not being good enough felt fresh and hot in that moment, causing me to lose connection to the target and my ventral window of tolerance. I faked a few more rounds and then found a way to end the session. I couldn't get out of her office fast enough, as my flight response was in full force. I felt too triggered and unsafe to give her feedback, let alone practice with her again. That experience left me with a vulnerability hangover, and I felt uncomfortable around her for a few months after.

My colleague was going through the motions of EMDR but forgot the most important ingredient: the relationship. Our mantra to "trust the process" and the mechanics of Phase 4 are not invitations for you to check out or turn on autopilot. While this phase can feel robotic and discourages talk therapy, you must remain connected and present. Though we are taught in EMDR training to get out of the way in this phase, refraining from talk therapy interventions, recognize that "get out of the way" doesn't mean "leave the room." Recall that neuroception is constantly scanning for cues of safety or danger. Cues of presence (see Chapter 6) inform neuroception and maintain connection and safety. Checking out in a session will be felt by the client's nervous system, potentially triggering vulnerability, shame, anger, or hurt.

Here are some of the common ways I see therapists disconnect and leave the room in Phase 4:

- They focus their attention out the window, on their worksheet, or anywhere other than on the client.
- They check their phone, email, or watch repeatedly.
- They don't offer the client cues of presence through tone of voice, eye contact, facial expressions, and cues of empathy. There is a flatness in the therapist's facial expressions and tone of voice.
- They lack vocal prosody at check-in.
- They don't use minimal encouragers as cues of presence (e.g., "Mmhmm. Just be curious. You got this. It's old stuff. I'm with you").
- They check out and daydream.
- They fail to track the client's physical process.
- They turn their body away from the client or lean away from the client.
- The therapist commonly experiences this phase as boring.

Phase 4 is a journey for your client, and you have negotiated a first-class ticket to tag along. It is a gift and an honor to be invited along for this ride and witness the client's process. Though the steps can feel robotic, the actual process is far from it. As compared to talk therapy, we must shift away from the role of an active doer to an active observer, which requires therapeutic presence. Active observing requires you to be present with your whole being, tracking, observing, and supporting. This phase asks you to move away from the intellectual and toward embodied presence. Cues of presence are vital in this phase, serving as the primary connection point between the client and therapist.

The nervous system responds to verbal and nonverbal cues to appraise safety. In talk therapy, therapists typically rely on the active listening skills of open and closed-ended questions, paraphrases, summaries, and reflections to establish and maintain connection and rapport. Cues of presence are more important in this phase than the active listening skills of talk therapy. Here are some ways you can integrate cues of presence into desensitization:

- Use your breath to convey compassion, empathy, and connection.
- Maintain your focus on the client.
- Remain present with the client in the moment. Distractions should be short and minimal.
- Use body language to convey presence.
- Use prosody and tone of voice to convey compassion.
- Use minimal encouragers at check-ins and within passes of BLS as appropriate. These include short phrases such as, "Mmhmm. You got this. You're doing great. Notice the shift. Just be curious. It's old stuff. Watch it change. I'm with you."
- Track the client's autonomic responses.
- Practice humility, looking to the client as the expert in their experience.
- Where and when appropriate, laugh with your client, celebrate progress, and offer enthusiasm and excitement as they notice the shifts and changes.

Although I talk significantly less in a desensitization session than in a talk therapy session, I am no less present or engaged. After practicing EMDR for more than 15 years, this phase still leaves me in awe every time. But I must communicate my engagement and my presence differently than in my talk therapy sessions. Cues of presence support the client to feel safe and supported while maintaining an open path for coregulation. If my client is working on a vulnerable memory, the care and connection they sense from my cues of presence can be coregulating and provide the support their autonomic system needs to process the target. Likewise, a lack of presence can trigger defenses, quickly leading to shutdown and disconnection.

Get out of the way, but don't leave the room.

TRACKING

Throughout desensitization, the autonomic and central nervous systems dance the dance of integration. Tracking the process requires that you track your client's neurophysiological state, tuning in to signs of ventral, sympathetic, and dorsal activation. Tracking the nervous system keeps you tethered to the client and informs interventions if the client loses dual awareness or processing becomes blocked. We track this phase based on the cognitive, emotional, and somatic material the client reports. You may return to Figure 3.1 (Autonomic States Graphic) to review potential signs and indicators of each autonomic state. Listen for the mobilizing qualities of sympathetic, the immobilizing qualities of dorsal, and the safe and connected qualities of ventral.

Let's practice tracking. As you read the following client check-in statements, what circuit(s) do you hear and track?

- "My heart's racing. I'm afraid"—sympathetic mobilization.
- "Nothing. I feel numb"—dorsal immobilization.
- "I can't move, but I'm so angry"—client says while making fists; mixed state of dorsal and sympathetic.
- "I'm calmer. I know I did the best I could"—ventral connection.
- "It's orange and big"—too little information to decipher; this could be any state.
- "I can't really see it. The image is gone; I feel calmer, but I notice something like anxiety still in my chest"—mixed state of ventral and sympathetic mobilization.
- "I don't feel my body"—dorsal immobilization.
- The client is breathing fast and shallow, and their face is red; they can't put words to their experience—sympathetic mobilization.
- The client looks blank; their face is flat and they can't put words to their experience—dorsal immobilization.

Tracking keeps the nervous system front and center, as it remains the focus of assessment and target of intervention. While you don't need to know definitively at every check-in where the client is, you do need to track the overall process, remain attentive to stuck points, and be responsive at times of client overwhelm. If the client loses connection to ventral, states of sympathetic or dorsal activation will overload the system and impair memory integration.

Tracking states, therefore, allows you to quickly select an intervention or interweave and get the processing back on track.

If you've seen one client process, you've seen one client process. After practicing EMDR desensitization a few times, you have probably learned that people can vary wildly in how they process. Some clients process with a significant amount of emotional or somatic content. Others report substantial intellectual and cognitive content, which can make tracking challenging. Their check-ins focus on narrative, images, scenes, or storyline and lack feelings and sensations. In these circumstances, it's helpful to periodically inquire, "What do you notice in your body?" or "What feelings and sensations go along with that?" Doing so maintains connection to the autonomic process. Clients could be reporting the narrative because the memory has integrated, and there's no remaining distress. They could be telling the narrative because they dissociated from the feelings and sensations held in the body. Or they could be telling the narrative because they have gone numb. Because the autonomic process is part of the stored experience, we must be sure we don't lose connection with it. Periodically checking in with feelings and sensations when they've been absent in the process does not detract from the protocol. It is rather a method to sustain connection to the autonomic process necessary for adaptive integration and resolution of the target.

ANCHORING

Anchoring is a technique I use to manage my client's activation level and maintain connection to the ventral circuit. Anchoring uses short and brief statements to increase or sustain connection to the present. This skill may be used proactively or in the moment, amid desensitization or at check-in. For example, if the client tends to move toward sympathetic overwhelm or dorsal collapse, you may use anchoring statements proactively. On the other hand, if the client demonstrates strong activation of defensive states during reprocessing, you can use anchoring in response.

Anchoring statements ask the client to maintain dual awareness by reminding them of their physical body or the physical environment. The intention is to maintain connection to ventral. Statements such as "Remember you're in my office. Wiggle your toes. Feel your feet on the floor. Take a moment and look around the room. Feel your seat in the chair" are quick, subtle reminders that direct your client to keep their awareness anchored in the present. Anchoring statements are short, brief statements used to anchor the client to dual awareness.

Anchors can be internally or externally focused, asking the client to notice their body or environment. Using the body as an anchor includes asking the client to notice things such as feeling the feet, wiggling the toes, feeling the back of the chair, noticing the breath, or remaining dually aware of their body in the room. Anchoring statements can also ask the client to remain aware of their present environment by looking around the room, taking a sip of water, opening their eyes for a moment, or sensing your presence. The focus of the anchoring statement is the anchor, rather than the statement itself.

Here are some potential anchoring statements. Notice that while each has a slightly different focal point, they all anchor to something in the present.

- Notice your feet and maybe wiggle your toes (anchors to the body).
- Remember, I'm right here with you (anchors to connection with the therapist).
- Remember where you are now; that was then, and this is now (anchors to present time and place).
- Notice the couch underneath you and the pillow on your lap (anchors to the sense of touch).
- Notice your dog by your side (anchors to connection).
- Perhaps open your eyes for a moment just to reconnect? (anchors to the environment).
- How about a breath here? Perhaps another intentional breath to stay with it? (anchors to breath).
- Would you like to stand or move in any way for a moment? (anchors to the body).
- Would you like a tissue or a drink of water? (anchors to the body and physical sensation).

Anchoring can help manage autonomic arousal without getting in the way of reprocessing. Anchoring statements should remain subtle and nondistracting, refrain from overly directing the client, and be invitational in nature. Reminding the client of dual awareness with anchoring statements does not risk cutting off channels of association but does reduce the likelihood of abreactions and overwhelm. Anchors anchor the client to dual awareness and support the process.

INTERWEAVES

Picture a fidget spinner. The fidget spinner represents the nervous system. When the fidget spinner is spinning, the mind and the nervous system are integrating, processing, and assimilating information in an adaptive manner. Sometimes, however, the fidget spinner stops spinning or the nervous system gets stuck or blocked, and the experience cannot integrate. This is an analogy of blocks and loops that can impact reprocessing, in which cases you should use an interweave strategy to jump-start reprocessing and get things going again (Shapiro, 2018).

Interweaves are a cognitive strategy to get processing back on track, developed by Shapiro (2018) to work with blocks and loops in processing. Interweaves are short, brief statements that should be used when the material is not generalizing, when processing is stuck or blocked, or when adaptive shifts are not taking place. Let's review a few examples.

1. The client is processing a memory of witnessing her father abuse her older brother and is stuck on "I should have done something." An interweave may ask, "What could an 8-year-old do in that moment?" This interweave seeks to expand the client's awareness around what is normal and possible for a child.
2. The client is processing a memory of a car accident and is stuck on the thought, "I'm going to die." An interweave may include asking the client "Did you?" This interweave expands the client's awareness to what really happened, which is that they survived.
3. The client is processing a memory of a traumatic birth. They are stuck on a feeling in their abdomen. "What does that sensation need to know?" This interweave helps to increase connection to the stuck point and allows the client to connect with the adaptive information the body may be missing.

Shapiro (2018) describes cognitive interweaves as strategies to jump-start blocked processing and support memory integration. Interweaves may introduce new material or link the client to information they already know but aren't aware of in the moment. Interweaves can be used proactively when processing is blocked or looping. They are used to foster a natural, adaptive resolution of the stored memory by shifting the client's perspective, somatic responses, or points of personal reference.

Interweaves are not that radically different than the interventions you already provide in talk therapy. Interweaves need to be aligned with the client's process and the autonomic process the clinician is tracking. The real difference between interweaves in EMDR and talk therapy interventions is that interweaves should be brief and to the point, and the clinician should return to passes of BLS as quickly as possible. Interweaves are not opportunities to slide into talk therapy. Their intention is to support the system to get unstuck so the experience can integrate.

Shapiro (2018) outlines several helpful interweaves in her text. A few specific PV-EMDR interweaves are outlined below.

- *Whose narrative is that?* As previously discussed, narratives change depending on autonomic states. Stories about the self, others, and the world take on different tones depending on which autonomic circuit has the most energy. If the client is stuck in a maladaptive narrative, you can bring awareness to the narrative and invite curiosity. For example, you may ask, "Which part of your nervous system does that story belong to? What might the story of [insert client's name for their ventral state] be?"
- *Which state is that?* This interweave can be used to bring awareness to the autonomic process, which can increase curiosity and the client's ability to notice and name. "Which state of your nervous system does that feeling/sensation/thought/experience belong to?" You can then follow up with a question oriented to actively engaging neuroception, which is, "Is that the response needed right now?"
- *Movement:* Movement and changing posture is a way to exercise the vagal brake (Porges & Carter, 2017). Humans are movement-oriented creatures, and our movements and postures can influence autonomic states and neurophysiological processes. Inviting movement into stuck points, blocks, or loops offers the client an avenue to get curious and connect with the somatic experience. You can invite movement as an interweave in several ways. You may ask, "Is there a

movement that feels appealing to you now? How might it be to stand or move your arms and legs here? I noticed you moved your hand there. How might it feel to notice that movement? What movement might help that stuck point? Is there a movement that feels like the antidote to that? What can you do with your body now that you couldn't do then?" There is a long list of options for inviting movement into therapy, with this list being far from comprehensive. The key to movement-focused interweaves is to invite curiosity and give permission.

- *Notice and name:* As reviewed in Phase 2, notice and name is a practice of interoception. To notice and name the internal experience allows the implicit to move to the explicit by bringing the experience into conscious awareness. This invites neuroception to investigate the experience, allowing unneeded defenses to resolve. You may ask, "What feelings and sensations are you aware of in this moment?" followed by a round of BLS. You can tag on a question to deepen awareness at the next check-in, asking, "How would you describe those feelings and sensations? What temperature, color, shape, sound, weight, or texture do they have?" followed by BLS. This interweave can support autonomic responses to metabolize as the internal world is brought into awareness.
- *Scanning for cues:* Scanning for cues is an interweave that engages the active pathway of neuroception, by asking the client to scan for cues of danger or safety. Scanning for cues may be useful if the client is stuck on a theme of danger from the past. You may ask the client something like, "Take a moment to scan for any cues of safety. Notice yourself in this moment. The room you're in, your physical body, and the space in between us. Are there any cues of safety here? Are there any cues of danger?" Once the client appraises their safety, return to BLS by saying, "Notice that."

Case Vignette

Erin (she/her) is a 38-year-old, white, heterosexual female. The client is processing a memory of abuse by an ex-boyfriend. The target for processing is a specific incident of violence in which he choked her. The client tends to move toward anxiety in sympathetic and sometimes dorsal collapse and numbness.

The following is how I would conduct a reprocessing session.

Target: This is the client's worst memory of the abuse. The target memory is "when he choked me, and I thought I was going to die."
Image: His face as he's choking me.
NC: I'm going to die.
PC: I'm safe now.
VOC: 4.
Emotions: Fear, numbness.
Body: Throat, chest, legs.
SUDS: 10.

I begin by reviewing instructions with Erin and ask if she has any questions. She says she doesn't. I start with some anchoring before we start reprocessing, increasing her connection to ventral. Because Erin tends to experience floods of autonomic activation, I start with this intervention to increase safety and support effective reprocessing.

Therapist (Tx): Before we begin, let's make sure you're grounded and present. I invite you to look around the room for a moment and just notice the space we're in. Notice the colors, the pictures, the light. [I pause as the client looks around.] Let your system know you're here with me in 2022. Are you here?

Client (Clt): Yeah. I'm here. I feel that.

Tx: How do you know? What tells you?

This is an intervention I utilize to support Erin to notice and name the experience of being present and connected.

Clt: I can hear the sound machine and feel the couch. I see you and I smell my lotion.

Tx: Good awareness. Now, let's bring up that memory. Bring the image to mind, along with the words "I'm going to die." Notice the feelings and sensations. Are you ready to start?

I ask Erin permission again, offering her choice before beginning BLS. She nods that she is ready to start.

Tx: Go ahead and start tapping now.

She begins self-tapping on her legs. Her eyes close. I keep my focus on the client, watching for cues and maintaining therapeutic presence. After around 20 seconds, I cue a check-in.

Tx: Go ahead and pause when it feels right [waits for Erin to pause]. Mmhmm. Good work. What are you noticing?

Clt: I'm just thinking about the apartment we lived in, where it happened.

Tx: Okay. Just notice that, and when you're ready, tap again.

She begins tapping again. Around 30 seconds pass, and I cue a check-in.

Tx: When you're ready, find the place to pause. What do you notice?

Clt: I am thinking of the argument we had. He told me I wasn't pretty and that he hated me.

Tx: Mmmmm. Can you go with that?

I maintain prosody in my voice and say this in a soothing, empathic tone.

Clt: Yes.

Tx: Okay. Go ahead and start tapping again when you're ready.

Erin adds another round of BLS. I notice a slight tightening in her face and a grimace as she clearly feels something painful.

Tx: You got this. Just notice it [a cue of presence].

Erin continues tapping and tears up.

Tx: When you're ready, go ahead and pause.

She pauses and takes a deep breath. I notice her take a breath, and I take a breath alongside her, cuing presence.

Tx: Nice breath, Erin. What's coming up?

Clt: My heart is racing, and my throat feels tight [with tears, voice choking up].

Tx: Can you notice all of that?
Clt: Yes.
Tx: Tap again when you're ready. You got this.

I provide encouragement, and Erin adds another round of BLS. I add cues of presence while Erin is tapping, saying in a soothing voice, "Yeah . . . mmhm . . . just notice it." Erin begins to cry.

Tx: Pause when you're ready, Erin.

Erin pauses and wipes her eyes. I pause in a moment of silence to allow her to wipe her tears. I pause to slow things down a little and titrate the work.

Clt: I thought I was going to die. I really did.
Tx: Mmhmm, yeah. I know this is tender. Can you do another round with that?

I ask this with empathy and tenderness, communicating with my voice that I hear how scary that must have been.

The client nods and begins tapping again.

Tx: Just notice and remember you're here with me now.

I use an anchoring statement by reminding her that this memory is in the past. Erin returns to BLS and then pauses without my cuing this time.

Tx: What's coming up now?
Clt: The same. I'm just thinking of that moment.
Tx: Can you go with that?

Erin nods and starts tapping again. I stay focused on her and connected. I invite her to pause when ready, and she checks in.

Tx: Where's all that now?
Clt: I thought I was going to die.

This is the third time she has checked in with the same material and appears to be blocked. I have tracked that Erin has physically moved very little in the last few check-ins, and her body appears to be frozen. It's time to provide an interweave.

Tx: Mmhmm. Is there a movement that would let your nervous system know that you didn't die? That you survived?

Erin thinks about that for a moment.

Tx: Just be curious about what that might be or what your body needs to know. You can tap again when you're ready. Move if that feels appealing while you do.

This is a movement-focused interweave. Erin begins tapping and then starts to move her head around and take big deep breaths, followed by audible sighs, letting her body know she survived. She moves her shoulders and her head, appearing to connect with her neck.

Tx: That's it, Erin. Let that happen.

I offer encouragement and attunement in this statement.

Erin continues to be with the somatic process, and eventually, the movement slows after around 40 seconds. She pauses.

Tx: Where's all that now?
Clt: I didn't die. I feel that now. But that thought is still there.
Tx: Okay. Nice shift. Notice the difference. I wonder if you can look around the room for a moment while you also notice that insight that you didn't die? If you want, you can add a round of taps while you do that.

I offer a polyvagal-informed interweave by asking the client to notice the internal narrative while cueing neuroception to scan the environment. She pauses on her own.

Clt: Yeah, I didn't die. I'm here. I lived.

Tx: Nice. Notice that.

The client begins to tap again.

She sits back on the couch; her shoulders drop slightly, appearing to relax. Her jaw unclenches As she pauses.

Tx: What are you aware of?
Clt: I just got a little calmer inside. Like my body is starting to get the message.
Tx: Good. Notice that.

She returns to tapping. I track that her face softens, and her shoulders relax. Her breathing regulates.

Tx: When you're ready, find the spot to pause.

Erin pauses.

Tx: What do you notice?
Clt: I'm thinking about the argument.
Tx: Go with that.

She nods and begins tapping. Her face scrunches, and her breathing becomes shallow. I add a cue of presence:

Tx: Yeah, just notice that. You got this.
Clt: I'm still thinking about it.
Tx: Notice all that, and notice your feet on the ground. When you're ready, tap again.

I provide another anchor here by cuing awareness to her "feet on the ground." Erin adds another round of BLS.

Tx: Pause when you're ready.
Clt: The cops came. A neighbor called because they heard a lot of noise. I didn't want to tell them the truth.

Tx: Mmhmm. Can you go with that?
Clt: Yes.

Erin begins tapping again and then pauses on her own to check in.

Clt: I am thinking about my conversation with one of the cops.
Tx: Notice that, and when you're ready. . . .

Erin taps again. I observe that her affect has lessened. There is now a flatness to her facial expression, and she is very still. She has reported no affect or sensation in the last four check-ins.

Tx: When you're ready, find the point to pause.
Clt: I'm thinking about what we had for dinner that night.
Tx: What feelings and sensations are you also aware of right now?

I ask for feelings and sensations here, as the last few check-ins have been specifically about the narrative. I want to keep the autonomic process online, so I ask for feelings and sensations.

Clt: Nothing.
Tx: Can you describe nothing to me?
Clt: There's an absence of feeling. I'm numb.
Tx: Numb. Can you notice the numbness and everything else coming up for you?

She nods and begins to tap again. Through tracking, I have observed that dorsal collapse is leading the way. I have asked for clarification of her statement, "Nothing." This is a method to help the client notice and name. The question identifies that "nothing" is numbness. Because my client has not reported sensation or feeling for multiple rounds, and I've tracked an increase in dorsal energy, I have specifically asked for feelings and sensations.

Erin tears up again with a swell of sympathetic activation. Her neck and jaw tighten as she takes a deep breath and holds it. Her face turns red.

I take an audible breath to convey my presence and possibly cue her to breathe.

Tx: Yeah, it's tender. Ride the wave if you can and pause when you need to.

This statement appears to support her, as she nods and allows herself to cry. I am right there with her, bearing witness and intently focused on her process. I say a few minimal encouragers in this time, with a soft and soothing voice: "Yeah . . . mmhmm." A few sobs come from her, and eventually she pauses. This set goes on for around a minute as she rides the autonomic wave.

Erin pauses, opens her eyes, and grabs a tissue.

Tx: Yeah, take a moment. Take as long as you need here.

She dries her eyes and takes a deep breath. I give Erin space to attend to her needs as another form of anchoring, as she notices the need for a tissue, dries her tears, and takes a breath.

Tx: Good breath there. How would it feel to do that again, and take another breath like that?

She nods and takes two more deep breaths. I mirror my breath to hers and breathe with my client. This is a method to anchor and maintain therapeutic presence.

Tx: Where's all that now?

Clt: Whew, that was intense. I was just thinking about how he always used to tell me I deserved it. I feel so hurt. Just an overwhelming hurt that's squeezing my heart. And right when I paused, I heard this voice inside my head that said, "No, you didn't." And I recognized it to be true. I didn't fucking deserve any of that.

Erin says this with some conviction. I see a shift and can hear some empowerment in her process here. This is adaptive and a big healing insight for her to gain.

Tx: Wow! That's a big insight! You most certainly did not deserve it! Can you go with that?

I respond with enthusiasm and excitement to align with the power of this moment. I am so thrilled for my client right now, and humbled to be a part of her healing journey.

Clt: Yeah.

She starts tapping again.

This short snippet from a desensitization session integrates the concepts reviewed in this chapter. As you may observe, I was engaged with Erin every step of the way, tracking her process and maintaining presence. I take a very active stance in EMDR processing but stay out of the way. My interventions were subtle, nondirective, invitational, and focused on the embodied somatic process. I never left the room, and I conveyed my presence with my body and my words. I used anchoring statements to help Erin maintain dual awareness. Also notice the variety of polyvagal-informed techniques outlined in this session. I remained active and attuned, tracking my client's process and offering support along the way, which allowed me to quickly utilize simple interventions to support her processing.

As reviewed in this chapter, Phase 4 of PV-EMDR is not passive. You are an active observer, gently supporting the process while holding space for your client. The skills of tracking and cues of presence keep you and your client tethered and maintain an open channel of connection and coregulation. The use of anchoring and polyvagal-inspired interweaves supports the autonomic nervous system to maintain enough connection to ventral and work through blocks effectively. The integration of Polyvagal Theory into Phase 4 brings this phase to life, and you may witness the power of this phase through a new and exciting neuro-informed framework. The Polyvagal Theory also supports the successful resolution of targets and reduces the likelihood of abreactions and challenging reprocessing sessions.

Chapter 11

PHASES 5 AND 6: INSTALLATION AND BODY SCAN

Phase 5, Installation, and Phase 6, Body scan, are the final two phases of memory reprocessing. I think of these phases as the icing on the cake, as they solidify the adaptive integration of the experience. While often short and brief, these phases are no less important, as they ensure that the autonomic defenses have been resolved and the experience is integrated. They are also necessary for cognitive restructuring and integrating the memory with adaptive networks (Shapiro, 2018). As the memory desensitizes, associated autonomic defenses subside, and the client eventually experiences the memory with the ventral circuit leading the way. Installation and body scan are a means to assess and double-check the work and connect the experience to the resolved and adaptive autonomic state. The final two phases of reprocessing are prime opportunities to integrate Polyvagal Theory, as determining completion of these phases is based on the autonomic nervous system.

One of our guiding principles of PV-EMDR is that the nervous system is the mechanism of assessment, intervention, and outcome of psychotherapy. Phases 5 and 6 are a means to measure adaptive integration of the memory by assessing the state of the nervous system following desensitization. Additionally, as memories are not just thought but also felt, these phases assess the implicit qualities of the memory as your client assesses their felt sense of their new narrative and their body. These two phases are all about the autonomic process and assessing the adaptive resolve of the memory.

I sometimes hear clinicians' desire to skip these phases. Sometimes our clients don't want to complete these phases either, because they feel better and want to move on to the next thing. But remember, EMDR is an evidence-based therapy, and keeping to its fidelity is important. If we don't maintain fidelity, we can quickly find ourselves practicing outside of the bounds of EMDR. Phases 5 and 6 are typically quick. In fact, sometimes they only take a few minutes. While often short and sweet, recognize that they are not opportunities to skip phases or important parts of the work. Skipping these phases puts you in a place where you are out of alignment with fidelity, and your client misses a meaningful part of the healing process. I have found that whenever I encourage a client or a clinician to just hang on a little longer and finish these steps, the feedback is always positive and grateful for having completed the phases.

PHASE 5, INSTALLATION OF THE POSITIVE COGNITION

Shapiro outlines the steps for installation of the positive cognition (PC) as part of the standard EMDR protocol (Shapiro, 2018). Once the target is reprocessed to a SUDS of 0 (or 1 or 2 in times of ecological validity), and remains 0 after a few additional rounds of BLS, you can transition to Phase 5, Installation. This phase focuses on "the full integration of a positive self-assessment with the targeted information" (Shapiro, 2018, p. 151). The PC and target memory are linked with passes of BLS, and the clinician uses the validity of cognition (VOC) scale to install the PC to a VOC of 7.

You will begin this phase by checking the PC, originally identified in Phase 3, Assessment. In my professional experience, I have found that 90% of the time or more, the PC changes from the original assessment. The client is no longer imagining what they believe. Instead, they have a genuine new belief, or internal narrative, as an outcome of desensitization. As Phase 4 desensitizes the target memory and the associated autonomic defenses, a new narrative takes shape, and the experience is understood through the experience of the ventral circuit.

As we've reviewed, the autonomic nervous system shapes our perception of ourselves, others, and the world. The narrative takes on one flavor when ventral is leading the way, and when sympathetic or dorsal leads, that narrative is considerably different. Negative cognitions such as "I can't trust myself," "I'm not lovable," or "I'm powerless" are informed by the autonomic state elicited when the memory is stimulated. These are not statements from the state of ventral. These are statements told by sympathetic or dorsal circuits. Upon successful reprocessing, the memory is experienced from the safe and connected state of ventral, producing an adaptive statement that supports growth and resiliency. Positive cognitions such as "I am a good person," "I did my best," or "I can be trusted" are experienced as truths from the ventral circuit.

To begin this phase, the clinician asks the client, "As you think of the experience now, do the words [repeat original PC] still fit, or is there another positive statement that fits better?" The new adaptive belief may be general, though it is often personalized. For example, rather than "I'm a good person," the client may say, "I'm a caring and compassionate friend." Instead of "I'm capable," the client may say, "I'm strong and I know how to fight back." I get so excited when clients can find their adaptive truth in their own unique words because it indicates the memory has reconsolidated to a point of adaptive resolution and is now an adaptive network that supports resiliency. A personalized and unique PC from the client's perspective is much more powerful than a generic PC on a list.

The PC should be self-referencing and stated in the positive. The PC is also specific to the target memory rather than a statement the client believes in every facet of their life. There is no rush, so take the time the client needs to identify the correct cognition, as it is an opportunity to connect to their new, adaptive narrative. I often find it beneficial to take a moment to pause and get curious about the new narrative. Sometimes clients need a moment to talk it out and try on a few potential statements to find the most fitting one. In these moments you may reflect some of your observations or client reports from processing, though refrain from telling the client what their PC should be. The following is an example of taking a moment to get curious.

Alana (they/them) is a 28-year-old, heterosexual Pacific Islander who has just finished targeting a memory related to a breakup with a friend.

Tx: As you think of the experience now, what positive belief goes along with it? When we set up this target, you stated you wished you could believe "I'm a good person." Does that still fit, or is there something that fits better?

Clt: [pauses for a moment and considers] That one's okay, but I think there's a different statement. I don't know what it is though.

Tx: That's okay. Let's pause here and get curious. This is new, so it makes sense we need to explore this. Take a moment and look inside. As you think about the experience now, what beliefs go along with it? Take as long as you need here to reflect.

They take a minute or two and look inward to explore this question.

Clt: I feel like it's more about being a good friend, even when things don't work out. Like I'm not a bad person because of this experience. We just weren't a good fit as friends.

Tx: That's a really great insight. As you think about that . . . being a good friend even when things don't work out, that you're not a bad person because of the experience, you just weren't a good fit, I wonder what all of that says about you as a person. Is there an I statement that captures that?

Clt: I'm a good friend, even though I'm not her friend.

Tx: Wow! That's a great statement. Let me just repeat that back and check inside if that feels right. "I'm a good friend, even though I'm not her friend."

Clt: Yes, that's it. Though I feel like I'm missing something about boundaries. Like I'm a good friend, but I can also set boundaries.

Tx: Really good. So we have "I'm a good friend, even though I'm not her friend." And you also said, "I'm a good friend, but I can also set boundaries." Does one of those feel more true than the other?

Clt: No. They're both true.

Tx: Amazing. You can certainly have more than one truth. Shall we keep them as they are, or do you want to try to combine them into one statement? What feels most appealing to your nervous system?

Clt: Ooooh, I like the combo. Let's combine them. Like, "I'm a good friend, and I can set boundaries."

Tx: Woooo! That's good stuff. Okay, let me make sure I got it right. "I'm a good friend, and I can set boundaries." Is that it?

Clt: Yeah, that's it.

Tx: And on a scale of 1 to 7, with 1 being false and 7 being true, when you think of the memory and the words "I'm a good friend, and I can set boundaries," how true do those words feel now?

Clt: A 6.

Tx: Great. Hold the memory and those words, "I'm a good friend and I can set boundaries," and follow my fingers.

I proceed to install the PC to a VOC of 7 with the client's preferred form of BLS, which was eye movements.

As you can see in this client excerpt, I take my time and allow my client space to look inward and get curious about the new narrative. Their positive cognition is likely a new experience, and new experiences may need a moment to be explored with curiosity. In essence, we are inviting neuroception to actively reappraise the narrative of the memory, as it is now adaptively stored.

Once the PC has been identified, the clinician proceeds to check it with the VOC scale. Scaling the PC is an opportunity to make the implicit explicit through quantification with a scale. The clinician asks, "When you bring up the original experience, how true do the words [repeat the PC] feel to you now on a scale of 1 to 7, with 1 being completely false and 7 being completely true?"

If the client reports a low VOC, meaning below 4, take a moment to explore potential misunderstandings, feeder memories, or blocks. Frequently, a low VOC is simply due to the client misunderstanding the scale and the question. Therefore, first and foremost review the question and the accuracy of the PC, and clarify the VOC. Sometimes clients need more time to home in on the most fitting PC, or they are trying to apply the PC to their entire life. The PC is not necessarily a statement they believe in every situation of their life. It is specific to the target memory as experienced in the present.

A low VOC may also indicate that the client's nervous system does not experience the memory with enough connection to ventral. A PC that does not feel true may be experienced as false because the autonomic nervous system experiences continued activation of sympathetic or dorsal circuits when the memory is recalled in the present. This may be the case if Phase 4, Desensitization, was not completed, or in the presence of feeder memories or blocks.

Double-check your work first by checking the SUDS of the target memory.

If the SUDS remains a 0, then you have confirmed the memory is desensitized and can move on to exploring feeder memories and other potential blocks. If the SUDS is above 0, or an ecological 1, return to desensitization.

If you suspect that a feeder memory or block may be impacting this phase, ask additional questions to explore and get curious. Some questions I may ask when I suspect a block include these: "What keeps this belief from being more true? Is there another memory that keeps this from being true? Are there any opposing beliefs that prevent this statement from being true? Notice what feels untrue about this statement and float back in time. Are there any other memories that feel similar or relevant? Is there any part of you that won't allow this belief to be true?"

Once the PC that feels true or somewhat true has been identified and the VOC is assessed, BLS is added to integrate the statement and the memory network. The clinician asks that the client "hold the original experience in mind along with the statement [repeat PC], and just notice," and begins rounds of BLS. Pairing fast and long BLS, around 20–30 passes, supports memory integration and cognitive restructuring. In this phase, BLS is still fast and long, as this is a reprocessing phase focused on rewiring the memory network. Clinicians often feel the intuition to install with short and slow BLS, similar to resourcing exercises taught in Phase 2. Recognize that this phase is still focused on reprocessing and adaptive resolution of autonomic defenses versus enhancing a state change strategy. Hence, BLS is fast and long.

The clinician checks the VOC repeatedly after each set and continues to add BLS until the VOC strengthens to a 7 or an ecological number. Ecological numbers are represented in those times when the VOC will not install to a 7 for a relevant reason. This may be the case for specific targets and situations, for situations that are ongoing in the present, or for targets that are part of a large cluster of related experiences, to name a few.

You can use interweaves in this phase to support any stuck points. When the client reports a VOC of 7, I recommend adding two to three more rounds of BLS to support the nervous system to resonate and internalize the new narrative. There's no risk in adding a few extra rounds to seal the deal.

Phase 5 is an opportunity for your client to resonate with the new narrative held in the autonomic nervous system and integrate that narrative into the memory network. You may add a few questions here to enhance the autonomic story and create a strong, embodied connection to the PC. For example, you might ask, "What in your body tells you this statement is true? What do you notice inside as you repeat those words? What feelings and sensations are you aware of as you think of the memory and those words?" These statements focus on the client's somatic process related to the PC, which invites the autonomic nervous system to connect more deeply to the experience. Questions that enhance the felt experience can strengthen the PC quickly and allow it to resonate in a more meaningful way for the client.

PHASE 6, BODY SCAN

Once the PC has installed to a VOC of 7 or an ecological number, the next phase is the Body scan (Shapiro, 2018). This phase is typically short, though nonetheless important. The Body scan checks the memory network and the client's autonomic experience held in the somatic body. Checking the body is a way to ensure that autonomic states are resolved, and the memory is experienced from the state of ventral.

The instructions for Phase 6 are to ask the client, "With your eyes open or closed, think of the original experience along with the statement [repeat the PC]. Scan your body from head to toe and let me know of any disturbance you are aware of." If the client reports disturbance, the clinician asks them to notice the disturbance and pairs rounds of fast and long BLS. Any remaining disturbance can typically resolve in this phase with a few additional rounds of BLS. However, the Body scan offers a means to double-check the work, potentially revealing feeder memories, blocking beliefs, fears, or other aspects of the memory that need desensitization for the experience to integrate fully.

As we reviewed for Installation, it's important to remain curious about any stuck points and explore them with a floatback or additional questioning to conceptualize and plan intervention. If disturbance remains in the body after a few rounds of BLS, the clinician can ask, "Notice that sensation, and all of its qualities. As you notice that, float back in time. Are there any other memories that stand out with a similar sense?" If the client reports a memory, you can say "Go with that" and add a few rounds of BLS to desensitize. If the memory clears, you can return to the body scan. If the memory does not clear, this is a likely indicator that you will need to desensitize the memory, starting at Phase 3.

Sometimes the body is experiencing distress that is outside of the context of the target. For example, if a client reports feeling tension in their back after a hard workout, or they feel scratchiness in their throat after being sick, those sensations may not be related to the target. You may ask the client, "Does that feel like it's about the target?" to clarify and proceed accordingly (Porges, 2011).

Because the autonomic nervous system is 80% somatic based, the body scan serves as a final assessment to ensure that the autonomic experience lines up with the cognitive experience. As the client thinks about the memory and the positive thought, the somatic experience serves as an outcome measure for the work. When the mind and body are in agreement, the memory has integrated to a point of adaptive resolution. The absence of distress or disturbance indicates that autonomic defenses are not activated when the memory is recalled, paired with the positive cognition.

Chapter 12

PHASE 7: CLOSURE

Closing sessions requires skill, intentionality, the Three Cs, and coregulation. Phase 7, Closure, happens at every session, no matter which phase of PV-EMDR you and your client have focused on for the day. The objective of this phase is to support the client transition away from the work and ensure connection to ventral. "The clinician should never allow the client to leave the office in a high level of disturbance or in the middle of abreactions" (Shapiro, 2018, p. 155). Closing sessions mindfully and intentionally not only ensures your client is regulated but also fosters safety in the therapeutic work and clinical relationship. Our clients need to trust that they won't be left feeling dysregulated after vulnerable sessions, which would create distrust for the therapeutic process and for you, the therapist. The client also needs to know what to expect following reprocessing sessions, an objective that is prime for integration of the Three Cs.

The interventions provided and the length of Phase 7 depend on the focus of the clinical work and the client's neurophysiological state at the end of a session. If you and your client have just reprocessed a memory to a 0 SUDS, VOC of 7, and the Body scan is clear, the client may be anchored to ventral and feeling amazing, needing very little time in closure. If the session has been challenging and activating, however, you should leave ample time to wind down and coregulate your client back to their window of tolerance.

Recognize that closure can facilitate the growth of new neural networks and adaptive connections, especially when the client is feeling activated at the end of a session. By supporting a client shift away from points of distress using skills that increase access to ventral, you facilitate trust in a few key areas. First is trust in the relationship. Taking time to support a client to soothe their internal world teaches the client that you reliably and dependably will keep them emotionally safe in therapy. No one likes a vulnerability hangover, and Closure teaches the client that you aren't going to make them feel worse and send them out into the world blown open and dysregulated.

Second, Closure teaches the client that they can feel and flex. If the client ends the session in heightened states of dorsal or sympathetic activation, the use of strategies cued by the therapist shifts the autonomic state toward ventral. As the client experiences the shift and the change in their level of distress, they learn that it is possible to feel distress and not spontaneously combust. They learn that there are tools and techniques that soothe and shift them back toward a state of safety.

Third and perhaps most impactful, Closure can help clients learn to trust the process. Feeling yucky feelings and thinking about hurtful memories is hard. It is normal for clients to have ambivalence and avoidance toward EMDR therapy, or any trauma therapy for that matter. Closure can therefore be an intervention that helps clients build courage and confidence in the process of therapy. If closure is done right, the client learns to trust that they can step into their pain and not get buried by it. They learn that they can feel hard feelings and think about uncomfortable memories and have the skill to put it all aside when they need to. They learn that they can control their internal world, rather than feeling like their internal world controls them.

NEW TRUTH

One of my favorite strategies for closing impactful sessions is to install a new truth. I use this strategy when the client has made significant progress in the session, though reprocessing is incomplete. I typically use this strategy for incomplete targets, especially when the client's work has been hard and tender. I start closure with the new truth, as it's powerful to go immediately to this intervention for incomplete targets, and then move on to the other tasks for closing a session.

The new truth connects to the changing internal narrative, allowing the client to pause and explicitly connect to the evolving story of the ventral circuit. This technique asks the client to reflect on their process and identify a new truth or positive insight that resonates with them. For example, "Given the incredible work you've done here today, is there a new truth or helpful insight that you can take from today's work?"

"I can do this; healing is possible; I'm a good person; I believe in myself" are potential new truths. A new truth could also be a feeling word, a body sensation, or even a powerful image. While a new truth can take the form of a positive cognition, it is often unique and specific to the client's experience. I do not try to tweak their new truth to fit into a perfect PC, as that is not the intention of this intervention. Instead, the intention is to support the client to recognize the progress they've made and connect to the evolving story of the memory as it reconsolidates without strong autonomic defenses. A new truth is only possible when the client can access enough ventral to feel and cognitively experience the narrative of this circuit.

Once the client has identified a new truth, you will ask, "And as you say those words [repeat the new truth], what do you notice in your body?" This question connects the client to the felt sense of the statement and invites the autonomic nervous system into the process. Once the client has identified the new truth and the body sensations, you may cue short and slow BLS, similar to that used in resourcing techniques. I typically have the client add four to eight passes of slow BLS, whether that be swaying, eye movements, tactile, or tones.

You should pause after four to eight passes and ask the client, "What do you notice?" If the experience is growing and new adaptive material is coming up, you can simply say, "Notice that," and cue another round of BLS. You may continue to pair short and slow BLS with adaptive material that arises, typically around three to five rounds total or until the material reaches a point that indicates the client is moving on. If the client reports negative material, you may need to ask the client to stay focused on the statement and body sensations, or the statement may need to be modified.

The new truth can be a beautiful way to wrap up a charged and challenging session. It connects the client back to their window of tolerance and helps them recognize their progress. It can also strengthen adaptive memory networks, support ego strength, and foster self-efficacy.

TUCKING IN

I use the terminology "tucking in" for this phase. The goal is to support the client to regulate or coregulate back to their ventral circuit. Consider the bedtime routine of a small child. They need a specific amount of time to complete their bedtime routine of goodnights, brushing teeth, and changing into jammies. There are often rituals like a bedtime story or a lullaby. The experience of being tucked in should be comforting, soothing, and nurturing as the system transitions from the day to sleep. Similarly, this phase offers structured transition time and should be nurturing and regulating for the client as they transition away from potentially vulnerable work in the session and prepare to continue with their day.

Remain mindful of your work for the day, and leave enough time to wind down the session. I base the amount of time I leave at the end of the session on my knowledge of my client, the focus of work for the day, and where they are in the process. Some clients can transition and flexibly maneuver back to ventral with ease. Others take more time to transition. Because each client is different, some need only a brief closure and others a more extensive one. Do not short your client on time to make this transition. The work of Phase 7 ensures they are tucked in or connected to ventral and contributes to their nervous system learning to feel and flex. Closure is a clinical intervention that can support the adaptive integration of maladaptive memories and defensive states and can be an exercise in engaging the vagal brake.

This phase begins with the clinician offering instructions to transition. I usually say, "We're getting to the end of our time together. You've done amazing work today. Let's be sure we take enough time to ensure you return to your day feeling grounded and connected. How does that sound to you?"

The Three Cs can be easily integrated into this phase and help guide the process. As reviewed in Chapter 6, the Three Cs are context, choice, and connection (Dana, 2018). The clinician begins this phase by offering context. Therapy time is ending; it's time to transition. A client may have been so engrossed in the work that they have lost track of time, and therefore, failing to offer context can be startling. I also always provide praise. Praise creates context, as many clients wonder, "How did I do? Did I do this right?" It's essential to cheerlead and celebrate the vulnerable work clients engage in, to build ego strength and self-energy. Therefore, I always offer praise as we wrap up.

I ask my clients how they're feeling and what feels appealing to them. I may say something such as, "On a scale of 0 to 10, with 0 being neutral or pleasant and 10 being the most disturbance you can imagine, where are you right now?" Note, I'm not asking for a SUDS of the memory. I'm specifically asking for the client to assess their level of autonomic arousal in general in that moment. Scaling and naming provide another opportunity to make the implicit explicit and can inform the intervention(s) I provide in this phase. If the client reports a high number on the SUDS scale, I know I need to offer coregulation, and I may need to use a few strategies. If the SUDS is low, I know that transitioning and tucking in may take only a few minutes, and the client may not need coregulation.

Always offer choice by inquiring what feels appealing to the client to wrap up. Containment and safe/calm place can be excellent interventions to close the work. However, I offer my clients a choice, with a few options based on what I know they prefer and the flavor of autonomic distress. For example, if the theme has heavily leaned toward sympathetic activation, I will look for skills to increase parasympathetic engagement and downregulate a hyperaroused system. Conversely, if the theme for the work has been the dorsal circuit and hypoarousal, I will offer skills to help them move out of collapse, toward connection and safety.

When I offer my clients choice in the closure process, I have found that sometimes clients choose safe/calm place, and many times they choose other skills that uniquely appeal to them. Many clients select somatic-focused interventions like mindful movement or breath work. Some clients enjoy grounding techniques such as scanning the room for cues of safety or grounding to their senses. Others enjoy connecting to a resource we developed through ego state interventions or their ventral resource as described in Chapter 8. Support the client to remain empowered in their process by allowing them to choose versus choosing them.

Tucking in also requires that the clinician review what to expect after a reprocessing session, which also creates context. If the work for the day has focused on memory reprocessing, it's important to remind the client that processing will continue. I often say something such as, "You've done amazing work today. As we wrap up, know that your nervous system is still winding down and processing the memory. You may feel tired or introspective today. You may have interesting dreams, notice other memories, or be in your feelings. Or you may not feel any of that and feel peaceful, calm, or even energized. Everyone's experience is different. Take care of yourself and use your skills when you need to. You might write down or journal anything that especially stands out to you. Reach out if you need. Do you have any questions?"

It is common for clients to feel the urge to engage in verbal processing at the end of a reprocessing session. It is also common for clinicians to feel an urge to ask questions and a desire to clarify the client's experience. Shapiro (2018) notes that the therapist should avoid verbal processing, as doing so can influence integration and reconsolidation. If clients feel the desire to share their insights and experiences, I let them share. After all, it is their experience, and sharing is important for some clients and nervous systems to feel connected. In these situations, I refrain from asking process-oriented questions, responding instead with simple statements of validation and positive regard. "I noticed that shift too; yes, that is interesting; mmhmm, that seemed powerful; yes, something to think about" are some ways I respond to clients who share. I do not ask open-ended questions such as, "What do you make of that? What do you think that means? How does that remind you of your past? What emotions are there as you share that insight?" Process-oriented questions can slide the session into talk therapy, influencing AIP and the client's process. Be mindful of this slippery slope.

Case Example

Glen (he/him) has been reprocessing a memory of neglect as a child. He is a 55-year-old, gay, white male. He has made a good deal of progress in the session; however, Phase 4 is not complete, as Glen has not processed the memory to a SUDS of 0. The following reviews the process for closure or "tucking in" and the installation of a new truth.

Glen has his eyes closed, as he has been self-tapping. I see that there are 12 minutes left in the session and move to closing the target.

Tx: Glen, you've done amazing work here today. I'm just noticing the time, and we have about 10 minutes left in our session. I want to be sure we have enough time to shift gears and put this away. Would that feel okay to you to shift right now?

I provide my client with context, choice, and connection here. I start by praising Glen for the work he's done, which offers connection. I then provide context by informing him of the change and invite his consent to move to closing.

Clt: Oh wow. That went fast. Yes, let's wrap up.

Tx: Wonderful. Before we leave this memory, I would like to offer you a moment to reflect on the work you've done here. You've come a long way today. And while there's still some work left to do on this experience, I wonder if you have a new truth or a helpful insight about yourself or this experience that you didn't have when you started? What can you take away from this work you've done today?

Clt: [considers this for a moment] Yes. I'm resilient. That really stands out to me now as I think back to this time.

Tx: That's incredible. Yes, you sure are. As you say those words in your mind, "I'm resilient," what do you notice in your body? Where do they show up?

I ask this question to connect Glen to the felt sense held in the autonomic nervous system with this adaptive narrative.

Clt: In my chest. It feels warm and my jaw tingles a little.

Tx: I'd like you to repeat those words in your mind, "I'm resilient," and notice where you feel them in your body. And as you do that, add some slow taps here.

He closes his eyes again and begins to add slow taps. I invite him to pause after five passes of slow BLS. Note that BLS here is slow, as we are enhancing the positive state rather than installing a PC as we do in Phase 5.

Tx: Pause when you're ready. [Glen stops BLS.] What do you notice?

Clt: I feel strong. I'm telling my little self that.

Tx: Beautiful. Can you repeat those words again, and notice all of that, and tap?

Glen taps again, adding short and slow taps of BLS. He pauses on his own this time and checks in.

Clt: I was also just thinking that I'm really proud of myself for doing this work.

Tx: Wow, that's big! How about one more round just noticing all of that?

He adds one more round of BLS and looks contented and calm.

Tx: Good work. As you check in with yourself now, on a scale of 0 to 10, how much distress or disturbance do you notice?

I ask this question to gauge Glen's overall autonomic state. Note that this question is not asking about the memory itself. It is a question aimed at assessing how much dysregulation Glen is experiencing, which helps inform me about how much tucking in he might need.

Clt: I'd say a 3.

Tx: Okay. Let's do a little more to calm your system before we say goodbye today. Is there anything that feels appealing to you right now? Perhaps your safe/calm place, the breathing activity you enjoy, or the calm lake?

I offer my client context with instructions and then a short menu of skills to increase his connection to ventral. These options are all skills that I know Glen likes. The "calm lake" is the specific cue word and image that he uses for his resourced ventral state, reviewed in Chapter 8.

Tx: Allow yourself to get comfortable and bring to mind the state of your calm lake. Give yourself permission to go there and leave this stuff behind, knowing you'll come back when the time's right. Bring to mind the sounds, smells, temperature, and images of the calm lake. Take a moment and let me know when you get it.

I give Glen time to pause here and connect inside. He nods, indicating he's there.

Tx: Great. Tell me what you're noticing inside.

I ask for feedback from the client to track his process and his autonomic response.

Clt: I see the still water and can feel the coolness of the air. It's quiet, and cool, and I smell grass.

Tx: That sounds lovely. What do you notice in your body as you connect to that?

It's important to always check in with the felt sense as clients do these exercises. Just because they see it doesn't mean they feel it. The felt sense is more important than the visual experience. Therefore, always ask to track and confirm that your client is experiencing the intervention as intended.

Clt: I feel calm and quiet everywhere. Kind of weightless, like I'm in water.

Tx: Very nice. As you hold all those sights, temperatures, and sounds, notice the sensations, and go ahead and tap again, slow.

Glen adds a round of BLS, approximately six passes, and I cue a check-in by saying, "Pause when you're ready." Glen pauses.

Tx: What do you notice?

Clt: A quietness in my head. I can feel my legs getting heavy, and I feel relaxed.

Tx: Notice that as you think of the calm lake, and go ahead and tap again.

He adds another round of slow taps, about eight passes this time, and I cue him to check in.

Tx: What are you aware of?

Clt: The same. I just feel really relaxed and peaceful. I think I'll go sit by the pond by my house on the way home.

Tx: That's great. How about one more round, just noticing all that good stuff?

Glen adds one more round of taps, about six passes again, and then opens his eyes.

Tx: Wonderful. How are you doing now?

Clt: Fantastic. I feel great. I think I could take a nap.

Tx: Yes. You certainly can, and that is a common side effect from this work. How are you on that 0–10 scale now?

Though Glen is reporting that he is well connected to ventral, I add one more check-in here to ensure the client is tucked in.

Clt: Zero. I feel great.

Tx: Well done. Good work today! I'm so proud of you! I just want to remind you that the process will continue and to be gentle with yourself after your session. You might feel tired or energized, you might have some interesting dreams, you might have some feelings come up or memories, or you may feel totally fine and not notice a thing. Reach out if you need to.

Clt: [nods in agreement and understanding] Got it. Can you do the same time next week?

Tx: Yes. I have you down. See you then!

Chapter 13

PHASE 8: REEVALUATION

Phase 8, Reevaluation, is the final phase of EMDR therapy, and a phase of every therapy, for that matter. At the beginning of a counseling session, it is customary to conduct a brief assessment or reevaluation with the client to gather relevant and meaningful updates. You may ask something like, "How have you been since we last met? What changes have you noticed since our last session? What is important for me to know as we get started today?" These are all ways to begin a session and the phase of Reevaluation. Checking in with progress, life events, and relevant changes informs the session's focus and provides important qualitative outcome data to track progress and setbacks.

Shapiro (2018) notes that Reevaluation should open each session, no matter what phase of EMDR therapy you have been engaged in with the client. There are two levels of reevaluation for the PV-EMDR therapist. One is a global reevaluation, and the other is specific to PV-EMDR. A global reevaluation is broad in scope and encompasses the many dynamic layers of the client and their unique life. A global reevaluation may explore day-to-day stability, housing, employment or school, relationships, family life, and current events. Think of a global reevaluation as a global reexamination of the client's present-day life and circumstances. A PV-EMDR-specific reevaluation zooms in, and on a microlevel examines the state of the client's nervous system. Because the nervous system is the focus of assessment, intervention, and outcome, reevaluation examines relevant neurophysiological correlates, incorporates changes into the working case conceptualization, and refines treatment accordingly.

In Chapter 7 we reviewed Phase 1, Safety and Case Conceptualization. Recall that case conceptualization is an ongoing process, beginning with the first client interaction and ending at termination. Phase 8 is a continuation of the material gathered in Phase 1, with a focus on changes, transformation, and resiliency. As in Phase 1, relevant data to examine include cues of safety, autonomic functioning, dual awareness, dissociation, defensive strategies of accommodation, and clinical themes as related to maladaptively stored memories. While we can consider Phase 8 to be a continuation of Phase 1, this phase focuses on changes related to clinical interventions and refines technique and treatment plan accordingly.

In Phase 8 of PV-EMDR, there are four key reevaluation categories you should keep in mind:

1. Macro-reevaluation
2. Micro-reevaluation
3. What's next
4. The therapeutic relationship

REMODELING A HOME

Have you ever remodeled a home or been part of a remodel? Or maybe you have a friend or loved one who has? As I write this book, my home has gone through two recent remodeling projects, one chosen and the other unplanned though necessary following a water leak. Remodeling is a mixed bag. On the one hand, you feel excited to think about the end product and how nice your place will be when you're done. "I'll have so much storage! I can't wait to take a bath in that tub! It will be so nice to put a fresh coat of paint on these walls." You start the project with some likely avoidance, some dread, but also hopefulness, excitement, a timeline, and a plan.

The remodel starts, along with a number of unexpected surprises. You pull out the cabinet and find water damage and mold. You tear down the wall and find there's something wrong with the electrical wiring. You start to paint and realize you're a terrible painter and don't like the color you chose. There's dust everywhere, your space is in complete disarray, you can't find anything, and the process is taking way longer than you expected. That's how my projects went anyway. Can you relate?

Treating toxic stress and trauma is like remodeling a home. It's a process; it's messy; and there are surprises along the way. Trauma healing is a remodel of the soul. It's not clean; it's messy. It's not easy; it's hard. It's not an upward, linear trajectory of improvement. It's a couple of steps forward, and a few steps back.

Healing requires that we confront painful parts of ourselves and our lives, which can feel embarrassing, shameful, and threatening. Healing requires us to live differently, to learn new adaptive strategies for regulating, and to change our relationships. In the process of healing, symptoms can sometimes get worse as feelings and sensations that have been compartmentalized or dissociated for a very long time become conscious. The client who gains the insight "I sabotage relationships because I'm terrified that if I get close to someone, they will abandon me, just like my mom did" has just found a water leak behind their sink that they didn't know was there. The client who takes responsibility and says "I have a problem with pills and alcohol and I'm afraid of living sober" has just knocked down a wall to find termites. While yes, these insights are helpful, they also uncover additional wounds that must be healed. Now, instead of relying on the defensive strategy of interpersonal sabotage, a client must learn to sit with the vulnerability that comes with getting close to someone. Or instead of numbing out with drugs and alcohol, they have to not only learn to survive cravings and urges but also deal with everything they've been chemically suppressing. It's good to discover these things so that repairs can begin. But it doesn't mean the repair is easy or painless. In fact, the repair is sometimes the most painful, tender part of it all.

Remodeling is a marathon, not a sprint. Clients may present with ambivalence or avoidance for any phase of the work. They may need to take breaks from reprocessing to pause and catch their breath. Sometimes there's a flare in symptoms with a different flavor because they are moving through the autonomic ladder on the way to ventral. Clients can regress into old maladaptive coping strategies, and sometimes people decide EMDR or therapy overall is just too much. This is all normal and par for the course. When I was remodeling my home, I thought about quitting and selling. I needed to dissociate at times because my environment became chaotic and overwhelming. I felt exhausted with contractors constantly in my space, making a muck and finding more problems that needed to be addressed. It's hard work, and we need to acknowledge this with our clients.

There are times when clients get worse because of our mistakes. If we are not practicing with integrity, if we've skipped phases, if we have moved too fast, or if we are dysregulated and absent in the work, we can overwhelm our client's nervous system and trigger increasing distress. When things get worse, we need to check ourselves and our work. Therapists have a responsibility to self-assess alongside the client assessment and seek out consultation, supervision, or additional training accordingly. It's normal to make mistakes, as you too are human. Take responsibility to make corrections and practice with integrity. But hold the duality of the process in your awareness as you assess, remaining curious as to what is in your power and control as the therapist, and what is simply part of the healing process. When it's hard to tell what's what, seek some feedback and get to consultation.

MACRO-REEVALUATION

I typically begin my reevaluation on a macro level. I ask a broad, open-ended question and allow the client to take the lead, reporting on what's most important to them. Clients may check in on changes to their relationships, political and sociological events, how they're handling a recent stressor, changes at work or school, or physical health, among others. A macro-reevaluation takes a zoomed-out snapshot of the client's life. This check-in guides the session's focus.

It is common, especially in today's world, for life events to focus the session away from EMDR-specific interventions. Political, environmental, and societal unrest bombard our lives and continuously challenge our hearts and minds. Clients come to therapy for a sounding board and support just as much as they do the in-depth, personal transformation work. Because we are social creatures, the experience of venting and getting basic emotional support is an intervention in safety and connection. It feels good to talk through a problem you're having and get emotional validation from someone you trust. Safety and connection is an intervention.

Sometimes clients present with the crisis of the week. It seems that every session there is some new drama, crisis, or blow-up on a macrolevel that needs attending to. One week they are going through a breakup, the next they have a medical scare, and the next they are getting evicted. While sometimes the crisis of the week can be an avoidance strategy, sometimes this is just the client's reality. Remember, the most important factor of therapy is the relationship. Even in times when it seems you can't get to deeper layers of clinical work, the therapeutic relationship is still medicinal.

MICRO-REEVALUATION

In addition to significant events and changes in the client's life, we must also assess the microchanges a client reports. These can be understood as neurophysiological changes that indicate nervous system functioning.

Psychotherapists treat the nervous system. Accordingly, we must always be tracking changes in nervous system functioning as we evaluate the effects of treatment and memory reprocessing. Shapiro's (2018) reevaluation factors include assessing for activation of associated material that needs to be addressed and tracking for adaptive assimilation. These two domains for reevaluation are tracked through neurophysiological correlates. Tracking symptoms and autonomic states provides insightful data on the effects and pacing of treatment, and the assimilation of maladaptive memories. As adaptive integration takes place, the client reports less activation of defensive states, and more health and wellness. Additionally, if associated memories have been activated, there are new crises or challenges, or treatment is not meeting the client's needs, the nervous system will communicate this through changes in autonomic states. Reexamination of the nervous system will inform your case conceptualization and treatment plan. It also refines the work and directs the session.

Connection to ventral is a component of the window of tolerance, and where health and wellness reside. With reliable, flexible, consistent access to the ventral circuit, overwhelming and distressing symptoms subside. Reevaluation therefore examines the client's growing capacity to access this state of their autonomic nervous system. Whether the work has been focused on developing therapeutic rapport and safety, learning skills to navigate the preparation hierarchy, or reprocessing memories, accessibility to ventral is a marker of progress and outcome of healing.

As reviewed in Phases 1 and 2 of PV-EMDR therapy, tracking outcomes can be accomplished by gathering hard and soft data points. You may ask your client about specific symptoms that have been a theme in their presentation.

You might revisit their map of circuits and explore changes to autonomic states. Or you may readminister a formal assessment to assess for changes. There is no single way to track or assess changes.

As you and the client engage in the tender and precarious work of healing and transformation, changes to autonomic states are normal and expected. While the goal is for clients to have increased access to ventral, achieving this feat is often challenging. Clients may move up and down the autonomic ladder as they learn skills and examine aspects of their experiences that have not been explored until now.

For example, with desensitization of a target memory a client may report an increase in dorsal activation between sessions. Dorsal may have been their response at the time of the trauma, or it may be protecting them in the present from feeling other emotions and sensations. This can be the case when clients present with ambivalence or avoidance of the work and memory reprocessing. A client may alternatively move from dorsal to sympathetic as they move up the autonomic hierarchy toward ventral. For clients who have been living in chronic states of dorsal disconnection, moving up the autonomic hierarchy requires movement through sympathetic activation. Your client may report that instead of feeling sad and shut down, they have been feeling increasingly angry, irritable, and agitated. Neither case is necessarily an indicator that therapy needs to alter course, or that you're doing EMDR "wrong." Sometimes these changes are indicative of healing.

As you track changes and autonomic responses, recall the concept of dual awareness. This is one foot in the past and one foot in the present, or in Polyvagal terms, one foot in the stress response and one foot in ventral. If a client reports an increase in defensive states with decreased capacity to access ventral, you will likely need to refine your approach to increase their connection to safety. Losing dual awareness and connection to ventral is an indicator that increased connection to safety is needed. If, however, the client is maintaining dual awareness, stay the course.

As a memory integrates, giving the client more access to ventral, this can also trigger its own challenges and vulnerabilities. For some, connecting to ventral may be met with fear, hesitation, or discomfort. Learning to feel peaceful and regulated can be a strange experience for clients who have lived in dysregulated, defensive states for long periods of time. Sometimes clients don't trust the state of ventral. Feeling safe may be a cue associated with danger, if their perpetrator was someone who caused harm but also kept them safe (such as a parent or a caregiver). Feeling safe may not be trustworthy to the client, triggering hypervigilance on the lookout for the other shoe to drop. A client may have blocking beliefs that tell them they don't deserve to feel safe, or that they aren't worthy of feeling better. It may even be that ventral feels boring to those who have lived in chronic states of sympathetic arousal. Remain curious if your client demonstrates resistance, avoidance, or fear of ventral. Bring this into conscious awareness and explore it together. "What's it like to feel safe/calm/regulated? Could there be any beliefs inside that prevent you from feeling happy and peaceful? What was it like to feel safe when you were younger? Is it safe to feel safe?" are potential questions to further explore this relationship. Sometimes this exploration may even identify additional targets or treatment plans to address with PV-EMDR.

It's important to also track the client on the preparation hierarchy, reviewed in Chapter 8. Because the nervous system is constantly being shaped and reshaped, things can change quickly. Clients can move up and down the preparation hierarchy in response to life events. While one does not suddenly or magically lose or gain autonomic resiliency overnight, life events can drastically alter the functioning of the nervous system. After all, that's what it's designed to do. Injuries, accidents, medication changes, medical events, sleep and diet, and new life stressors or traumas all impact the functioning of the autonomic nervous system. If your client presents in session stating they have felt overwhelming anxiety because their partner was just diagnosed with a terminal illness, changes to their autonomic state are to be expected. Additionally, if your client sustained a concussion in a recent car accident, they're probably off their baseline.

While clients can move up and down the preparation hierarchy in response to life events, resiliency gained is never lost. That is, skills your client has acquired are not suddenly forgotten or erased from the nervous system. The autonomic nervous system is wired to respond to present-day events, stressors, and traumas adaptively and defensively. Clients may not be safe enough in their life and environment to feel. They may struggle to notice and name or feel and flex because survival states are activated by very real threats. But skills learned and developed are not erased or obsolete. They just might be hard to access. Trust that with more access to safety, along with coregulation and support, they'll be able to get back to what they've learned in the past.

WHAT'S NEXT?

Based on the macro- and micro-reevaluation, you and the client must identify the next step and focus for the day. This question asks you to keep track of your progression through the PV-EMDR phases and focus the session based on the client's needs. It's important to ask the client what they need from the session and agree upon the work: "What feels most important for us to focus on today? A few options for our work include returning to reprocessing the EMDR target we started last time, or we can focus on this recent stressor you shared. What feels right?" These are some potential questions. It's important to give the client choice and context as you focus the session, and it can also be helpful to review some options as related to their goals and treatment plan.

Avoidance and flooding are the hallmarks of trauma and toxic stress, and we must be careful not to recreate these dynamics in therapy. If we do not ask a focusing question and instead allow the client to check in and ramble for the entire session, we will never get through the eight phases nor make much progress on specific treatment goals. Clients are not going to say, "Can we go back to learning neural exercises? I think it's time to install safe/calm place," or "Let's move on to installation of the positive cognition, as that memory is now a SUDS of 0." You must find a balance between letting the client lead while also providing some structure and direction. If we don't, we can foster avoidance. Likewise, it's important we give the client choice so as not to create an experience of powerlessness. If we move too fast or without the client's choice, we can recreate the dynamic of flooding.

It is not uncommon in psychotherapy to have to return to earlier states of work to increase stability and build additional coping skills. PV-EMDR therapy is no exception. Returning to the analogy of remodeling a home, expect the unexpected. If you have been reprocessing a target and a new layer of work is uncovered, you may need to return to Phases 1 or 2. For example, a client reprocessing a memory suddenly recalls an aspect of the experience that was forgotten or dissociated. They recall another layer of trauma or hurt, and it creates significant distress. Or, as you desensitize a memory, defensive ego states are activated, and there is an increase in maladaptive coping as the client loses connection to dual awareness. These are both common scenarios indicating the need to return to Phases 1 and 2 to increase safety and stability, and build additional resources.

EMDR is not a strict, scrupulous therapy. It is a client-centered approach. Polyvagal Theory emphasizes the importance that clients have context, choice, and connection at every clinical juncture. Therefore, the next step in therapy is dynamically informed by a macro- and micro-reevaluation, as well as the client's choice. Remember that the nervous system is the pacesetter of therapy. We cannot rush or force healing if the nervous system is not ready or lacks resources. Remain flexible and adaptive, and remember that healing is not an upward, linear trajectory.

HOW'S OUR RELATIONSHIP?

In Chapter 5 we reviewed the importance of a healthy therapeutic relationship and tending to the therapeutic soil. The state of the therapeutic relationship must be continuously reevaluated and tended to. As reviewed in previous chapters, the human nervous system thrives in safe connection. The therapeutic relationship supports the clinical work at every session, and therapeutic presence must be in place every step of the way.

While developing the relationship is often the focus in the beginning stages of work, maintaining the relationship must remain a priority. Phase 8 is the perfect phase, and a reminder, to check in on the health of your client-therapist relationship, make repairs when necessary, and explicitly ask for feedback. I like to check in with my clients every two or three months and ask for feedback on their thoughts on therapy and the health of our relationship. Examples of questions I may ask to gather feedback include, "How is this going? How is our therapeutic relationship? How can I support you better?" Taking time to pause and ask for feedback gives the client permission to share and demonstrates that you value their input. While some clients are bold and have no problem speaking up, most of our clients will not share feedback unless given the opportunity. Be open and nonreactive to any critiques and make repairs and adjustments where necessary.

While it is not necessary to explicitly ask for feedback on the therapeutic relationship at every session, the state of your therapeutic relationship should always be in your awareness as you reevaluate. Relationships can be thought of as a living, breathing energetic process. All close relationships in our lives require care and tending to. Because the therapeutic relationship is so special and unique, its health and wellness are vital for positive treatment outcomes. Its value and contributions to the work cannot be diminished.

REEVALUATION CASE SCENARIOS

Below are a few case scenarios of Phase 8, Reevaluation. In each case I note the relevant macro- and micro-data, identify the next step, and reevaluate the therapeutic relationship. Phase 8 is typically quick, though encompasses a lot of data. As you reevaluate, you are incorporating new data into your current case conceptualization.

Michael (he/him) is a 26-year-old, Black, gay, trans male. Michael has been working on a treatment plan related to a severe medical illness he had as a child. You've been working with Michael for four months, and he has developed several coping skills and is prepped in relation to the preparation hierarchy. The previous session focused on reprocessing a target from your EMDR treatment plan. Today Michael reports feeling especially anxious and disturbed due to recent antitrans legislation passed in his state. He's feeling unsafe, isn't sleeping well, and is hypervigilant. This recent political event is understandably a cue of danger to Michael's neuroception and is all he can think about right now. You offered a formal check-in on your relationship a few weeks ago and assessed that your therapeutic relationship remains supportive and safe for Michael. This appears to remain intact and true today. You ask Michael, "Given everything you just shared, what feels most important for our time today? We can focus on these disturbing things happening in the world, go back to EMDR, or focus on something else. What feels like the right thing to you?" Michael says he needs support with present-day stressors. You provide support and increase connection to ventral with emotional validation and a regulating breathing technique. You also help Michael develop a protective ally, and install with bilateral stimulation.

Lee (he/him) is a 34-year-old, Chinese American, hetero male. To date, the focus of the work has been in Phases 1 and 2. You have spent ample time with Lee building skills to manage symptoms and increase stability. At check-in, Lee reports that he is doing "really good." He says that his sleep has been much better. He's felt happier, has more energy, and is spending more time with family. These are big shifts for Lee, who was previously isolated and stuck in a shut-down, depressive dorsal state. On a macrolevel, Lee is very stable, and he reports no significant changes at today's check-in. Reexamination of Lee's functioning on a micro- and macrolevel indicate it is an appropriate time to explore progressing to reprocessing target memories. "I'm so impressed with the leaps and bounds you've made in the time we've known each other. Does it feel like time to start exploring memories for EMDR, or is there something else you'd like to focus on today?" The clinician offers Lee connection in the form of celebratory praise for the growth Lee has experienced, context for treatment options, and choice. Lee says he wants to focus on EMDR today and reprocessing memories. Before proceeding, you check in with Lee on the relationship: "Before we get started, I wanted to check in with how therapy is for you. I like to get a client's feedback from time to time to make sure I'm being as helpful as possible and to make sure our relationship feels supportive. How are things going, and how is this relationship feeling for you?" Lee says he's been happy with the progress he's made and that he feels comfortable with you. You move on to treatment planning with Lee following this reevaluation.

Kris (they/them) is a 45-year-old, queer, Black client. They just started reprocessing a target for the first time in the last session. The chosen target was related to chronic pain, and reprocessing was complete, with a 0 SUDS, 7 on the VOC, and a clear body scan. At your next session, you ask a few questions, including, "How have you been since we last met? What's new in your life? What did you notice after EMDR?" Kris reports that they felt "so much better" after that session. Their pain has significantly decreased; they have felt calmer, less anxious; and sleep has improved. They report feeling worried about their auntie who has been sick with COVID, and they've been dealing with an annoying situation at work. You ask, "What feels right for our session today? Does it feel like returning to our EMDR work is the best fit, or should we focus on something else?" Kris says they'd like to return to EMDR. They recently provided you positive feedback on the relationship. You check in with their experience with reprocessing: "What was our last EMDR session like for you?" Kris shares that they really like EMDR and thought it was very "different" as a therapy: "I don't really understand what I'm supposed to notice though. When you tell me to notice, I don't know what you're talking about" This is helpful feedback that Kris's nervous system needs a bit more context about desensitization. You follow up on their feedback by validating: “That makes sense. I know that language can feel really vague. Let me explain more and see if that helps.” You give Kris a bit more instruction and information on the process of desensitization, after which they look more confident and relaxed.

REEVALUATION OF A TARGET

If your previous session was focused on reprocessing, you will need to reevaluate the target (Shapiro, 2018). Whether or not reprocessing was complete, it’s important to reevaluate the current state of the memory. Some targets that were fully reprocessed to a 0 SUDS, 7 VOC, and a clear body scan may need to be reengaged for further reprocessing as some additional distress surfaces between sessions. Other targets that were not reprocessed may now be resolved. Because the nervous system is in constant transformation, targets typically change from one session to the next.

To reevaluate the target, you may ask the client, “If you think about the memory we last worked on now, what do you notice? What has changed?” The client responds with a broad check-in on the target, and you tune in to significant changes, indications of adaptive integration, stuck points, or blocks. If the client’s report is adaptive or neutral, the next step is to check SUDS. If the SUDS is a 0, then proceed to the installation of the positive cognition, followed by the body scan.

If the target is incomplete, as indicated by a SUDS higher than 0, the next step is to reengage the target for reprocessing (Shapiro, 2018). It is typical, especially with adult clients, for a target to require multiple sessions of desensitization before the autonomic distress resolves, reaching a SUDS of 0. With highly complex targets, or when working with complex PTSD, memory networks can be vast, and there can be many layers of distress to process through. While EMDR tends to work faster than other therapies, it is not magic, and reprocessing takes time.

REENGAGING AN INCOMPLETE TARGET

As reviewed in Chapter 9, Phase 3, Assessment, is often short. The objective of the target assessment is to activate the central and autonomic nervous system and transition into desensitization. To reengage an incomplete target, the clinician asks a few brief questions.

Below is an example of a script to reengage a target:

Tx: As you bring that experience to mind, what's the worst part of it now?
What image represents the worst of it now?
What emotions and body sensations do you notice as you think of it now?
On a scale of 0 to 10, with 0 being no disturbance or neutral and 10 being the greatest disturbance you can imagine, how disturbing is it now?

After asking these questions, the client is ready to transition back into desensitization. Return to the standard processes of desensitization, installation, and body scan to fully reprocess the memory to a point of adaptive resolution. The process of reengagement is quick and brief, as the goal is to access and stimulate the memory and move into reprocessing.

THE THREE-PRONGED PROTOCOL

As outlined by Shapiro (2018), the EMDR standard protocol focuses on three prongs, which are past, present, and future. All three prongs should be assessed and included in case conceptualization and included in a comprehensive treatment plan. Shapiro recommends that reprocessing begins on the past prong, as past maladaptively stored memories inform the present. Once past targets have been reprocessed, the therapist moves on to the present prong, targeting present-day triggers and related fears. Finally, the therapist explores the future prong by assessing if desired outcomes have been achieved and assesses for potential anticipatory events to desensitize.

Comprehensive treatment focuses on the three prongs and begins reprocessing targets from the past first. Sometimes, however, you may take a modified approach and invert the prongs, beginning with the present or future prong first. This may be appropriate when the client has a tight time frame and needs quick relief from a present or future stressor. This can also be appropriate when there is not enough stability to target the past, but the client could manage to reprocess a present or future trigger. Additionally, the client may explicitly say they aren't ready to reprocess the past and want to focus on the present or the future.

In any clinical situation, there are multiple choice points and ways forward. There is rarely one right way to intervene. You, as the therapist, may identify benefits in targeting the past, present, or future prong. Always return to the importance of the Three Cs (from Chapter 5) and offer your client choice and context. This is their therapy and their healing journey, and their system often knows best.

THREE-PRONGED CASE SCENARIOS

> Tara (she/her) is a 26-year-old, Black, hetero female. She was sexually assaulted last year by an acquaintance. She reported the crime, and the case is going to trial in two weeks. Tara is experiencing a flood of sympathetic activation, reporting increasing levels of anxiety, hypervigilance, flashbacks, and nightmares. You offer Tara some options and discuss the potential use of EMDR to target present-day triggers such as flashbacks and nightmares or the future anticipatory event of the trial in two weeks. Tara decides to target her future fear, and you proceed to target the future prong. The target for reprocessing is the future fear of seeing her perpetrator in the court room.
>
> Jason (he/him) is a 21-year-old, white, questioning male. He had an adverse medical event two years ago in which a routine procedure turned into a traumatic near-death experience. He has to go to the doctor to get a physical to try out for basketball and is terrified to enter a medical building. He dissociates and goes mute when he enters a medical office. He is having nightmares and is increasingly anxious. He presents with a mixed state of dorsal and sympathetic activation. You offer Jason potential options for using EMDR to create relief. You explore with Jason the option of targeting the past event, as he has a month until his physical is scheduled. You also explore the option of targeting present-day nightmares and anxiety, as well as targeting his future fears of going into medical offices. Jason decides he wants to start by targeting his nightmares, and you begin with the present prong. The target for reprocessing is a specific recurring nightmare.

Note that in both case scenarios, you could begin with any prong, and meaningful work would happen. Your client would likely experience the benefit of

EMDR and relief from symptoms wherever you started. Shapiro recommends that reprocessing begin with the past prong, whenever possible and appropriate (2018). Present- and future-pronged targets are directly linked to the past experiences, and therefore symptoms will not fully change until the past is integrated. However, the prong to target is ultimately determined by the client and informed by your well-rounded case conceptualization. Clients may not be prepared or feel ready to target the past. Remember that our mantra in EMDR is "trust the process," and trusting the client's preference and intuition are ways to integrate this wisdom in the direct clinical work.

Chapter 14
THE EMBODIED THERAPIST

Throughout this book, we have explored a comprehensive framework for integrating Polyvagal Theory into your EMDR practice. We have reviewed key concepts and points of clinical intervention throughout the eight phases. We have also outlined the undeniable contribution of your nervous system to your client's therapeutic journey. Your nervous system and the clinical interventions you provide are not distinctly separate. In fact, your nervous system needs to embody the spirit of your teachings for clinical interventions to be deeply effective.

I'm sure that you have probably had the experience of booking a room or hotel sometime in your adult life. When you reserve or rent lodging, you likely take some time to examine the online pictures and reviews. You probably aren't drawn to places that look grimy, unsafe, or run-down. I would guess you find spaces that look clean, safe, and well cared for to be most appealing. Why would you pay good money to rent an inhospitable place?

In a way, clients rent your nervous system when they come to therapy. Just as you wouldn't want to rent a dirty hotel room, you probably wouldn't want to seek counseling from a dysregulated therapist. Receiving therapy from someone who is flooded with sympathetic overwhelm, collapsed in dorsal shutdown, and hijacked by their own unresolved adversities quite simply is not a healing experience. We can't show up to our profession with messy nervous systems, as it's not therapeutic and it poses the risk of doing more harm than good.

Our jobs as psychotherapists are unique and special, because of the specific instrument at the heart of our work: the therapist's nervous system. Your nervous system is your clinical instrument through which you provide interventions. If your nervous system is consistently dysregulated, it's unlikely you will be able to establish a safe and supportive space for your clients. Your nervous system is your magic wand that you lend to your clients each day you sit in your counseling chair. If you're going to be good at helping people heal, you have to start by getting your nervous system healthy and regulated. You have to be an embodied practitioner.

The *Merriam-Webster Dictionary* defines "embody" as a verb, meaning to "give a body to a spirit; to make concrete and perceptible; to represent in human form" (Merriam-Webster, n.d.). To be embodied requires you to integrate and incarnate your knowledge and teachings of the human nervous system into your day-to-day life and therapy practice. You have a wealth of knowledge, compared to the average civilian, on interpersonal neurobiology. You know the power of the social engagement system, the therapeutic effects of safe connection, and the importance of supportive relationships as contributors to resiliency. You know that health and wellness come from practicing skills to manage stress responses and integrating maladaptive memories. Such knowledge comes with the responsibility to integrate and personify.

I too often see examples in the counseling field of disembodied therapists and experts who don't practice what they teach: professionals who don't apply the information they teach to clients to their own personal or professional lives. The therapist who knows they're overwhelmed and burned out but won't take a day off or acts like seeing eight clients every day is a badge of honor. The leader who focuses on productivity over people, creating a toxic work environment and distrust in their employees. The professor who doesn't create safety in the classroom for role-plays or vulnerable conversations, leaving students feeling shamed and triggered. The supervisor who is too scattered and busy to be present or helpful to their supervisees, creating a culture of busyness and crisis. The expert who lectures with a big ego and gets defensive about feedback, creating an unsafe environment and deterring people from learning skills to help their clients. These are common examples of a disembodied professional, behaving in ways that reduce safety, connection, and opportunities for healing. Their actions are in complete contradiction to what they know to be true about health, wellness, boundaries, self-care, and interpersonal connection. These are examples of professionals who talk the talk but fail to walk the walk.

We've all probably been there at some point (Simionato & Simpson, 2018; Yang & Hayes, 2020). Maybe you're reading this now and feel called out because I just described a behavior that you actively engage in. It's okay. You're not a bad person. But it's time to do better. I used to live a disembodied life. I started out in the nonprofit world, where I learned some bad habits and internalized dysfunctional beliefs from a toxic work culture. I used to employ unhealthy coping skills to create a faux window of tolerance in attempts to manage my own unresolved trauma. I used to revel in my busyness and overwhelm and viewed them as indicators of my importance and worth. I used to have a big therapist ego. I used to have a lot of unhealed personal stuff that regularly triggered my defensive autonomic states. Heck, I still do these things sometimes. I bet you do too! You're human; you have probably experienced adversity in your life; you have been trained in a field that doesn't truly value the importance of therapist wellness; and you live in a society that puts money ahead of sanity. None of us are immune to these disembodied ways of living. But we have to change the paradigm and stop practicing against neurobiology if we hope to have integrity and to be truly effective healers.

If we can't embody what we preach, we are nothing more than arrogant imposters. We set ourselves up to practice as if we are omnipotent by acting as if the rules don't apply to us. Our behavior conveys that we believe ourselves to be exceptions to the truths of neurobiology, Polyvagal Theory, and AIP. This creates a dangerous culture for clinicians working in a high-burnout field to overwork and overextend. When we try to defy the rules of our physiology and interpersonal relationships, we do harm to ourselves, our colleagues, our loved ones, and our clients. There is nothing that makes you so special that your nervous system doesn't operate under the same processes as everyone else's.

Burnout is a real issue in the psychotherapy field. The demand is high, the job hard, and the resources few. A 2020 Gallup poll found America's mental health to be at the worst it had been in two decades (Brenan, 2020). It is no secret that the pandemic and events of the last few years have taken a toll on people, leading to increases in addiction, depression, anxiety, and suicide. With additional demands placed on the system, we are facing a shortage of therapists. Many clinicians find themselves overwhelmed, with full caseloads, long waitlists, and no reprieve in sight. This increases our risk of burnout and compassion fatigue. A study by Summers et al. in 2020 identified that 78% of counselors they surveyed reported high levels of burnout. More than three-quarters of our profession is fried!

The burnout risk in this profession is real (Simionato & Simpson, 2018; Yang & Hayes, 2020). Burnout is a stress response and a sign of chronic autonomic activation. Most of us went into this job knowing it's not an easy one. Additionally, we all move in and out of ventral throughout the day in response to life demands and the many existential threats we face from environmental, societal, and political crises. Yes, it is hard to stay resilient and maintain your connection to ventral at this time in history. But the fact that it's a hard job and a hard world are not excuses to let your self-care and self-regulation go to the wayside. In fact, these statistics beg us to up the ante if we have any hope of staying in this field and maintaining therapeutic presence for our clients and those we serve. Remember that self-care is intentional self-regulation. You cannot light yourself on fire for the sake of others and remain sustainable. You are not stress proof.

What kind of nervous system do you hope to lend to your clients and your professional community? A fried, exhausted, depleted, activated sympathetic or dorsal system? Or a regulated, connected, safe, energized ventral system? I'm sure you answered the latter. To do so requires intentional effort and regular practice of skills that support your health and wellness. To show up from a place of ventral, you, my dear colleague, have to do your work and practice. It requires making a commitment to embody what you teach and take care of your own biology. It all starts with you.

Start by taking a personal inventory of the state of your nervous system. How well do you take your own therapeutic advice? Where do you fall on the preparation hierarchy? Are you frequently hijacked by maladaptively stored memories? Do you show up to your work with ventral leading the way? How well can you notice and name, and feel and flex? How healthy is your nervous system? It is only when we get honest with ourselves about our growth edges and pain points that we can identify a pathway forward. Without self-reflection, there can be no self-correction.

It can be helpful to develop a list of anchoring and regulating skills that help you to increase your connection to ventral. These are ways to foster regulating resets, as we reviewed in Chapter 5. After all, when we get overwhelmed and lose access to ventral, it can be hard to identify what we need and what might help us. Creating a list can serve as a cheat sheet when your biology is outside of its capacity to problem solve.

I like to divide the skills I use into five categories. While many skills overlap, the five categories help me to develop a diverse list of options. These five categories are physical, emotional and social, spiritual, intellectual, and workplace. Below are some examples of my favorite go-to's.

- Physical: take a walk; sit still and breathe; sing; get the amount of sleep I need to feel good (for me that's 8 hours a night); eat healthy food; abstain from alcohol and no more than one cup of coffee if any (they really dysregulate me); eat chocolate and ice cream.
- Emotional and social: have a coach or therapist; acknowledge my feelings; practice self-compassion; cry when I need to; moderate my news exposure; practice mindfulness; check out when I need to with a show or a movie; play and snuggle with my pets; spend time with my husband and friends; spend time alone when I need it.
- Spiritual: sit in nature; meditate; read inspirational books by spiritual leaders; attend spiritual talks and lectures; talk to my higher power; look for wonder and beauty when I feel hopeless.
- Intellectual: have a variety of books I'm reading at once (clinical, business, motivational, spiritual, fiction); listen to podcasts; talk about hard and complex issues when I have the bandwidth; take workshops and trainings; take a break from learning and my intellect when I need it.
- Workplace: set boundaries with my schedule and try my best to respect them; say no when I need to; schedule breaks; always schedule lunch; hold time for administrative tasks; take new trainings that inspire me; take time off; call out when I'm sick or outside of my ventral circuit; keep flowers and plants at my desk.

As you develop your list, be honest. Don't judge yourself, what you need, or what helps. And don't write down skills that you think you should do but know you won't do. Let's be real. Sometimes you eat the carrots, and sometimes you eat the cake. Sometimes you go for a walk, and sometimes you dissociate on social media or binge-watch a show. It's not about creating a list of ideal skills; it's about creating a list of real skills.

This list is a work in progress. You will find new skills along the way, and others may lose effectiveness. You are in constant transformation, as is your nervous system. Therefore, it's understandable that your list will change and evolve along with your neurons and memory networks.

The more you practice noticing, naming, flexing and feeling, the more habitual the practices will become. You will learn to quickly catch yourself in your personal and professional life when autonomic responses and maladaptive memories hijack you. You will be able to engage skills with greater ease and more fluidly as you develop autonomic resiliency. It may feel like work at times to employ these techniques, but with time and repetition, it will become second nature. After all, practicing your skills repeatedly not only builds vagal tone but also wires adaptive memory networks.

The stronger your connection to ventral, the more resiliency you will have in your nervous system, and the more equipped you will be to support your clients. This is the path of the embodied therapist. To recognize that, you must both talk the talk and walk the walk. You have to practice what you teach and integrate your knowledge into your own life if you are to have integrity and authenticity. Get to therapy and heal those wounds. Practice those skills to tame your autonomic dragon. Set boundaries and push back on burnout culture. You too are resilient and can heal and grow, just like your clients. When we make a commitment to become embodied, we pledge to resign ourselves from the status quo of toxic systems and unhealthy workplace norms. Embodiment takes practice and regular tending. It isn't easy, and it can certainly feel hard, vulnerable, and scary. But remember that the better you are, the better everyone else is around you. Be courageous and brave, if not for yourself, then for your clients, fellow professionals, your loved ones, and humankind.

Healing others begins with healing you.

Appendix

ATTACHMENT INTERVIEW

1. Who were your primary caregivers when you were growing up?
2. Did your primary caregivers experience any of the following: divorce or separation, mental or physical illness, substance use, incarceration, service deployment, death?
3. What are five words that describe each of your caregivers?
4. What were your relationships like with your caregivers as a child? Did those relationships change as you grew up?
5. Did you ever feel any of the following with your caregivers: criticized, unsafe, ignored, unimportant, abandoned, afraid, humiliated, or terrified?
6. Was there violence in your home growing up?
7. Were your physical needs cared for?
8. Were your emotional needs cared for?
9. Did you receive praise? If so, how were you praised? Were you
10. Did you get in trouble much as a child? How were you consequenced or punished?
11. What were you told as a child, about yourself, others, and the world?
12. What were you like as a child? What were you like as a teenager?
13. Did you have any medical issues growing up (illness, surgery, injuries, etc.)?
14. What do you know about your development and birth?
15. Who were your major supports in childhood?
16. How have your experiences in childhood impacted you today?
17. What did you learn about feelings and emotions as a child?
18. How did your caregivers manage feelings and emotions? What were their coping skills like?
19. Were you soothed and regulated by your caregivers when you were upset or scared?
20. What is your relationship like with your childhood caregivers today?

PROGRESSIVE RELAXATION SCRIPT

This progressive body relaxation exercise is to help the body and the mind experience a deep sense of relaxation and ease. It is inspired by the practice of yoga nidra.

I begin by inviting my client to get comfortable. They may want to sit or even lie down. This exercise can be very calming, and sometimes clients may even drift off to sleep. I invite them to get a pillow or a blanket and to find a truly comfortable way to be. I make certain they know what we are doing and have context and give them the choice to stop at any time.

As you read through the script, pause after naming each place in the body for three to five seconds. Give the client's attention just enough time to rest on that spot but not linger. Keep a smooth, soft, and soothing voice as you read this.

Script

This is a progressive relaxation exercise. We will be focusing on helping the body relax and feel peace. I will briefly name a point of the body, and as I do so, simply bring your awareness to that space and release any tension you may be holding there. Bring attention to each place without judgment. Just notice your experience.

Top of the head
Third eye
Right brow, right eye, right temple, right cheek, right side of jaw
Left brow, left eye, left temple, left cheek, left side of jaw
Chin
Throat
Back of the head
Back of the neck
Collarbones
Right shoulder, right bicep, right elbow, right forearm, right hand
Right thumb, right pointer finger, right middle finger, right ring finger, right pinky, right palm
The entire right arm

Left shoulder, left bicep, left elbow, left forearm, left hand
Left thumb, left pointer finger, left middle finger, left ring finger, left pinky, left palm
The entire left arm
Chest
Right side of the chest
Left side of the chest
Right side of the body
Left side of the body
Abdomen
Top of the spine
Middle of the spine
Lower spine
Pelvis
Right hip, right thigh, right hamstring, right knee, back of the right knee, right shin, right calf
Right ankle, right foot, right arch of the foot
Right big toe, right second toe, right middle toe, right fourth toe, right pinky toe
Bottom of the right foot
Entire right leg
Left hip, left thigh, left hamstring, left knee, back of the left knee, left shin, left calf
Left ankle, left foot, left arch of the foot
Left big toe, left second toe, left middle toe, left fourth toe, left pinky toe
Bottom of the left foot
Entire left leg
Pelvis
Torso
Head
The entire body

Check in with your client: "What do you notice?"

If your client reports qualities of ventral and adaptive material, you may cue short and slow rounds of BLS to enhance their experience.

To transition your client out of this state, move very slowly. Read the following script very slowly so as not to jar their nervous system.

Start to come back by deepening your breath.
Before you open your eyes, wiggle your fingers and toes.
Stretch if that feels right.
Slowly, very slowly, make your way back.

References

Applegate, J. S. & Shapiro, J. R. (2005). *Neurobiology for clinical social work: Theory and practice.* Norton.

American Psychiatric Association. (2017). *Diagnostic and statistical manual of mental disorders* (5th ed.). American Psychiatric Association.

Arnsten, A. F. T., Murray, Raskind, M. A., Taylor, F. B., Connor, D. F. (2015). The effects of stress exposure on prefrontal cortex: Translating basic research into successful treatments for post-traumatic stress disorder. Neurobiology of Stress, 1, 89–99.

Badenoch, B. (2008). *Being a brain-wise therapist: A practical guide to interpersonal neurobiology.* Norton.

Bergmann, U. (2020). *Neurobiological foundations for EMDR practice.* Springer.

Beutler, L. E., Malik, M., Alimohamed, S., Harwood, T. M., Talebi, H., Nobel, S., & Wong, E. (2004). Therapist variables. In M. J. Lambert (Ed.), Bergin and Garfield's handbook of psychotherapy and behavior change (5th ed., pp. 227–306). New York, NY: Wiley.

Bowlby, J. (1988). *A secure base: Parent-child attachment and healthy human development.* Basic Books.

Brenan, M. (2020, November 20). Americans' mental health ratings sink to new low. Gallup. https://news.gallup.com/poll/327311/americans-mental-health-ratings-sink-new-low.aspx

Brodal, P. (2016). *The central nervous system.* Oxford University Press.

CDC. (2022). Adverse Childhood Experiences Centers for Disease Control and Prevention. |Violence Prevention Injury Center| CDC. (2022, August 22). Retrieved from https://www.cdc.gov/violenceprevention/aces/

Chamberlin, D. (2019). The network balance model of trauma and resolution - Level 1: Large-scale neural networks. Journal of EMDR Practice and Research, 13(2), 124–142.

Connor, K. M., & Davidson, J. R. (2003). Development of a new resilience scale: The Connor-Davidson Resilience Scale (CD-RISC). *Depression and Anxiety, 18*(2), 76–82.

Corrigan, F., Fisher, J., & Nutt, D. (2010). Autonomic dysregulation and the Window of Tolerance model of the effects of complex emotional trauma: Journal of Psychopharmacology, *25*(1), 17–25.

Courtois, C. A., & Ford, J. D. (2013). *Treatment of complex trauma: A sequenced, relationship-based approach.* Guilford.

Cozolino, L. J. (2014). *The neuroscience of human relationships: Attachment and the developing social brain.* Norton.

Cozolino, L. J. (2017). *The neuroscience of psychotherapy: Healing the social brain.* Norton.

Dahlitz, M. J. (2015). Neuropsychotherapy: Defining the emerging paradigm of neurobiologically informed psychotherapy. International Journal of Neuropsychotherapy, 3(1), 47–69.

Dana, D. (2018). *The polyvagal theory in therapy: Engaging the rhythm of regulation.* Norton.

Dana, D. (2020). Polyvagal exercises for safety and connection: 50 client-centered practices. Norton.

Dana, D. (2021). *Anchored: How to befriend your nervous system using polyvagal theory.* Sounds True.

DeAngelis, T. (2019, November). Better relationships with patients lead to better outcomes. *Monitor on Psychology, 50*(10), 38. https://www.apa.org/monitor/2019/11/ce-corner-relationships

de Jongh, A., Resick, P., Zoellner, L., Minnen, A., Lee, C., Monson, C., Foa, E., Wheeler, K., Broeke, E., Feeny, N., Rauch, S., Chard, K., Mueser, K., Sloan, D., Gaag, M., Rothbaum, B., Neuner, F., Roos, C., Hehenkamp, L., Rosner, R., & Bicanic, I. (2016). Critical analysis of the current treatment guidelines for compex PTSD in adults. Depression and Anxiety, 33(5), 359–369.

Delgadillo J, Saxon D, Barkham M. Associations between therapists' occupational burnout and their patients' depression and anxiety treatment outcomes. Depression Anxiety. 2018 Sep; *35*(9): 844–850.

Drexler, S. M., & Wolf, O. T. (2017). Stress and memory consolidation. In N. Axmacher & B. Rasch (Eds.), Cognitive neuroscience of memory consolidation (pp. 285–300). Springer International Publishing.

Felitti, V. J., Anda, R. F., Nordenberg, D., Williamson, D. F., Spitz, A. M., Edwards, V., & Marks, J. S. (1998). Relationship of childhood abuse and household dysfunction to many of the leading causes of death in adults. *American Journal of Preventive Medicine, 14*(4), 245–258.

Gauhar, Y. W. (2016). The efficacy of EMDR in the treatment of depression. *Journal of EMDR Practice and Research, 10*(2), 59–69.

Geller, S. M., & Greenberg, L. S. (2012). *Therapeutic presence: A mindful approach to effective therapy.* American Psychological Association.

Geller, S. M., Greenberg, L. S., & Watson, J. C. (2010). Therapist and client perceptions of therapeutic presence: The development of a measure. *Psychotherapy Research, 20*(5), 599–610.

Geller, S. M., & Porges, S. W. (2014). Therapeutic presence: Neurophysiological mechanisms mediating feeling safe in therapeutic relationships. *Journal of Psychotherapy Integration, 24*(3), 178–192.

George, C., Kaplan, N., & Main, M. (1985). Adult Attachment Interview. Unpublished manuscript, Berkeley, CA: University of California.

Gibson, J. (2019). Mindfulness, interoception, and the body: A contemporary perspective. Frontiers in Psychology, 10.

Goddard, A. (2021). Adverse childhood experiences and trauma-informed care. Journal of Pediatric Health Care, *35*(2), 145–155.

Henry, W. P., Schacht, T. E., & Strupp, H. H. (1990). Patient and therapist introject, interpersonal process, and differential psychotherapy outcome. *Journal of Consulting and Clinical Psychology, 58*(6), 768–774.

Herman, J. L. (2015). *Trauma and recovery: The aftermath of violence, from domestic abuse to political terror.* Basic Books.

International Society for the Study of Trauma and Dissociation. (2011). Guidelines for treating dissociative identity disorder in adults, Third Revision. Journal of Trauma & Dissociation, *12*(2), 115–187.

Kain, K. L., & Terrell, S. J. (2018). *Nurturing resilience: Helping clients move forward from developmental trauma, an integrative somatic approach.* North Atlantic.

Kalmakis, K. A., & Chandler, G. E. (2015). Health consequences of adverse childhood experiences: A systematic review. Journal of the American Association of Nurse Practitioners, *27*(8), 457–465.

Kiernan, J. A., & Barr, M. L. (2009). Barr's the human nervous system: An anatomical viewpoint. Philadelphia, PA: Lippincott Williams & Wilkins.

Knipe, J. (2014). *EMDR toolbox: Theory and treatment of complex PTSD and dissociation.* Springer.

Kok, B. E., & Fredrickson, B. L. (2010). Upward spirals of the heart: Autonomic flexibility, as indexed by vagal tone, reciprocally and prospectively predicts positive emotions and social connectedness. *Biological Psychology, 85*(3), 432–436.

Korn, D. L., & Leeds, A. M. (2002). Preliminary evidence of efficacy for EMDR resource development and installation in the stabilization phase of treatment of complex posttraumatic stress disorder. Journal of Clinical Psychology, *58*(12), 1465–1487.

Kuiken, D., Bears, M., Miall, D., & Smith, L. (2001). Eye movement desensitization reprocessing facilitates attentional orienting. *Imagination, Cognition and Personality, 21*(1), 3–20.

Laborde, S., Mosley, E., & Thayer, J. F. (2017, February 20). Heart rate variability and cardiac vagal tone in psychophysiological research—recommendations for experiment planning, data analysis, and data reporting. *Frontiers in Psychology.*

Linley, P. A., & Joseph, S. (2005). The human capacity for growth through adversity. American Psychologist, *60*(3), 265–267.

Luke, C. (2016). Neuroscience for counselors and therapists: Integrating theory, practice, and neuroscience. San Diego, CA: Cognella Academic Publishing.

MacCulloch, M. J., & Feldman, P. (1996). Eye movement desensitisation treatment utilises the positive visceral element of the investigatory reflex to inhibit the memories of post-traumatic stress disorder: A theoretical analysis. *British Journal of Psychiatry, 169*(5), 571–579.

Manfield, P., Lovett, J., Engel, L., & Manfield, D. (2017). Use of the flash technique in EMDR therapy: Four case examples. *Journal of EMDR Practice and Research, 11*(4), 195–205.

McIntyre, C. K., McGaugh, J. L., & Williams, C. L. (2012). Interacting brain systems modulate memory consolidation. Neuroscience & Amp; Biobehavioral Reviews, *36*(7), 1750–1762.

Merriam-Webster. (n.d.). Embody. In *Merriam-Webster.com dictionary.* Retrieved June 24, 2022, from https://www.merriam-webster.com/dictionary/embody

Monnat, S. M., & Chandler, R. F. (2015). Long term physical health consequences of adverse childhood experiences. The Sociological Quarterly. *56*(4), 723–752.

Newman, L., Sivaratnam, C., & Komiti, A. (2015). Attachment and early brain development—neuroprotective interventions in infant–caregiver therapy. *Translational Developmental Psychiatry, 3*(1), 28647.

Nijenhuis, E., van der Hart, O., & Steele, K. (2010). Trauma-related structural dissociation of the personality. Activitas Nervosa Superior, *52*(1), 1–23.

Ogden, P., Kekuni, M., & Pain, C. (2006). *Trauma and the body: A sensorimotor approach to psychotherapy.* Norton.

Park, G., & Thayer, J. F. (2014). From the heart to the mind: Cardiac vagal tone modulates top-down and bottom-up visual perception and attention to emotional stimuli. *Frontiers in Psychology, 5.* https://doi.org/10.3389/fpsyg.2014.00278

Payne, P., Levine, P. A., & Crane-Godreau, M. A. (2015). Somatic experiencing: Using interoception and proprioception as core elements of trauma therapy. Frontiers in Psychology, 6.

Pereira, V. H., Campos, I., & Sousa, N. (2017). The role of autonomic nervous system in susceptibility and resilience to stress. *Current Opinion in Behavioral Sciences, 14,* 102–107. https://doi.org/10.1016/j.cobeha.2017.01.003

Petruccelli, K., Davis, J., & Berman, T. (2019). Adverse childhood experiences and associated health outcomes: A systematic review and meta-anaylsis. Child Abuse & Neglect, 97.

Puhlmann, L. M., Derome, M., Morosan, L., Kilicel, D., Vrtička, P., & Debbané, M. (2021). Longitudinal associations between self-reported attachment dimensions and neurostructural development from adolescence to early adulthood. Attachment &Amp; Human Development, 1–19.

Porges, S. W. (2022). Polyvagal Theory: A Science of Safety. Frontiers in Integrative Neuroscience.

Porges, S. W. (2020). *Clinical applications of the polyvagal theory.* Lecture presented at PESI. https://catalog.pesi.com

Porges, S. W. (2003). Social engagement and attachment. *Annals of the New York Academy of Sciences, 1008*(1), 31–47.

Porges, S. W. (2011). *The polyvagal theory: Neurophysiological foundations of emotions, attachment, communication, and self-regulation.* Norton.

Porges, S. W. (2017). *The pocket guide to polyvagal theory: The transformative power of feeling safe.* Norton.

Porges, S. W. (2021b). *Polyvagal safety: Attachment, communication, self-regulation.* Norton.

Porges, S. W., & Carter, C. S. (2017). Polyvagal theory and the social engagement system: Neurophysiological bridge between connectedness and health. In P. L. Gerbarg, P. R. Muskin, & R. P. Brown (Eds.), *Complementary and integrative treatments in psychiatric practice* (pp. 221–240). American Psychiatric Association.

Porges, S. W., & Dana, D. (2018). *Clinical applications of the polyvagal theory: The emergence of polyvagal- informed therapies.* Norton. Presti, D. E. (2016). *Foundational concepts in neuroscience: A brain-mind odyssey.* Norton.

Shapiro, F. (2001). *Eye movement desensitization and reprocessing.* Guilford.

Shapiro, F. (2007). EMDR, adaptive information processing, and case conceptualization. *Journal of EMDR Practice and Research, 1*(2), 68–87.

Shapiro, F. (2018). *Eye movement desensitization and reprocessing (EDMR) therapy: Basic principles, protocols, and procedures*. Guilford.

Shapiro, R. (2010). *The trauma treatment handbook: Protocols across the spectrum*. Norton.

Shapiro, S. L., Brown, K. W., & Biegel, G. M. (2007). Teaching self-care to caregivers: Effects of mindfulness-based stress reduction on the mental health of therapists in training. *Training and Education in Professional Psychology, 1*(2), 105–115.

Siegel, D. J. (1999). *The developing mind: Toward a neurobiology of interpersonal experience.* Guilford.

Siegel, D. J. (2020). *The developing mind: How relationships and the brain interact to shape who we are.* Guilford.

Simionato, S., & Simpson S. (2018). Personal risk factors associated with burnout among psychotherapists: A systematic review of the literature. Jounral of Clinical Psychology, *74*(9), 1431– 456.

Simionato, G., Simpson, S., Reid, C. (2019). Burnout as an ethical issue in psychotherapy. Psychotherapy (Chic). *56*(4), 470–482.

Smith, B. W., Dalen, J., Wiggins, K., Tooley, E., Christopher, P., & Bernard, J. (2008). The Brief Resilience Scale: Assessing the ability to bounce back. *International Journal of Behavioral Medicine, 15*, 194–200.

Sokolov, E. N. (1963). *Perception and the conditioned reflex.* Oxford.

Solomon, M. F., & Siegel, D. J. (2003). *Healing trauma: Attachment, mind, body, and brain*. Norton.

Söndergaard, H. P., & Elofsson, U. (2008). Psychophysiological studies of EMDR. *Journal of EMDR Practice and Research, 2*(4), 282–288.

Souza, G. G., Magalhães, L. N., Cruz, T. A., Mendonça-De-Souza, A. C., Duarte, A. F., Fischer, N. L., & Volchan, E. (2013). Resting vagal control and resilience as predictors of cardiovascular allostasis in peacekeepers. *Stress, 16*(4), 377–383.

Souza, G. G., Mendonça-de-Souza, A. C., Barros, E. M., Coutinho, E. F., Oliveira, L., Mendlowicz, M. V., Figueira, I., & Volchan, E. (2007). Resilience and vagal tone predict cardiac recovery from acute social stress. *Stress, 10*(4), 368–374.

Stickgold, R. (2002). EMDR: A putative neurobiological mechanism of action. *Journal of Clinical Psychology, 58*(1), 61–75.

Summers, R. F., Gorrindo, T., Hwang, S., Aggarwal, R., & Guille, C. (2020). Well-being, burnout, and depression among North American psychiatrists: The state of our profession. *American Journal of Psychiatry, 177*(10), 955–964.

van der Hart, O., Nijenhuis, E. R., & Steele, K. (2006). *The haunted self: Structural dissociation and the treatment of chronic traumatization*. Norton.

van der Kolk, B. A. (2014). *The body keeps the score: Brain, mind, and body in the healing of trauma.* Penguin.

Vojtova, H., & Hastro, J. (2009). Neurobiology of eye movement desensitization and reprocessing. *Activitas Nervosa Superior, 51*(3), 98–102.

Yang, Y., & Hayes, J. A. (2020). Causes and consequences of burnout among mental health professionals: A practice-oriented review of recent empirical literature. Psychotherapy (Chic). 57(3), 426–436.

Zernicki, B. (1987). Pavlovian orienting reflex. *Acta Neurobiologiae Experimentalis, 47*(5–6), 239–247.

Index

Note: Italicized page locators refer to figures.

About the Author

Rebecca Kase began her counseling career in 2005 as an MSW student. She is from St. Louis, Missouri, and resided in Denver, Colorado for many years. She now calls Gig Harbor, Washington home with her husband and fur babies. A yoga instructor and practitioner since 1998, Rebecca believes in infusing science and spirituality in her teachings and clinical practice. She is the owner of Kase & CO, an EMDR training and consulting business. Her company values creating shame-free, inclusive, and embodied spaces for therapists to learn EMDR therapy and heal trauma. A trauma survivor herself, Rebecca believes in the importance of embodying the lessons we teach as healers and has a unique way of bridging the gap between the academic and the "woo woo/woo hoo." She believes healing is a task everyone is faced with in this lifetime, and that the most powerful paths for transformation lie in doing your own inner work.